Churches and Urban Government in Detroit and New York 1895–1994

African American Life Series

A complete listing of the books in this series can be found at the back of this volume.

Series Editors

Churches and Urban Government in Detroit and New York 1895–1994

HENRY PRATT

Preface by
Ronald Brown

Wayne State University Press Detroit

Manufactured in the United States of America.
08 07 06 05 04 5 4 3 2 1

Library of Congress Cataloguing-in-Publication Data

Pratt, Henry J., 1934–2000
Churches and urban government in Detroit and New York, 1895-1994 /
Henry Pratt ; preface by Ronald Brown.
p. cm — (African American life series)
Includes bibliographical references (p.) and index.
ISBN 0-8143-3172-6
1. Christianity and politics—Michigan—Detroit—History—20th century. 2. African American churches—Michigan—Detroit—History—20th century. 3. Christianity and politics—New York (State)—New York—History—20th century. 4. African American churches—New York (State)—New York—History—20th century. I. Title. II. Series.
BR563.N4P72 2004
332'.1'0974710904—dc22
2003017637

∞The paper used in this publication meets the minimum requirements of the American National Standard for Information Sciences—Permanence of Paper for Printed Library Materials, ANSI Z39.48–1884.

For Hilary and Betty Cunningham

Contents

Foreword

Throughout his academic career, Henry Pratt was intrigued by the dynamic and reciprocal relationship between political interest groups and public policy formation. In an introduction to *Gray Agendas,* a cross-national study of the relationship between old-age interest groups and public pension formation, he notes, "I have been fascinated for a number of years by the social and cultural settings that have proved conducive to interest group formation, and to later reorientations of groups' accustomed modes of social action" (Pratt, *Gray Agendas,* 1993: 9; see also *The Gray Lobby,* 1976). Although perhaps best known in gerontological circles for his pioneering work in interest group formation and influence among older adults, he returned in his later years to a previous study of the relationship between church-based interest groups and urban politics. The present book is thus the product of a long-standing scholarly inquiry, which he first explored in his 1962 Columbia University doctoral dissertation on "The Protestant Council of the City of New York as a Political Interest Group."

A Detroit native, he fell in love with New York City during his first year as a graduate student at Columbia. As a native New Yorker myself, I was particularly thrilled to hear of this evolving interest in one of his many letters to me during our engagement. In November 1958, he wrote: "I supposed there are some studies which are best carried out on a secluded and restful campus among what is sometimes referred to as a community of scholars. But for the student of metropolitan government the intellectual reinforcement (which contributes to any kind of scholarly effort, regardless of subject) may flow in large degree from the place in which he finds himself. In New York City, data is the very soot of the air and clang of the fire bell." Always fascinated by the nitty-gritty of urban politics, he became a "runner" for the Riverside Democratic Party and once found himself inadvertently doing errands for Tammany Hall. He also immersed himself in the life of urban churches, attending services at St. John the Divine, Riverside Church, and other politically influential churches all over the city.

He returned to Detroit in the early 1970s to accept a position at Wayne State University, a move that rekindled his interest in the political continuities and transformations of his native city. During the 1970s he became curious about the role of ethnic loyalties as they interact with organized religion to influence community solidarity and political interventions in Detroit, which led to his edition of a collection of essays on *Ethno-Religious Politics* (1974).

Throughout his life, Henry also invested himself personally in a number of political "callings," including a variety of political campaigns, the Civil Rights movement, opposing religious persecution, and a number of feminist causes. He was thus personally invested in the role that individuals, acting alone but particularly in groups, can play in American life and politics. Henry remained fascinated by the role played by church organizations in urban politics. While at Columbia, he agreed with Reinhold Niebuhr's realistic approach to politics and his application of theology to both national and international political affairs. So, in the innocent, indefatigable way anyone who knew him would immediately recognize, he went to Professor Niebuhr's office and introduced himself as someone interested in religion and politics. By the time I arrived back in New York shortly before our marriage in 1960, he was Professor Niebuhr's research assistant, doing library runs for him and enjoying Sunday luncheons at his apartment. During the late 1960s, we returned to New York City for him to undertake the interviews and archival research for a book on the National Council of Churches, which Wayne State University Press published in 1972 as *The Liberalization of American Protestantism.* In this first book, he analyzed how the National Council responded to the political and ethical challenge of the Civil Rights movement by becoming more liberal. He demonstrated how the council emerged from "political quiescence" to insist that "major social issues be confronted by the churches," demonstrating the crucial role of "pressure group activity aimed at social reform goals" (Pratt, *The Liberalization of American Protestantism,* 1972: 265).

The present book, therefore, represents the final outcome of a set of passions and interests, both scholarly and personal, that Henry developed and elaborated on throughout his career. His particular excitement about the relationship between church political interest groups and urban politics, and the depth of this interest based on a lifetime of study, are what sustained him in writing this book during the last three years of his life.

Annis Pratt
with Faith Pratt Hopp

Preface

Henry Pratt's premature death on May 7, 2000, prevented him from fully addressing reviewers' concerns about black church confederations in chapter 6. Our common interest in the connection between religious institutions and local political culture led to countless discussions about this matter. Henry largely believed that black clergy placed more emphasis on the establishment of biracial coalitions because of their minority status. In contrast, I suggested that black religious nationalism or the belief in religious-group autonomy played an equally significant role in the development of strategies by black clergy. In the 1999 fall semester, Henry offered an undergraduate course on religion and politics, which he had developed; I was a guest speaker in his class. This was the last intellectual exchange that we had about the religion and politics nexus. The discussion centered on the contemporary affect of religious black nationalism on the political mobilization of African Americans in the city of Detroit. More specifically, we focused on the influence of the Shrine of the Black Madonna on grassroots political efforts in the city of Detroit. Henry had begun to explore more closely this dimension of black church life; however, he was unable to incorporate much of it in his chapter on black church politics.

After a discussion with Annis Pratt, Faith Pratt-Hopp, and Arthur Evans, then director of Wayne State University Press, I agreed to finish chapter 6. This chapter uses the pluralist-regime theoretical framework to describe how a black nationalism/integration political framework affected the political choices of progressive black activists. More to the point, I use Henry's interviews, newspaper articles, and new primary sources from the Wayne State University Reuther Library and the Bentley Historical Library at the University of Michigan to describe the black nationalism/integration political worldview of black activists. This information is used to describe how and why progressive black clergy were influenced by the black power ideology of the 1960s and 1970s. Black power, or the pursuit of personal and collective autonomy, led them to organize their collective resources in the pursuit of political power at the local level. Chapter 6, centering on the pluralist-regime theoretical framework that guides the book, argues that black religious nationalism, expressed largely by Malcolm X, Rev. Cleage, and to a certain degree by Adam Clayton Powell, affected black church politics in the early 1970s.

The idea of black nationalism—or collective autonomy and self-determination—would catch fire in both cities largely because of political discontentment at the mass level that would erupt in northern urban insurrections in the late 1960s. This is best illustrated by the fact that C. L. Franklin, an organizer of the March Down Woodward in 1963 that featured Martin Luther King, would, by 1968, have such sympathy for black nationalism that his church, New Bethel, would be the site of a controversial shoot-out between Detroit police and the Republic of New Africa. Furthermore, black nationalism in Detroit always had an interest in regime change. The idea of black nationalism within a pluralist system would echo itself in the formation of the Michigan Freedom Democratic Party in 1963, which consisted of black nationalist, Marxist, trade unionist, and civil rights activists. Finally, the black nationalists were part of the initial electoral campaigns of Coleman Young, David Dinkins, and Jesse Jackson, all of which are discussed in chapter 6. Essentially, what we hope to show is that a pluralistic-regime framework can be used to describe black church federation politics from the late 1960s through the early 1990s.

I do not think that Henry would disagree with this approach. He makes the point in the introduction that regime theory and pluralism both underscore the possibility that various non-regime institutions may, under certain conditions, exert a sustained influence on urban government. Black churches sought to adapt to a "newly emergent political environment" by using a black power ideology, rooted in black religious nationalism.

Ronald Brown

Acknowledgments

Professor Ron Brown, a colleague in the Political Science Department at Wayne State, was most generous in his willingness to serve as coauthor of chapter 6 following Henry's death. The depth and specificity of this chapter owe much to interviews undertaken by Sabrina Williams and by Carolyn L. Heartfield, to whom we owe special thanks. We were most grateful to Arthur Evans, the past director of the Wayne State University Press, and to the current director, Jane Hoehner, for providing encouragement and feedback on the manuscript to both Dr. Brown and to Henry's family. We are aware that numerous others assisted Henry with gaining interviews with prominent church leaders in New York and Detroit, although, given his death before he could write his own acknowledgments, we regret that we cannot thank all of these people personally.

Finally, we appreciate Henry's colleagues throughout the Wayne State University community and his students, who sustained and encouraged his intellectual interests throughout his thirty-year career at the university. The publication of this book three years after Henry's death represents a true scholarly and personal collaboration, and I hope that the outcome of its publication will be the kind of intellectual and scholarly discussions and debates that Henry most enjoyed during his lifetime.

Introduction

This is a book about city hall and the church, and more especially about the linkages between citywide ecumenical church structures, on the one hand, and officials of large municipalities and their respective states, on the other. The book's emphasis on big cities, as opposed to cities generally, is premised on the view that America's major metropolitan centers are of special importance, both symbolically and materially. Admittedly, the post–World War II mushroom growth of non-central-city communities—suburbs, satellite cities, and other urban places—is a development of major significance. Yet their emergence has not wholly eclipsed the large metropolises, which continue to play a unique role in the nation's life and imagination. The book's emphasis on religious bodies citywide, as opposed to congregations and parishes, is grounded in the fact that the former are the chief mechanism for church pronouncements on moral and social issues, and the primary instrument for church efforts to influence city hall. While it is true that parish spokespeople—including, among others, local pastors and priests—do occasionally lobby local officials and politicians, such activity is typically on matters of narrower compass as compared to the broader concerns of their citywide counterparts. Obviously, any full discussion of the relationship between church and city hall would need to consider the local church dimension. Yet the present study treats it only tangentially—in the behavior of church federations and hierarchies responding, in part, to parish-based initiatives.

I gave careful thought before deciding to focus upon the two cities New York and Detroit. My interest centers on citywide church organizations and the factors that may have contributed to their sustained political involvement since being formed in either the closing years of the nineteenth century (the New York case) or the opening years of the twentieth (the Detroit case). It is clear from preliminary investigation that the church organizations in question are similar in some respects but dissimilar in others. One can hypothesize that this contrast is in some fundamental way related to a contrasting urban governance style in the two settings. From a research standpoint it is an advantage, not a disadvantage, that New York and Detroit are, in most respects, closely akin. Both these cities (1) have long-standing "liberal" political cultures, (2) exercise metropolitan dominance over a hinterland that encompasses much of their own state in addition to portions of others, (3) are diverse in terms of ethnicity and race, and (4) contain large numbers of Catholics and Protestants (New York, of course, also has a large Jewish population). By holding constant such background characteristics, one can more easily test for the possible significance of the known variable, namely the form and style of urban governance.

Analysts sometimes apply a general model, deductively derived, to a range of cases to illustrate that the theory "fits" the cases. To do this, however, one would need to apply the model to all known instances of the phenomenon in question to establish that every instance follows essentially the same rule. Yet as Ann Shola Orloff observes in her discussion of state pension policy development in the industrialized nations, such an approach "may well push the analyst away from the direct involvement with the cases which is so important for untangling the complex causality inherent in macro level social and political processes" (Orloff, 1993: 28). Following both Orloff and Theda Skocpol (1984), I opt for a strategy of analyzing the causal regularities, hoping to "account for important historical patterns within specific and significant sets of cases" (Orloff, 1993: 28). For the same basic reason that Orloff adopts a "most similar nations" strategy, under which variation among control or background variables is minimized while variation along potentially explanatory dimensions are maximized, so this study, by focusing on two cases that are similar in most respects, aims to assess the significance of one key area of contrast.

The most salient area of contrast presented by the two cases relates to their forms of municipal government and their related political ethos. On the one hand, New York is historically a machine city in which party organizations offering inducements, both symbolic and material, to their supporters were for many years central to the city's politics. This picture has altered somewhat of late. Tammany Hall, the traditional symbol of party control in the city, began to fade as a political force beginning around 1950 and is now but a shell of its powerful position in the 1920s. Still, traditional political organizing continues to figure in New York City mayoral contests, and various elements of the old regime remain securely in place (McNickle, 1993: 325). Detroit, on the other hand, has been governed on the basis of reform principles for most of the twentieth century. "Reform" is part of a larger Anglo-Saxon middle-class ethos, and its abiding goals consist of eliminating corruption, increasing efficiency, and making local government in some cases more democratic (Banfield and Wilson, 1963: 138–39). Detroit was perhaps the first large American city to accept the reform package essentially in its entirety: nonpartisan, at-large municipal elections; the initiative, referendum, and recall; the short ballot; the municipal reference bureau and the citizens' association; and (especially since the revised city charter of 1974) the strengthening of the power of the mayor. Among all the reforms brought together by the National Municipal League in 1916 as its "second municipal program," and then promoted nationwide as orthodoxy, Detroit elected to reject only the council-manager form of government, as have essentially all American big cities (Banfield and Wilson, 1963: 141).

Machine dominance in a given city tends to shape the political environment in which interest groups of all kinds, urban church federations included, must operate; "reform" tends to produce an equally distinct environmental impact. The question for research, then, becomes one of trying to identify the contrasting patterns of church political behavior in Detroit, with its reform tradition, and in New York, with its equally traditional machine orientation.

The premise that church representatives are potentially a source of influence and pressure in large-city governance is one unlikely to arouse much controversy. Churches are generally recognized as having an "interest"—moral, spiritual, and material—and, as is true of pressure groups generally, their interest is one that can serve as the basis for organized, concerted action. The urban politics literature of the past quarter century, while seldom mentioning churches as such (a point returned to below), does underscore the role of pressure groups and lobbies, and often employs an implicit "demand-pressure" model in accounting for public policy outcomes.

The present discussion is sensitive to the possibility that a church demand-pressure model may apply to one or the other of the cities during all or some of their twentieth-century histories. Churches may make "demands" in the form of formal pronouncements or other public policy statements. They may then apply "pressure" aimed at insuring that such statements receive full consideration. Assuming a positive response from government, the church groups would then logically monitor the situation to guarantee that outcomes roughly coincide with the original intent.

Yet the research is also sensitive to a second possibility, one that includes, but goes beyond, the demand-pressure model. Under certain conditions municipal officials and citywide church leaders may become partners in what amounts to an interdependent, symbiotic relationship. Leaders of both "church" and "state," I suggest, may on occasion participate in a trading relationship, with each party exchanging resources that the other considers useful, even critical, to its own functioning. ("Resources" here is intended in its broadest sense, denoting both symbols and tangible, material assets.) While there is no presumption here that such symbiosis has in fact taken place in either of the two settings, it may now (or may recently have) occurred, and the research needs to be sensitive to that possibility.

Relationships between church organizations and city hall, whether in the simple demand-pressure mold or in the more complex symbiosis pattern, occur in the context of this country's tradition of church-state separation. That tradition restricts the ability of church leaders and city officials to collaborate overtly with one another, as is often the case in other public policy spheres—for example, in urban land-use development where business groups and government officials often act jointly in furtherance of municipal projects. Federal and state courts are invoked from time to time in giving legal definition to the church nonestablishment clause and also the religious "free exercise" clause of the First Amendment. In that process, the courts play an important role in big-city church-state relations. Given the peculiarities of First Amendment concerns, the nexus between city church groups and city government probably has no exact counterpart elsewhere in urban governance, where interest groups of other types seek to influence public policy outcomes.

In exploring the linkages between church organizations and urban governance structures, I take into account the two approaches that together have dominated late-twentieth-century theorizing about American urban politics, namely "regime theory" and "pluralism." Each of these merits a word of explanation. A "regime" has been defined as an informal yet relatively stable group with access to institutional resources that enable it to have a sustained role in making governing decisions. Participants are likely to have an institutional base, a domain of command or power (Stoker, 1995: 58). There is no formal hierarchy that serves as the focus of direction and control. Instead, regime theory posits a "network," premised on solidarity, loyalty, and trust, through which cooperation is obtained and governing capacity is achieved. Regime theory, as Stoker remarks, "is concerned with the process of government interest group mediation," including "the internal politics of coalition building" (Stoker, 1995: 50). Churches are unlikely to be included within any city's regime, given the emphasis placed on church-state separation, the scarcity of disposable church resources, and church leaders' absence of real "command" over the resources nominally at their disposal. Yet there remains the possibility that churches are involved in the mediation process in their efforts to influence one or more areas of pubic policy.

Studies reveal that a number of North American cities are governed by regime in a classic, highly developed form. Atlanta, in the decades beginning in 1945, is a leading case in point (Stone, 1989). Detroit has been found to lie at the other end of the continuum: a city with a limited and weak regime-building capacity (Stoker, 1995). Still, despite such wide city-to-city variation, regime-theory analysts consistently report that social complexity is a fundamental aspect of American big-city politics, and that fragmentation and the absence of consensus characterizes most urban systems (Stoker, 1995). Interest groups of all types benefit from this pattern, since fragmentation normally enhances their ability to achieve and maintain governmental access.

"Pluralism," a somewhat older analytic tradition, dates from the 1960s and early '70s, and to the writings of analysts such as Robert Dahl, Raymond Wolfiner, and Nelson Polsby. Two of its leading propositions are: (1) power is fragmented and decentralized, and (2) there are dispersed inequalities, insofar as all groups have some resources to articulate their case, even if their demands are not necessarily or specifically acted upon (Judge, 1995: 14). Since receiving its classic expression forty years ago, the pluralism tradition has metamorphosed to the point that its recent expressions have been labeled "neo-pluralism." Thus, for example, Douglas Yates reformulates Robert Dahl's original query, "who governs?" into the question "does anybody govern?" Yates's "street fighting pluralism" emphasizes the wide diversity and complexity of interests and decision games (Yates, 1977). Policy making, in this view, involves direct and well-crystallized conflicts about urban goods and services (Judd, 1979: 24). To a far greater extent than classical pluralism, neo-pluralism is sensitive to the social context of policy formation—spatial, temporal, and socioeconomic. In this respect it has come increasingly to overlap concerns central to regime theory, in which social context is also underscored. Consequently, the earlier intense debate between pluralist and elite approaches has now considerably abated (Judge, 1995: 30).

Regime theory and pluralism, then, both underscore the possibility that various non-regime institutions may, under certain conditions, exert a sustained influence on urban government. Are churches and church leaders one such source? It is an aim of the present study to find an answer. It would be wrong, of course, to prejudge the issue. Conceivably, churches and other religious organizations are only occasional, fairly minor urban actors. Yet contemporary theory gives no reason, a priori, to exclude them as important, especially considering that church leaders—often socially notable and prestigious—are recognized as a source of pronouncements on social-policy issues: gambling, vice, public assistance needs, racial discrimination, and so on. To repeat, regime theory and pluralism, while starting from very different assumptions, are in agreement on at least this point: even though business leaders and elective government officials together usually comprise the core of the big-city governing elite, the regime's behavior is typically attuned to a variety of outside forces. These "other voices" are generally regarded as worthwhile for the elite to consider and to accommodate to the extent possible. The present question, then, is the degree to which, if at all, churches are a significant facet of that larger political environment.

The present study seeks to extend a long-standing theme in my research, namely the close linkages that can develop between interest groups and government. In my recent book, *Gray Agendas: Interest Groups and Public Pensions in Canada, Britain, and the United States* (Pratt, 1993), I trace the complex and interdependent relationship between government programs and lobbying organizations in the three countries. Documented there is how public policies have sparked the creation of organized senior-citizen groups, which, in turn, through their intensified political clout, have been able to shape subsequent public policy.

My thinking on this matter has been enriched by the writings of other scholars. An early exponent of this view, Theodore Lowi, maintains that the activist administrations of John F. Kennedy (1961–63) and Lyndon Johnson (1963–69) led to the nationalization of the government's police power—that is, power relating to the health, safety, and morals of the community—and thus presented social problem-solving as a positive good for various interest groups to pursue, even in the absence of a crisis like a depression or war. Lowi refutes the usual view that the turning point for such a change occurred several decades earlier, under Franklin Roosevelt, and points out that the Roosevelt New Deal was an emergency program designed for emergency circumstances whereas the changes enacted under Presidents Kennedy and Johnson have mostly survived over time (Lowi, 1978). In short, in the Kennedy/Johnson years, government initiatives deeply impacted interest group behavior.

Other analysts incorporate this theme as an element in their empirical research. For example, Anne and Douglas Costain, in accounting for the reemergence of the women's movement in the 1960s and early '70s, provide evidence of major "interaction" between movement organizations and Congress. "It seems reasonable to conclude," these authors observe, "that pressure from social movements elicits a response from Congress and that Congressional response in turn affects the subsequent behavior of the movement" (Costain and Costain, 1985: 22). In a still more recent writing, the same authors employ a similar logic to account for the recent reemergence of America's environmental movement (Costain and Costain, 1992).

The 1990s witnessed a surge of published writings dealing in part with the capacity of government to influence church-based, faith-based, and other social action groups. Timothy Byrnes, for one, reaches the following conclusion regarding the political activity of the National Conference of Catholic Bishops (successor to the National Catholic Welfare Conference): "The Catholic bishops' activity over the past two decades illustrates that the role of American churches and religious leaders is also a function of the structures and procedures of the American political system. A substantial shift in governmental and policy initiative to Washington, D.C. led the bishops to adopt a more collective, national approach to public policy matters" (Byrnes, 1991: 127). In a similar vein, the church historian Robert Wuthnow points out that in the post–World II era public policy impacted all religious bodies, and that government programs came to exert "a decided impact on the religious environment, if not directly then indirectly" (Wuthnow, 1995: 8). The present study incorporates this church-state interaction theme and builds upon it. My aim is to pay special attention to local government–church group interaction employing a comparative, cross-city framework.

One should take note of the fact that church-state relations in the nation's cities are not a topic significantly addressed in the recent urban politics literature. Recent scholarship on that topic, as reflected in the bibliographies and indexes appearing in urban textbooks authored by leading political scientists including Bryan Jones (1983), Dennis Judd (1979), Paul Peterson (1981), Clarence Stone (1986), and James Q. Wilson (1968), evidence the fact that urban research, while treating other types of pressure groups—for example, labor unions and civil rights organizations—pass over in silence any possible role for churches and other religious institutions; all these texts are silent on this particular topic. I am aware of only one recent book, authored by two sociologists, that treats this precise area (Demerath and Williams, 1992).

It was not always so. In an earlier era, urban scholars often referenced pressure-group activity by churches and religious groups. For example, a political scientist of the post–World War II era, Harold Zink, devoted four pages in a two-hundred-page book to "churches" among several "important pressure groups in [U.S.] cities" (Zink, 1948). A decade later, Wallace Sayre and Herbert Kaufman, in their classic study, *Governing New York City* (1960), commented repeatedly on religious-group activity in that metropolis, while Robert Dahl's celebrated study of New Haven, *Who Governs* (1961), devoted a three-page discussion to "the church." Other writings from the pre-1970 period, while not referencing "churches" as such, did underscore—more so than their more recent counterparts—the importance of religious voting in city elections (for example, Reed, 1934; Gosnell, 1937; Kneier, 1947).

While intending no criticism of the more recent textbook authors, I find this more than a little surprising. The same post-1970 period that saw the apparent diminution of scholarly interest in church involvement in urban politics witnessed a surge of interest in religious action nationally—lobbying, petitioning of the U.S. Supreme Court, and the formation of religious-group political coalitions. Several political scientists have been prominent in this regard: Robert Booth Fowler, Allen D. Hertzke, Ted G. Jalen, A. James Richley, and Clyde Wilcox, among others. It is worthy of note that the religion and politics section of the American Political Science Association is presently the largest such interest group of any in the association.

One could make an argument that the declining recognition of churches in the urban politics literature is a logical reflection of the churches' diminished political importance there. Such an argument offers food for thought. Yet it is ultimately unpersuasive in my opinion. It is true that citywide organizations with an historically white middle-class support base, including especially city church federations, have often experienced a loss in political clout in the years since 1970. Such decline can be attributed in part to the membership losses experienced by the nation's mainline Protestant churches, historically such federations' chief source of support: the United Presbyterian Church, a loss of 21 percent; the Episcopal Church, a loss of 15 percent; the United Methodist Church, 10 percent; and so on (Richley, 1985: 278–81). The decline is also attributable in part to large-scale middle-class migration to the suburbs, where the strength of liberal Catholics, Protestants, and Jews, once fairly concentrated in inner-city ethnic enclaves, becomes scattered and divided, with negative effects for their urban power potential. One recent author, Paul Djupe of Denison University, has developed this theme at length (Djupe, 1996).

It is conceivable, nevertheless, that any such declines in white-church collective strength have been offset, at least to some degree, by newly formed church bodies comprised of African Americans and other racial minorities. Furthermore, the apparent decline in most urban church federations' political authority and influence, far from justifying their total disregard, might better be viewed as opening up potentially fruitful lines of research. What exactly caused this development? Was it simply a result of the above-mentioned decline in mainline Protestant membership and of middle-class migration to the suburbs, or may it also be rooted in alterations in the wider political environment? If so, that would serve to highlight the importance of political, not merely sociological, factors. The present study aims to explore that issue as well.

Variations over time in urban church power and influence, greater at certain times, less at others, is a subject worthy of thoughtful investigation. Rather than consider urban church groups at a single, fixed point, or possibly in a limited before-and-after view, the present study approaches them in terms of critical stages beginning with the outset of this century and moving on to the present. Available archival materials are mostly adequate to test hypotheses relevant to this approach. In the case of New York's church federation, presently named "The Council of Churches of the City of New York," but having other names at various points throughout its long history, a primary source for past developments is my (unpublished) Ph.D. dissertation, "The Protestant Council of the City of New York as a Political Interest Group," accepted by Columbia University four decades ago (Pratt, 1962). Also, a fairly complete set of archival records is available at the Walter Reuther Archives at Wayne State University, and at the organization's own headquarters, for "The Christian Communication Council of Metropolitan Detroit Churches." Leslie Tentler's superb historical treatment of the Detroit Catholic archdiocese is an invaluable source on that topic (Tentler, 1990). Unfortunately, the archives of the New York Catholic Archdiocese are not available for scholarly inspection, resulting in some inevitable gaps in the portions of this study relating to that religious institution. Yet even in that case, interviews with informants and attention to the published literature, however thin, lay a foundation for including the New York Archdiocese in this study with meaningful hopes of fruitful results.

The critical developmental phases of the urban church federations and diocesan hierarchies covered in this study are presumed to be a function of their need to cope effectively with an ever-changing, and potentially threatening, wider environment. While that environment obviously consists of various elements—economic, sociological, demographic, and so on—my hypothesis is that municipal government, and the urban "regime" of which it constitutes a primary element, are uniquely important in defining the environment in which churches function. Thus, as government's scope and authority grew from around 1900 onward, the church federations and diocesan hierarchies could possibly have responded by altering their behavior—not always immediately and directly, but always in time and in predictable patterns.

A leading political scientist, David Truman, hypothesizes that interest groups first form, and subsequently expand or contract, in response to various "disturbances" in the their environments (Truman, 1951: 26–43). In treating this point, Truman emphasizes especially depression and war as sources of disturbance. Yet he is also aware that government may serve as a source under certain conditions. In line with that thought, it is logical to imagine that the introduction of city agencies into an environment previously dominated by the church—for example, church social welfare programs—was initially perceived by church leaders as a "disturbance," and that the initial formation of church-supported interest groups is explainable as one response to that perception. One can also hypothesize that several decades later, at the point that big-city and state governments further enlarged their existing social welfare and educational programs, churches again typically perceived that expansion as a disturbance requiring a response on their part. That response consisted to a large extent of a reenergized church presence at city hall and among selected city agencies. It seems logical that the churches should respond in this manner, since, as Truman also points out, the overriding objective of groups disturbed in some manner is to stabilize the situation and to restore as much as possible of the preexisting harmony between themselves and the wider environment.

One final point deserves to be made before this discussion moves on to a chapter-by-chapter outline of its overall scope. The twentieth century has been aptly referred to as "the century of the state." Some people choose to view this development normatively. To them, growing governmental involvement in the lives of average citizens is regarded in a mostly positive light—as a progressive trend beneficial to the vast majority of citizens, the downtrodden especially. No such normative implication is intended here. In large metropolitan cities, often characterized as "liberal" cultures, of which Detroit and New York are examples, the twentieth-century increase in governmental power is quite apparent, more so perhaps than in rural areas and less-concentrated urban centers. Indeed, that reality helps to justify the selection of those two cities for study and analysis: the effects of governmental intervention on social institutions like churches are more obvious there. But I do not presume that this increase in state power is always and necessarily a good thing. Government welfare programs presumably do some things better, others not so well, as compared to church social service agencies. It is not the purpose of this discussion to weigh the relative merits of the two approaches nor to arrive at a normative judgment of the matter. I choose to regard the twentieth-century increase in state power in the United States as a simple fact, while leaving it for others to decide whether that development has been to the overall benefit, or the detriment, of American society.

In line with the above, chapter 1 of this study explores the relations between urban church groups and government in the period around 1900. In both Detroit and New York, this was a time when city and state governments were beginning to enlarge the scope of their social service efforts, though only to a limited degree compared to what would come later. The discussion explores the impact of expanding government programs on the urban churches, and the churches' organizational response. It takes account of a growing sense of threat experienced by church leaders related to mass European immigration, urban crowding, and sectarian rivalry. How did churches, both Catholic and Protestant, endeavor to cope with that political reality? The discussion tests the hypothesis that the initial twentieth-century stirring of urban church social and political action was responsive, in part, to the early impact of positive government combined with the anxiety experienced by many church leaders related to a rapidly changing, and somewhat menacing, wider environment.

Chapter 2 carries the above themes into the 1930s and the Great Depression era. To what extent were the Detroit and New York City church organizations affected by the large-scale increases at this time in the scope of government programs? How were these agencies affected, if at all, by the insecurities and anxieties endemic to the times, and how, if at all, did it affect their social and political behavior?

Chapters 3 and 4 move the discussion on to the next juncture in the development of citywide church activity in the two cities, namely the Civil Rights and Great Society/New Frontier era of the 1960s and early '70s. Positive government flowered nationally during this period, led by Democratic presidents John F. Kennedy and Lyndon Johnson, and later maintained, up to a point, by their Republican successor, Richard Nixon. These developments in Washington had their local-level counterparts, as municipal governments expanded efforts aimed at combatting racism, hunger, and poverty. While churches in northern urban centers were generally supportive of civil rights, their officials were often made uncomfortable as activists involved in various movements—

civil rights, welfare rights, and anti-Vietnam—now in some instances turned their anger against the church, targeting the church as part of the "problem" and not, as church leaders would have it, as part of the "solution." How did city church federations and diocesan hierarchies respond to this altered wider environment? Chapter 3 explores this topic with regard to Protestantism and Catholicism in New York and Detroit, while chapter 4 deals with New York Protestantism's attempts to influence appointments to city offices.

In chapters 5 and 6, the discussion moves to the last two decades covered in this study, 1975–94. These years saw the nation's established urban church structures forced to contend, to a degree never before encountered, with the suburban exodus of their traditional white, middle-class support base, and its replacement by local populations now heavily, in some cases predominantly, comprised of racial minorities. (Detroit, indeed, is now the largest majority-black city in North America.) This change has seriously stressed the traditional citywide church federations, although in both the cities under discussion they did manage to survive. Also affected have been the two cities' Catholic archdioceses. Chapter 5 explores the implications of those developments for church/city hall relations from the standpoint of the traditional Catholic and Protestant citywide religious bodies. Did city and state government continue to exert a major impact on these agencies as shown to be the case in times past?

Chapter 6 treats the same period from the standpoint of minority-based religion, especially the black church. To what extent did the black church in New York and Detroit adapt itself to the newly emergent political environment? What, if anything, was the impact on it of the election in both cities of African American mayors? Were the black ministers' councils the functional equivalent, for blacks, of the cities' traditional church federations, historically supported by mainline (mostly white) churches? In short, chapters 5 and 6 explore the coping strategies of church leaders confronted with a social landscape recently altered, almost beyond recognition, by population movement.

The conclusion ends the discussion by revisiting the themes introduced at the outset and by offering an overall assessment of the data against a broader theoretical background.

1

Urban Churches in the Progressive Era

It is not the conventional wisdom to suggest that American Social Christianity, from its inception in the last quarter of the nineteenth century to its eventual fading from the scene around 1920, was significantly impacted by municipal and state government. Social Christianity has been treated by several historians and sociologists, with special attention paid to its most prominent facet, the Social Gospel movement (Hopkins, 1940; Hutchinson, 1941; Abell, 1943; Yinger, 1946; May, 1949; Cavert, 1968). Others have treated the participation of the American Catholic Church (Abell, 1960; Roohan, 1976). In accounting for the movement's emergence and subsequent development, these authorities point with varying degrees of emphasis toward several factors: mass European immigration to U.S. cities, the rise of an industrial economy, the growth of labor unions and related anti-union campaigns by owners and managers, the prevalence of slums and urban congestion—all of them regarded by religious leaders as requiring an appropriate church response. Yet government, as such, does not figure in this literature. Government is not, of course, a wholly autonomous institution; it is responsive to wider societal forces including the kinds just mentioned. Still, one can plausibly suggest that in the period under discussion city and state government, having recently expanded in scale and visibility, was also to some degree an independent factor. Did government, therefore, constitute a "disturbance" in the eyes of church leaders, to be coped with in various ways, including the possible formation of new church-related agencies and institutions? And once formed, how did any such agencies and institutions seek to deal with their governmentally impacted urban settings? The present chapter explores these topics.

Municipal Government Expansion

"Government," two leading students of urban government remark, "is the city's central agency of change and conservation. It is the city's prime rule-maker, the omnipresent supervisor. Its officials are always important actors . . . [It] is often the innovator and provider of indispensable facilities and services for the city and its people" (Sayre and Kaufman, 1960: 32–33). Although made in regard to a particular city, New York, this comment also applies to large American cities generally. While government's role as innovator, conservator, and service provider is rooted in the past—the distant past in the case of older cities, the more recent past in the case of newer ones—one can usually identify a critical point in a given city's development when its government transcended an initially limited role, as one among several forces involved in urban life and not always very important, to become a central actor, always involved to one degree or another in major urban projects and decisions. In the case of Detroit and New York, one can make a case that that juncture came with the Progressive Era, which lasted for about a generation beginning around 1895. It would be misleading to suggest, of course, that the present-day functional importance of urban government was fully apparent at that point. Government's role would, in fact, continue to expand in the decades to follow, with new activities assumed and existing ones enlarged. Still, in broad outline the present-day picture was at that time first manifested.

In the case of Detroit, available statistics enable one to chart this transition with some precision. In 1890, just before the Progressive Era commenced, the city had a "tax budget" of $2,236,000, a municipal debt of $1,945,000, and a per capita debt of $15.50 (Upson, 1922). The number of city-performed activities stood at 108. Moreover, Detroit's government was reputed as generally inept, having "fallen under corrupting influences and . . . [ceasing] to be representative of the public interest, responsible to the people, or responsive to the public will" (Catlin, 1926: 592). Although city elections were partisan, in nether Detroit nor Michigan were the existing party organizations very effective. Instead, Detroit's partisan government was largely under the influence of two interests, liquor and the utilities, and they gave allegiance to no party (Ramsay, 1944: 113). Yet this municipal malaise evoked only occasional public outcries and no concerted effort toward systemic reform. City residents mostly accommodated themselves to the utility magnates, saloon keepers, bartenders, and men of no known occupation—referred to by their opponents as the "Vote Swappers League" and by themselves as the "Royal Ark Group"—who dominated city elections and government generally.

Within a generation after 1890, however, this picture of ineptitude and public apathy would dramatically change. By 1922, Detroit's tax budget had increased to $25.5 million (a 9-fold increase from 1890), its net debt to $26.7 million (a 14-fold increase), and its per capita debt to $26.9 (a 2.5-fold increase), while the city was now performing 265 "activities" (a 2.5-fold increase). In a 1922 essay reflecting upon Detroit's Progressive Era, Lent D. Upson, the director of the Detroit Bureau of Municipal Research, emphasized developments beginning in 1910. "During these twelve years [1910–22]," he remarked, "the cost of government has multiplied more than five times . . . [and the] newly established activities are now important city services . . . [such as] nutrition of school children . . . city planning, community centers, junior college, grade separation, vice control, hospitals, education of the blind, and civil service—to mention a few" (Upson, 1922: 318). In a later report on the same topic, Upson further elaborated: "By 1910 [Detroit's] twenty-four original activities [of 1824] had grown to 179. [Yet] only after 1910 did the city government feel the full effects of the machine age. Between 1910 and 1920 eighty-six new activities were added. . . . In a generation, the services rendered by the city to its citizens had increased by almost as many as in the previous three-quarters of a century" (Upson, 1942: 11).

Moreover, the change in Detroit government was as much qualitative as quantitative. The year 1916 saw the establishment of the privately supported Detroit Bureau of Municipal Research, and this reform-oriented agency soon developed a reputation for impartiality, objectivity, and insightful analysis. And as detailed below, the city soon thereafter dealt a decisive blow to its once-dominant bipartisan bartenders and saloon keepers coalition, replacing it in 1918 with a new city charter based upon reform principles. Bipartisan government now gave way to nonpartisan; ward-based city elections to at-large; a corrupt and incompetent Election Commission to one marked by honesty and competency. This profound alteration in city administration did not escape public attention and, indeed, was generally recognized.

One individual in particular, Mayor Hazen S. Pingree, stands out for helping to transform municipal policy issues, often fairly technical and undramatic, into matters of general interest to the public. Although not the only mayor of importance during Detroit's Progressive Era, Pingree more than any other was responsible for popularizing the concept of low-cost, clean, and competent city administration. During his six-year mayoralty, 1890–96, he waged an unrelenting campaign against the "interests," in the course of which he broke with some of the most prominent men in the city who had sponsored his nomination and helped to secure his election. Pingree steadfastly refused the blandishments and bribe offers from the city's traction magnates. Defying such pressures, he embraced the principle that the privilege granted to traction corporations to operate on the city's streets should be compensated in the form of low transit fares. Later on, he launched a campaign to bring the transit system, and likewise the city lighting system, under municipal ownership. His enemies exacted a heavy price for these perceived transgressions. The mayor, regarded as a betrayer of his class, was dismissed as director of a leading local bank (he had been a successful businessman before entering politics) and was forced out of his family pew in the Woodward Avenue Baptist Church where he was a member of long standing. In the depression of 1893–94, with hardship widespread in the city, the mayor proposed that the city's churches should contribute to a fund for the purchase of plows, implements, and seeds, and thereby allow the needy to grow their own food. The scheme ended up a fiasco, with total church contributions to Pingree's "potato patch plan" coming to a paltry $13.80 and with the pastor of a fashionable Presbyterian church ridiculing the plan from his pulpit (Holli, 1969: 52–53, 70–71).

In the course of being ostracized by Detroit's social elite, the mayor won the abiding loyalty of the city's working classes, Catholic and Protestant alike. Detroit's large foreign-born community had failed to produce leaders, but it provided a political base for Pingree. In the process, the mayor helped to dispel the notion that the Age of Reform must depend primarily upon native-born middle and upper classes, and that newcomers can have no important part in that process. From Pingree's service as mayor, and later as governor of Michigan, citizens in large numbers came to regard government as a force for social betterment—a legacy that would persist for years after his death in 1901 (Holli, 1969: 219–20).

The Progressive Era was a no less significant juncture in the history of New York. While there are, unfortunately, no precise figures on the expanding scope of New York government at this time, it is apparent that around the turn of the century the city entered upon a new era. The transformation involved several far-reaching policy developments: in 1896, the centralization of public education under a single Board of Education and a professionally trained Board of School Superintendents; in 1897, a vast enlargement in the city's population and physical size as a result of state legislation establishing the consolidated "Greater New York City"; in 1901, the revamping of the city charter in ways that restricted the unfettered power of the mayor, the party bosses, and the local party machine, and that has provided, in slightly modified form, the framework for city governance from that time to the present; and in the early 1900s, construction of New York's first rapid transit subway line, 722 miles long (exceeded in length only by the London Underground)—a system planned, financed, and constructed by the city. Worthy of note is the fact that all these municipal initiatives stemmed from proposals advanced and widely debated in the 1890–95 period. In that five-year time span, New York became a cauldron of policy discussion and controversy (Hammack, 1982).

In both Detroit and New York, the general public, church people included, were brought to consciousness of the civic issues at stake and the necessity for them to be satisfactorily resolved. Archival records for the period frequently reference civilly active religious people—clergy and lay; Protestant, Catholic, and Jewish—as a constituency whose support was considered helpful in facilitating possible expansions in municipal services. Nevertheless, group awareness is one thing, group political behavior is another. The question arises, did the increasing scale of government at this time affect the formation of new civically active church organizations? Moreover, did the enlargements in municipal services possibly foster redirection in policy among the two cities' more established religious organizations? The following discussion treats these matters. Before addressing them directly, however, it may be useful to consider the wider national picture.

Churches Confront the Industrial Age

In the late nineteenth century, the nation's Protestant and Catholic churches, while divided on matters of theology, forms of worship, and ecclesiastical structure, were alike in their sensitivity to the social realities of post–Civil War America. In the case of Protestantism, the initial mood after 1865 was one of general complacency, an attitude related to the final victory of the Union armies in the Civil War, which many northern-state residents viewed as vindication of the righteousness of their cause. The Union victory of 1865, combined with the assassination of President Lincoln that same year, prompted Republican leaders to forge an alliance between the GOP and corporate capital. This alliance endured for some years and was essentially sanctified by the nation's Protestant churches (Mead, 1956).

America's "Protestant establishment" responded to the stresses and dislocations of the Industrial Age in ways typical of established orders when confronted with novel, disturbing developments, namely by making common cause with the emergent social forces and by intensifying existing efforts along accustomed, well-tested paths. In the words of a leading historian, "American

Protestantism achieved during this period a striking ideological harmony with the modes of modern industrialized civilization, the free-enterprise system, and the burgeoning of [American] imperialism" (Mead, 1956: 14). For two decades after 1865, the churches' chief response to social disruptions related to the Machine Age consisted in expansions of church charity efforts targeted at the needy (Cavert, 1968).

Yet despite the general acceptance of laissez-faire and sanctification of the social status quo, dissenting voices began to be heard demanding a more collective, more compassionate response toward industrial society and urban ills. American Social Christianity was essentially a case of the transfer of European practice to the American setting, given that developments in England, Germany, and France preceded the U.S. movement by roughly a decade (Hutchinson, 1975). In time, the movement was to gain increasing Protestant acceptance. Although initially limited to scattered pulpit declarations and the publication of tracts and small books, it eventually achieved organizational expression through such groups as the Evangelical Alliance (beginning in 1886 when Josiah Strong became its general secretary) and the (Episcopal) Church Association for the Advancement of the Interests of Labor (CAIL), formed in 1887. The depression of 1892–95 helped accelerate the movement. In troubled times, its basic message now gained in influence and volume (May, 1949: 181).

Social Christianity never became dominant in any Protestant denomination but instead remained a minority tendency, its adherents successful only to the point of winning denominational approval of their objectives and official authorization to establish denominational boards, of which CAIL served as the prototype. Given the limits on denominational support, the movement's ability to influence urban-industrial America was dependent upon the formation of Social Gospel–oriented interdenominational councils at the local, state, and national levels. After fifteen years of preparatory work, the movement in 1908 achieved its institutional embodiment with the formation of the Federal Council of Churches of Christ in the USA (FCC). (This agency's work continues to the present time under its successor organization, the National Council of Churches of Christ, the NCC, formed in 1950.)

The FCC is a clear case of group formation in response to a perceived environmental disturbance. A carefully drafted policy statement adopted by the FCC's founding convention, "The Social Ideals of the Churches," placed the group firmly in support of Social Gospel objectives, including labor movement concerns such as reduction of the work week, abolition of child labor, and workers' compensation. As J. Milton Yinger observes, the "Social Ideals" and the FCC's own formation were reflective of a deeply felt anxiety among church leaders over the threatened loss of the urban working class and uneasiness over the widening gulf between Protestantism and organized labor. The FCC was an expression of the these leaders' defensiveness in a situation where traditional Protestant evangelism, fashioned on the frontier and in towns and villages across America, had come to seem irrelevant and inappropriate (Yinger, 1946: 138, 140).

Such developments nationally were paralleled at the local level. The first expression of local interchurch cooperation was the Christian League of Methuan, Massachusetts, formed in 1888 (Cavert, 1968). And the first such body in any large metropolis was the Federation of Churches and Christian Workers of New York City, formed in November 1895. From almost the moment of its inception, this group was widely influential, its existence serving to stimulate the formation of similar groups in other cities (especially Pittsburgh, 1899), and its leaders taking an active role in the formation of the Federal Council of Churches.

As was true of Protestantism, American Catholicism was deeply affected by the stresses and dislocations that marked the decades following the Civil War. The American Catholic Church—largely comprised at the time of European immigrants, and frequently the target of nativist, anti-Catholic abuse from the Know-Nothing Party, the Ku Klux Klan, the American Protective Association, and other such groups—responded very differently than "established" Protestant churches to the evolving national picture. Here there would be no informal political alliances, neither with the Republican Party, now dominant in most non-Southern states, nor with corporate capitalism, now ascendent in this, the Gilded Age. Nevertheless, the Catholic response to the emergent urban-industrial age did parallel the Protestant response in certain respects.

As the Catholic social conscience first began to awaken, there was a tendency to rely upon past strategies and traditional thought patterns. Catholicism's predominant response to urban vice, for example, took the form of exhortation, almsgiving, and works of mercy—an approach that left little room for exploration of the underlying economic or societal causes of moral degradation. Catholics "were content for the most part to seek social improvement within the framework of existing arrangements" (Abell, 1960: 27). Moreover, this mood was largely unaffected by the occasional hard times, such as the national depression of 1873–74. American Catholics' initially conservative response to urban squalor, dislocation, and industrial strife also applied to the interpretation given to the papal encyclicals of this period. For example, in May 1891, Pope Leo XIII, with a view toward healing certain rifts that had opened up among both European and American Catholics, issued *Rerum Novarum*—a major encyclical on the condition of labor. While the American response to this was not entirely uniform, the main body of Catholic opinion gave it a narrow, traditional gloss: poverty, no less than vice or crime, stems chiefly from ignorance and moral weakness, and the betterment of labor today, as in the past, required "a gradual evolution in which education, individual and social, rather than legislation, [is] to be principally stressed" (Abell, 1960: 77).

Yet, like Protestantism, American Catholicism did not long persist in such initial caution. Beginning the mid-1880s, a mood of social liberalism and reform increasingly came to the fore. It included a sympathetic attitude toward the labor movement, where Catholics were generally well received by labor leaders, including the AFL president, Samuel Gompers, in marked contrast to the reception given the Protestant Social Gospel movement, which labor generally viewed with suspicion. Catholic priests and laypeople participating in Social Christianity early on received no explicit direction or authorization from the Church hierarchy, so they acted essentially on their own in a noncanonical setting. Thus the American Federation of Catholic Societies, formed in 1901 and dedicated to champion social justice as defined by Leo XIII in *Rerum Novarum,* essentially paralleled the Protestant-led Federal Council of Churches but with the difference that it acted in the absence of any clear imprimatur from the American bishops such as that conferred upon the FCC by its constituent denominations. The same was true of most other Progressive Era Catholic responses: the Militia of Christ for Social Service (1910), the Social Service Commission (1911), and the National Conference of Catholic Charities (1915). Only with the establishment in 1917 of the National Catholic War Council—precursor to the National Catholic Welfare Conference (1919)—did the Catholic hierarchy formally commit itself to an organization dedicated to the cause of social justice and social service (Abell, 1960).

The apparent reluctance of American Catholic bishops to become involved in this area also typically applied at the local level. As elaborated upon below, in neither Detroit nor New York before World War I did the archdiocese establish city-church organizations dedicated to social reform and social service. While the two archdiocesan chanceries responded in various ways to the urgent economic and social demands of the age, such responses were generally unfocused and unsustained.

This Catholic-Protestant contrast in terms of church policy was reflective of a more fundamental contrast in terms of their social settings. Urban Protestants, caught up in one degree or another with "reform" and the cause of moral uplift, mostly embraced an idealist view, projecting no less than a transformation of American urban life. In a phrase popular among movement adherents, the aim was to "Christianize the social order" (Rauschenbusch, 1912). As historian Henry F. May remarks, "This moderately progressive school, often known as the Social Gospel (a term that did not become general until about 1910) achieved a position of great influence in the course of American social thought" (May, 1949: 170). Catholic leaders, on the other hand, adopted an essentially realist position. Confronting a wider society heavily imbued with nativist, anti-Catholic opinion, and acutely conscious of their still-insecure status in American life, the American bishops displayed little interest in appeals for social transformations or other similarly naive notions. Thus, while the Progressive Era Protestant church bodies were typically expansive and optimistic, America's Catholic chanceries were typically cautious and defensive in their approach toward the larger scene. That fundamental difference in outlook had implications for church social action.

Formation of the Detroit Council of Churches

Metropolitan church federations of this period, comprised chiefly though not always exclusively of Protestants, are referenced in essentially all published accounts of the Social Gospel movement. Yet, as suggested above, the last word has not been written regarding their formation and early development. One can, therefore, fruitfully examine their wider urban settings at the point just prior to and immediately following their inception for evidence of possible public policy impacts.

The Detroit Council of Churches of Christ emerged in the aftermath of World War I, "the Great War," interpreted by the DCC founders as signifying "the value and imperative need for co-operative effort and centralized direction. The Allied armies had the same supreme purpose in view—the winning of the war" (Gleiss, 1924: 5). Although the archival accounts relating to the council's inception are devoid of references to Detroit government and politics, there is indirect evidence to suggest that its leaders believed themselves engaged in a war of sorts in their wider setting. The council's early leaders could not have been unaware or indifferent, for example, to the fact that after 1910 major issues involving the liquor business in the city were being decided by the Detroit Common Council, and that in a typical year, 1916, the council issued twice as many saloon licenses as were legally allowable under state law (Ramsay, 1944: 26). The liquor industry, Protestantism's archenemy, exercised political influence over Detroit government far out of proportion to its numbers or of any positive contribution it might make to the local economy.

The Detroit church federation originated in a vote taken at the November 1918 meeting of the Pastors Union of Detroit "looking toward the formation of a comprehensive and aggressive council of churches" (Gleiss, 1924). The group's leaders thereupon engaged in intense discussions and ended up approving a church federation plan for submission to the constituency. In May 1919, representatives of nine mainline denominations met at the Woodward Avenue Baptist Church (the church attended during his lifetime by Hazen S. Pingree) for purposes of organizing the Detroit Council of Churches of Christ. After beginning operations, the federation quickly expanded: within five years' time its number of constituent denominations had increased to fifteen, and its annual budget, initially $10,000, to $54,000 (Gleiss, 1924: 11). Social Gospel goals were prominent on its agenda. Among the group's fourteen standing committees in 1924, the names of several convey a pronounced "movement" flavor: Social Service, Public Welfare and Law Enforcement, Industrial Relations (chaired, incidentally, by the then-obscure Rev. Reinhold Niebuhr), Race Relations and International Goodwill, and the Committee of One Hundred (a body dedicated to promoting "good citizenship and law enforcement"). A council board member in these early years, and the chair of its public affairs committee, was one Pliny W. Marsh, who would later become a civic notable.

It was perhaps not pure coincidence that the same month, November 1918, should see both the first decisive step toward formation of a Detroit church federation and a vote by the local electorate on a proposed new city charter. The charter referendum was approved by a wide margin, thus bringing to a close a period dating back to at least 1875 characterized by mediocrity and petty corruption in Detroit city government. Evidently, the public was intent on attacking the old order at its roots and on replacing it with a new regime that held out some prospect for fundamental civic betterment.

Spearheading the charter-reform effort was a group of socially elite Detroit citizens. In 1912, the Detroit Citizens League was founded at a meeting held at one of Detroit's more prominent Presbyterian churches. The group's initial leader was the president of the Cadillac Motor Car Company,

Henry M. Leland—a forceful, energetic, and highly intelligent individual. The league was originally a federation of Protestant men's clubs pledged to banishing the saloon influence from local politics and electing "good men" to public office. Its original name, "Detroit Civic Uplift League," was reflective of that religious backing. (This name was later abandoned in favor of "Citizens League" in the face of sarcasm and ridicule in the local press.) The league was managed in top-down fashion; its membership, which varied in number between three and five thousand, generally had little say in its policies and decisions. The membership policy was fairly restrictive, which later became a source of friction internally as some members charged the League with needless exclusivity and elitism (Fragnoli, 1980).

Yet the league never ignored or minimized one important constituency, the churches. From 1912 to 1915, church committees, consisting of three members each from contributing congregations, functioned in an advisory capacity. The league secretary, Pliny W. Marsh, was an ardent Republican, an active churchman, and a former attorney for the Michigan Anti-Saloon League (Lovett, 1930: 74). It was Marsh who in 1916 recruited to the staff William P. Lovett, a former Baptist minister and newspaper reporter who had served as publicity director for the Michigan "dry" campaign. Earlier that same year the state's "drys" had secured enactment of the Michigan prohibition amendment.

Determined to avoid the image of self-righteousness and exclusivity that had marked the league's first two years, Marsh steered the organization toward a broad program of charter reform and honest elections. (During this period Leland retreated into the background, focusing more on fund-raising than on strategy or daily operations.) Marsh and Lovett were insistent that the league should avoid the image of a purely business-oriented, "moral forces" focus but instead should stress the charter's potential benefit to all city residents. The charter's eventual adoption with broad support—Protestant and Catholic, immigrant and native-born—amounted to a vindication of that approach.

The Protestant churches were central to the league's campaign. In contrast to the cool, reasoned analysis used in appealing to the general public, the league's rhetoric in addressing church audiences was highly moralistic. "The fate of the movement," Lovett declared in one such setting, "depends on whether Christian citizens are alert or asleep. If we are at the polls we shall win—you can help God answer your prayers in that way" (quoted in Fragnoli, 1980: 127). Having legally banished the saloon (in the 1916 legislation), Lovett insisted that the "moral forces" in Detroit now must take the next logical step—

charter reform. It is arresting that the league's seven-member board of directors was chosen on the basis of Protestant denominational membership (Lovett, 1930: 81). The process thus paralleled that used in connection with the Detroit Council of Churches, whose board members were likewise denominationally decided.

The pattern of group influence in Detroit government established in the late 1910s would continue into the next decade and even somewhat beyond. The first group of city officials under the 1918 charter consisted almost entirely of reform-minded individuals from the previous government—the mayor a former reform-oriented police commissioner, and six of the nine council members former allies in the fight against the Vote Swappers League. In no case did a supporter of the old order achieve citywide office under the new charter. The Citizens League and other blue-ribbon civic associations—all comprised of native-born whites, well-to-do if not actually wealthy, mainly though not exclusively Protestant, and progressive in the tradition of Theodore Roosevelt—remained the largest source of outside pressure on city government (Ramsay 1944: 114, 295). The Detroit Citizens League and the Detroit Council of Churches maintained their close relationship, with both remaining committed to municipal reform principles (Ramsay, 1944: 129). From the outset, concern over the saloon and the entrenched sway of "wets" over Detroit municipal government was the common element linking the two organizations. That linkage would persist even after Congress's adoption of the Volstead Act (1919) and the subsequent ratification of the Eighteenth Amendment, which forbad the manufacture, sale, import, or export of intoxicating liquors.

The role of government in all this emerges as highly significant. Protestant concern over the power of liquor interests in Detroit government had existed for many years before 1910 without evoking much by way of a collective response. Beginning at that point, however, with the arrival of "positive" government in the city, what was once viewed as tolerable became less and less so. The churches roused themselves. Their eventual success came partially as a result of their own campaigning and partially on the basis of the ineptitude of the city's "old order." With charter reform dominating the local political scene in 1917–18, the Royal Ark group mounted but a feeble defense. The pro-charter movement was successful in all voting precincts, including heavily Catholic and Democratic ones where one might have anticipated that the "wets" would prevail (Ramsay, 1944).

Formation of the New York City Church Federation

The New York City counterpart to the above-described Detroit events occurred roughly two decades earlier, at the dawn of the Progressive Era. At a meeting held at the Alumni Club of the Union Theological Seminary in November 1895, representatives of New York Protestantism, including both churches and various lay-led Protestant welfare groups, voted into existence the "Federation of Churches and Christian Workers of New York City."

Two factors, one where government had indirect impact and the other more direct, underlay this initiative: European migration occurring on such a massive scale as to profoundly alter the New York social landscape and the effectiveness of New York City's municipal government. As brought out in an account written a decade later by the Rev. Walter Laidlaw, the federation's original executive director:

> In the ten years 1890 to 1900 the city added more population than the whole population of London in 1801. People with their eyes open saw this increase in progress when the Federation was started. They saw another thing: New York had more foreigners than any other large American city. . . . By 1900 New York's foreign born had grown to exceed all the foreigners of Boston, Baltimore, Philadelphia, Chicago and St. Louis put together, and New York was more foreign than any of them. (Laidlaw, 1906: 301)

The founders of the Federation of Churches were clearly dismayed by this picture. A 1906 account of the group's origins published in their house organ notes, "Protestantism has relatively lost ground in New York in recent years." The unsigned statement goes on to plead that the Federation of Churches should endeavor to "prepare the way to usher in a new era of success in reaching the shifting, heterogeneous population of its great metropolis, and ministering to their social and religious needs" ("Historic Sketch," 1905: 5).

As a means of achieving this objective, the founders resolved that the new organization should develop a plan of cooperation among New York's churches and Protestant institutions. The Council should undertake research aimed at determining the number and place of residence of the city's unchurched families and individuals, and should draw any appropriate conclusions. Walter Laidlaw, upon assuming his duties as staff director in September 1896, launched a series of "scientific surveys" of the New York City population. These pioneering studies identified for the first time the precise religious composition of the city, by neighborhood and by borough, and attracted much favorable attention both inside and outside the Council.

The expanding scope and content of municipal and state policy, especially the strong encouragement given by government to mass European migration, became a factor in the church council's, and especially Laidlaw's, early work. The overseas migration to New York City was neither entirely spontaneous nor entirely promoted by the business interests that stood directly to gain from the influx of persons willing to work for long hours at low wages. Government, especially state and municipal but also to some extent federal, was also involved. In the 1850s, about two million immigrants moved through the Port of New York. In 1855 New York State established an official immigration center at Castle Garden, an unused facility at the southern tip of Manhattan. At the same time, a new official entity, the New York State Board of Emigration, was established to oversee the Castle Garden operations and to eliminate the exorbitant charges and fraudulent practices that had colored the previous, entirely private, system. Castle Garden eventually proved inadequate, and in 1892 the state opened Ellis Island, the country's most famous immigration station. New York and some other states along the eastern seaboard sent agents to Europe to attract settlers. For its part, the federal government cooperated by permitting unlimited foreign immigration, save Chinese and Japanese migrants whose numbers were sharply limited through immigration restriction statutes enacted beginning in 1882. In short, governments at the state, local, and federal levels were involved in helping to enlarge, and indirectly to disrupt, New York City's preexisting population pattern.

A second motive was also evidently involved in the church federation's inception, although to document this point one must rely on indirect evidence. It is highly plausible that the founders were motivated in part by alarm over the ineffectiveness of city government in the months leading up to the group's inception. In 1894–95, the city's reform forces reached a peak of agitation and anxiety. One issue of great moment in their eyes was the condition of the city's public schools. A powerful reform coalition comprised of prominent individuals such as Seth Low and other (mostly Republican) leaders, and groups such as the New York State Chamber of Commerce, lobbied the legislature in Albany to centralize control over New York City's public schools under a board of education and a powerful, professionally trained board of superintendents. This action would, it was hoped, reduce if not entirely eliminate Tammany Hall's long-standing practice of using the school system as a source of patronage jobs for Democratic Party faithful. In April 1896, lawmakers in Albany acquiesced to this demand by authorizing the establishment of a new system of school administration for the city.

Some of New York's leading Protestant clergymen were active in this school-reform campaign. The Reverend Dr. Charles H. Parkhurst, an anti-vice crusader and arguably the city's most prominent late-nineteenth-century clergyman, charged in his organ, the *City Vigilant,* that the existing boards of ward trustees were "nurseries where political aspirants serve a novitiate" (quoted in Hammack, 1982: 263). Another Protestant publication, the *Critic,* used similar language to charge that the existing system served Tammany Hall's interests at the expense of an educated citizenry. Both the Protestant Episcopal Bishop of New York, Henry Codman Potter, and the Rector of St. George's Episcopal Church, William S. Rainsford, raised their voices to denounce the existing ward-based school arrangement (Hammack, 1982: 281).

The school issue represented a special case of a larger concern, namely the practice of installing unprofessional and ill-qualified Tammany Hall supporters into key posts in city agencies. While not a new practice—indeed, it dated back years, even decades—public agitation over the spoils system mounted as the scale of city government expanded, touching the lives of the average citizen in ways not previously experienced. It is no accident that 1895 saw the publication of the Rev. Mr. Parkhurst's polemic, *Our Fight With Tammany,* and that John D. Townsend's 1901 indictment of the existing order, *New York in Bondage,* concerned itself largely with events of the same 1894–95 period. In 1894, the Townsend group, which styled itself "The Independent Country Organization of New York City," filed a petition with the state legislature detailing allegations of graft and venality in no fewer than ten city departments. In a chapter of his book titled "1895," Townsend agonizes over the fact that the reform forces in the city, having succeeded in the elections of the preceding November in electing as mayor a reform-minded Republican, William L. Strong, had since fallen victim to apathy and disarray. "The strength that came with victory," he ruminates, "together with the immense power conferred upon our mayor by the legislature, seemed to have bred in reformers a confidence in their own strength utterly out of proportion. They were actually weak because in certain ways they had become strong" (Townsend, 1901: 208–9). Mayor Strong's time in office was brief, 1896–98, and during that single term he managed to infuriate both Tammany Hall, through his nonpartisan distribution of patronage and strict enforcement of Sunday blue laws, and his erstwhile reform supporters, who lamented his refusal to use the mayor's removal power in an aggressive way to weed out incompetents and time-servers in the municipal service. It appears that civic reformers were alarmed at this time as perhaps never before in the past, and that church leaders were aware of this mood, and to an extent involved in it.

It is, therefore, quite likely that the Protestant clergy and laypeople who assembled in November 1895 and created an interdenominational church council for New York City were animated in part by a shared concern over the poor quality of municipal governance and public morals in the metropolis. Their new organization would logically take up, as one of its primary goals, the cause of civic uplift and alleviation of the city's malaise. Support for this interpretation can be found in the church federation's "Historic Sketch," published a decade after its formation, which notes that the group was then operating through several departments, one of them devoted to "representing the city in regard to moral issues" ("Historic Sketch," 1905: 28).

New York and Detroit Catholicism in the Reform Age

As mentioned above, American Catholicism responded to the era of social Christianity partly through the formation of new, mostly lay-led, Catholic organizations and, in a more muted way, through actions taken by the nation's Catholic bishops. The literature on this topic hints at the possibility that these actions occurred in the wake of certain fairly aggressive government actions—state, local, and national. The discussion to follow explores this theme, beginning with Detroit.

In a highly illuminating discussion, Leslie Tentler observes that the devastating depression of the mid-1890s, which left as much as one-third of the Detroit workforce unemployed, had surprisingly little impact on the number and scope of parish-based Catholic charity efforts in the city. The burden of even token relief was simply too great for the average parish, and instead city government augmented its existing system of relief for the poor. "Many Catholics," Tentler notes, "were accustomed to turn to the city rather than the parish in times of need" (Tentler, 1990: 225). Still, the depression of the mid-1890s shook such people's complacency, and helped pave the way for a more sophisticated church effort in the areas of relief and social reform. Increasing numbers of Catholics came to believe that more was required of them than simply token assistance and good advice. This changing mood was embodied in 1906 with the formation of the St. Mary's Aid Society (the first truly interparochial group to appear in the city). The year 1913 witnessed the formation of the Barat Club, a Catholic response to the critical shortage of housing in the city (Tentler, 1990: 225–26). Of special interest is the case of the League of Catholic Women, a genuinely interparochial group formed in 1915 as a rechristening of the Weinman Settlement Association—formed seven years previously as an aid group for Italian and Syrian residents on Detroit's near east side. The League embodied the more humane impulses of the Progressive Era and was passionate in its commitment to the amelioration of social conditions.

Of special interest for present purposes was the League's heavy involvement with the Detroit Juvenile Court, where its members served as probation officers and oversaw the placement of children in foster homes (Tentler, 1990: 226–27). This court's existence gave the fledgling women's organization a sense of focus that it otherwise would have lacked. It is useful, then, to observe that this court was at the time a recent addition to the array of Detroit municipal services. The world's first full-fledged juvenile court had been created in Cook County (Chicago) in 1899. Though the creation of this new mechanism for dealing with juvenile offenders, child advocates hoped to avoid the stigma of a criminal conviction (Trattner, 1994: 127). Michigan was among the states that took an early and lively interest in the Chicago experiment, and in 1905 the Michigan legislature enacted Public Act 312, "To Regulate the Control of Delinquent, Neglected, and Juvenile Children and to Establish Juvenile Courts." This statute mandated that Michigan counties with populations over one hundred thousand should assign one judge exclusively to juvenile cases and should designate a "juvenile court" for their handling. Detroit acted promptly in compliance with this state mandate, appointing its first juvenile judge in 1907 and two years thereafter establishing a full juvenile court with an investigator and a probation officer (soon increased to four officers) assigned to it full time.

It is understandable that the League of Catholic Women should take keen interest in this newly formed unit of government. As early as 1911, 83 percent of the individuals brought before the juvenile judge, Henry S. Hulbert—most of them for offenses like truancy, larceny, and destruction of property—were children of foreign-born parents (*Detroit Saturday Night,* February 25, 1911: 3, 6). While the religious composition of this client population is unknown, the large proportion of immigrant parentage suggests that many, perhaps most, were of southern- and east-European heritage (that is, Polish or Italian), and therefore mostly Catholic. Had the League not acted as it did, the Detroit Association of Charities, a Protestant group, would most likely have assumed chief responsibility for the care and placement of juvenile offenders, Catholic and non-Catholic alike. While the Catholic

Women's League was far more than simply a satellite of the city juvenile justice system, and probably would have formed even in the juvenile court's absence, the group would not likely have achieved the prominence it did nor survived for so long after its reformulation in 1915 had the court not been in the picture.

Archdiocesan Caution in a Threatening Atmosphere

If response to an expanding government was reflected in the behavior of the religiously active Catholic laity of Detroit and New York, such influence can also be detected, though at lower intensity, in the behavior of the two cities' Catholic archbishops. The hierarchy's reaction to government was usually more reactive than planned and deliberate, and was usually not accompanied by any marked evidence of political sophistication. Yet government did "disturb" the archdiocesan chanceries in the two cities, as the following discussion documents.

For essentially all of the Progressive period, the Catholic Church in each city was ruled by a single individual: New York by Archbishop (later Cardinal) John Murphy Farley, who reigned from 1902 until his death in 1918 (between 1895 and 1902 he had served as Auxiliary Bishop of New York); and Detroit by Bishop John Samuel Foley, who served from 1888 until his death in the same year as Farley's. Even though both men were dedicated priests and reasonably competent administrators, neither displayed much originality nor courage, especially in the later years of their episcopates. Of Farley, Thomas Shelley remarks that "the last ten years of his administration in New York were played out in the shadow of *Pascendi* [a 1907 papal encyclical which denounced modernism in the strongest terms and condemned various unnamed Catholic "partisans of error"], with integrist reaction growing stronger every year" (Shelley, 1992: 360). In regard to Foley, Tentler concludes that he acted imprudently in case of three intra-Church disputes during his tenure: the 1893 case of Father Dominic Kolasinski, the pastor of St. Albertus (Polish) parish; the 1893 "Church Farm" case; and the 1896 case of Father Francis Kennedy, pastor of St. John's Church in Ypsilanti (Tentler, 1990: 126–36). While stressing that any judgement of Foley should be tempered in the light of various extenuating circumstances, Tentler still concludes that "these three cases reveal a side to Foley that was narrow, vindictive, and resistant to compromise" (Tentler, 1990: 135).

Given their cautious temperaments, it is not surprising that neither bishop reacted with any great vigor to the sectarian political struggles of the time and their menacing anti-Catholic overtones. As the decade of the 1890s opened, tensions mounted between Catholic representatives and their opponents in both the New York State and Michigan legislatures. Lawmakers there were approaching a showdown over the school question and the issue of whether or not Catholic and other sectarian schools should be allowed to survive. In New York, an energetic anti-Catholic organization, the National League for the Protection of American Institutions (NLPAI), led by its general secretary, the Rev. James M. King, pastor of New York's Union Methodist Episcopal Church, exerted considerable influence in Albany. The NLPAI's Michigan counterpart was the American Protective Association (APA), a group founded in Clinton, Iowa, in 1887 with fervent anti-Catholic objectives and that found in Michigan especially fertile ground (Pratt, 1967: chap. 9; Tentler, 1990: chap. 10). The details of the protracted struggles in the two legislatures need not concern this discussion. It does bear mentioning, however, that the NLPAI and the APA both ultimately met defeat and the interests of Catholic schooling were vindicated.

In these struggles, which went to the heart of the Catholic Church's political interests, one observes in both Farley and Foley an absence of sustained interest or commitment. The activities of the NLPAI stimulated Catholic organizational efforts in their own defense in the New York legislature, but Archbishop Farley was not notably involved (Pratt, 1967: 239). The Detroit chancery under Bishop Foley was somewhat more energetic, with a major chancery campaign, ultimately successful, mounted against the Jamison Bill. (That bill, introduced in 1895, would have stripped Catholic bishops of the right to hold church property in their own names, as was the traditional practice.) But to fight the suggested legislation, Tentler notes, "Bishop Foley had to overcome what was, given the times, an astonishing degree of political ignorance" (1990: 269). The bishop was not aware, and had to be told by state senator John Donovan, that there were but two Catholics in the Michigan legislature (Donovan and one other) and that only a single other member might be readily persuaded to embrace the chancery point of view. Furthermore, Foley was unable to secure unanimous support for his campaign among the priesthood. For example, Father Peter Baart, a Detroit priest known for his opposition to growing episcopal power, lobbied in support of Jamison's bill.

Both bishops were inclined to subordinate church access at city hall and the state house to the maintenance of their episcopal authority in cases where the two aims apparently conflicted. In the early 1900s, Cardinal Farley, alarmed over criticism directed at him from Rome over an alleged weakness in handling "modernist" tendencies in the New York Archdiocese, headed for safe ground. In 1903, he responded in a peculiar manner when the newly elected mayor of New York, George McClellan Jr., a reform-minded Democrat, asked him if he wished to recommend any Catholics for appointments as city commissioners. Farley responded that he would prefer the appointment of "fair-minded Protestants." This delighted the mayor, who hailed the prelate as "a very broad-minded, liberal, fine old man" (McClellan, 1956: 237–38). Commenting on this incident, Shelley remarks that the bishop's decision was not based on any precocious ecumenism but on a canny speculation that Catholics of the kind McClellan would appoint would bend over backward in their effort to avoid the appearance of favoring their own church, and the church would suffer as a consequence (Shelley, 1992: 361). The cardinal, it seems, had problems enough with members of his own flock without having to respond to, from his standpoint, burdensome independent-minded Catholics in high-level governmental posts. It did not mitigate the difficulty, apparently, that McClellan was prepared to accept whatever Catholics Farley might wish to recommend to him. Better to have Protestants.

Still, this wary stance toward the political order did not wholly insulate the bishops and their ecclesiastical interests from government-related disturbances. Beginning around 1900, New York State expanded its social welfare involvement and became increasingly concerned for the well-being of state-subsidized clients served by sectarian welfare institutions. In the last years of Cardinal Farley's New York episcopate, a series of highly critical state and city investigations into Catholic charitable institutions caused a crisis in the archdiocese. In a series of official probes that began in 1910, the City Department of Charities and the New York State Board of Charities unearthed evidence of widespread abuses at private charitable institutions. While Catholic institutions were not the only ones so charged, they were the largest single category. The charges were spelled out in a pamphlet written up and distributed by the commissioner of the city agency, John A. Kingsbury. Even though the Archdiocese of New York and the Diocese of Brooklyn both grew impressively in size at this time, the revelations rocked each ecclesiastical body. Largely in response to the scandals, Cardinal Farley's successor, Patrick Cardinal Hayes, in 1920 reorganized the several hundred charitable institutions and agencies in the archdiocese as the "Catholic Charities of the Archdiocese of New York." It proved a major turning point. The newly formed church agency soon developed a reputation for professionalism and went on to play an important role in the development of Catholic social service nationally (Sharp, 1954: 108; "Catholic Church," *Encyclopedia of the City of New York,* 1993).

Early Evolutionary Changes

Government influenced the above-described religious groups, not only in the period preceding their formation, but also in their fledgling stage to follow. Thus, the 1897 state legislation that provided for the establishment of Greater New York City indirectly prodded the [Catholic] Diocese of Brooklyn and Archdiocese of New York into closer collaboration. The increased amity was necessitated by the fact that Brooklyn and Queens, governed by the Diocese of Brooklyn, and Manhattan, the Bronx, and Staten Island, governed by the Archdiocese of New York, were now united as boroughs of the larger city. In Detroit, the Council of Churches and the Citizens League remained closely connected throughout the 1920s, thus maintaining a unity of civic purpose developed in the charter-reform crusade of the late 1910s. Yet the clearest case, perhaps, of public policy impact on religious-group behavior during a group's fledgling stage is the case of New York's Federation of Churches and Christian Workers.

Government policy impacted the New York church federation in several ways. In 1925, in line with the city's expanded boundaries, this group renamed itself "The Greater New York Federation of Churches." City consolidation also indirectly affected the scope of the church group's scientific surveys. The NYFCCW's first such survey, conducted in 1897, focused narrowly upon the Fifteenth Assembly District in Manhattan, and was thus restricted to "old" New York. Its subsequent surveys accepted no such boundary restrictions, but instead encompassed neighborhoods in all five boroughs—seventy-seven neighborhoods by 1902, including ones in Brooklyn and Queens.

Direct evidence is lacking, but it is highly probable that such vigorous expansion on the part of a group distinctly "New York" in its origins was viewed with trepidation by Protestants in Brooklyn, the self-identified "City of Churches" and home of the city's oldest Protestant church organization, the Brooklyn Church and Mission Society. Brooklyn residents had long resisted the late-nineteenth-century consolidation movement, fearing that, as noted in an early 1890s editorial in a local newspaper, the *Brooklyn Eagle,* it would "destroy the homogeneously Protestant character of the city" (quoted in "Consolidation," *Encyclopedia of the City of New York,* 1993). Interviews conducted with Brooklyn Protestants in recent years evidence considerable mistrust on their part over a perceived New York dominance of their purported equal partnership. Such feelings were quite possibly also present in this earliest period of Protestant organization, an atmosphere that, again, resulted indirectly from government's expanding role.

Moreover, the growing scale and sophistication of government indirectly impacted the scientific methodology employed by Laidlaw and his associates for their neighborhood surveys. In 1898, the church federation abandoned the laborious hand-count method of tabulating the information employed in its initial studies and in its place adopted a mechanical system involving the use of punched cards—an approach revolutionary for the times, and a predecessor of the modern computer. The story behind this technical innovation is instructive.

Visiting the NYC Board of Health one day to procure some routine information, Laidlaw noticed an electrical machine being used by a city employee, Dr. Roger S. Tracy, to tabulate New York City death rates. The federation director realized at once that his own tabulations might benefit from the use of this equipment. Following this visit, Laidlaw sent a copy of the federation's first report to Hermann Hollerith, the president of the Tabulating Machine Company, the machine's manufacturer, requesting that Hollerith let him know the terms upon which a similar machine might be placed at the federation's disposal. The response was gratifying. Not only would one be provided, but it would be free of charge. The church federation thus became the country's first private voluntary organization to employ this useful tool in its work.

The Hollerith machine had emerged through a series of events over several decades, and it is useful to observe that its development was government-inspired. The agency in this case was the U.S. Census Bureau, which sponsored Hollerith's early efforts beginning in 1881 and which he continued for another decade.

Conclusion

The Progressive Era constitutes a turning point in the histories of both New York and Detroit and in the environments of their churches, both Catholic and Protestant. The leading Protestant denominations in the two cities responded overtly to the new setting with the formation of well-funded, city-wide church federations. The Catholic response was more muted, with strong organizational reactions occurring among laypeople but with the two archdiocesan hierarchies remaining cautious and change-resistant. Whereas Protestant leaders were consciously aware of the unsettled and disturbed urban situation and acted accordingly, Catholic leaders, while aware of the wider changes, were inclined to regard the situation with greater equanimity, and dealt with the changes through various adjustments rather than policy innovations or structural alterations. Yet even they were not immune to the impact of expanding city and state government, as evidenced by the stresses experienced by the New York Archdiocese following the official probes of the city's Catholic charities and eleemosynary institutions.

It would be misleading, however, to apply the term "disturbance" to each and every instance of church-government interaction documented in this chapter, if by "disturbance" one intends a disruption to an existing institution and a felt need on the institution's part to restore a preexisting social balance. "Disturbance" in that sense applied to the formation of certain of the groups mentioned here: the Detroit Council of Churches, the [Detroit] Catholic Women's League, the Federation of Churches and Christian Workers of New York, and the Catholic Charities of the Archdiocese of New York. Yet in other cases government entered the picture in the role of facilitator, as a benign presence whose outputs were embraced by church leaders as a useful adjunct in the furtherance of their own self-defined objectives. An example of this interaction was the New York church federation following its formation in 1895.

The New York City and Detroit political environments at this time were basically akin. Both cities employed the partisan ballot in the election of mayors and city council members, both used ward-based or borough-based election systems, both embraced the party patronage (or "spoils") systems for appointment to city offices, and both occasionally elected reform mayors, such as Pingree in Detroit and McClellan in New York, who confronted the machine and resisted its intrusions, but who, after leaving office, were succeeded by others more amenable to the machine and inclined to do its bidding. Beginning in 1919 when Detroit's new charter went into effect, thereby launching a new regime in the city, the two cities' political cultures would begin to diverge, and more sharply so with the passage of time. Yet no clear contrast between the two cases marked the Progressive period as a whole.

2

Churches, Government, and the Great Depression

The Depression of the 1930s rocked America's urban churches to their foundations and called into question the adequacy of existing mechanisms for dealing with social problems and relating to city and state political institutions. In the preceding decade, the country's citywide church federations, while connected in certain ways to local and state governments, had dealt with them mostly episodically and from a distance. While it is true that religious groups were fairly assertive in expressing themselves on moral and ethical issues—with church representatives typically being given a respectful hearing when they approached city hall or the state capitol—there were limits to such involvement. In a survey of twenty-six urban church federations conducted in the last pre-Depression year, 1929, the sociologist H. Paul Douglass found voluntary organizations of this type to be involved with government in various ways. Their divisions of social welfare were in fairly routine contact with state and local authorities in the social service field, and the federations often took responsibility for helping to adjust the tripartite relations between local sectarian welfare agencies, government, and parish churches (Douglass, 1930: 384–409; see also Cayton and Nishi, 1955: 64). Outside the social service field, church groups often gave voice to the churches' "social ideals," with government—local, state, and national—serving as the usual target audience. "When the federations sound the slogan, 'the promotion of moral and social welfare,' Douglass commented, "they almost always mean attempts to influence government" (Douglass, 1930: 374).

Nevertheless, such linkages, while pervasive, remained mostly fragile and unstable. Did the Great Depression change that pattern in some essential way? While the American church history literature (for example, Smith, Handy, and Loetscher, 1963) treats the Depression and New Deal era in some detail, the standard sources are ambiguous as to whether the developments of this period affected the nation's urban churches in any long-term, fundamental sense. Indeed, this literature can be interpreted as suggesting that the effect was transitory and that church-state relations in the nation's urban centers and elsewhere returned to an earlier pattern with the passing of the national emergency and with the United States's subsequent entry into World War II. The New Deal, it should be noted, was mostly transitional: a very large proportion of the policies were justified by the emergency conditions of the time, and there was no intention of sustaining them beyond that point.

The present chapter tests a contrasting hypothesis: the possibility that a major watershed occurred in the 1930s with consequences for both churches and public authorities alike. In other words, the premise is that the Depression-related expansion of urban government was more than just temporary in the two cities under discussion, and instead involved a fresh mode of relating: one that would persist, in one form or another, over time. The concept of disturbance remains relevant in this context. I am sensitive to the possibility that in the 1930s externally generated disturbances may have affected religious-group behavior, especially among those religious structures not so secure or mature as to be invulnerable to Depression-related rather than government changes.

The Depression in National Perspective

The stock market crash of 1929, followed by the onset of the Great Depression in 1930, affected all segments of American society. The nation's index of factory employment reached a pre-Depression high of 110.3 in September 1929, from which point it plummeted: to an average of 92.4 in 1930, to 78.1 in 1931, to 66.3 in 1932 before finally bottoming out at 62.3 in March 1933 (Schneider and Deutsch, 1969: 294). By that year, over 15 million Americans, 25 percent of the total workforce, were unemployed. In March 1933, with the nation's entire banking system in danger of collapse, President Roosevelt declared a bank holiday, thus gravely threatening the life savings of millions of ordinary citizens.

The extent of change occurring at this time in municipal and state government can scarcely be overstated. Prior to the Depression, public welfare agencies had been involved only nominally in institutional services—chiefly in the maintenance of almshouses, poor farms, and county homes. They also provided pauper relief and, in some cases, old-age pensions—always at a bare subsistence level. Yet under the crisis conditions of the 1930s, governments were forced to become proactive. This decade saw the establishment of sixteen state departments of public welfare, nine boards of control, fourteen supervisory boards, and six state child-welfare agencies (Cayton and Nishi, 1955: 29–30). These new agencies, and their existing counterparts elsewhere in American state government, became the conduits for New Deal-generated federal relief funding.

The Depression era and its child, the New Deal, attracted the attention of the nation's church leaders and aroused much religious comment. Catholic leaders found the Depression compellingly important. "For the first time," one analyst notes, "the nation's bishops were faced with a national crisis for which a response was readily provided by Catholic social teaching" (Byrnes, 1991: 28). The National Catholic Welfare Conference provided a national platform to publicize the church's response to the crisis, and in 1933 the American bishops issued a pastoral letter applying Pope Pius XI's teaching, *Quadragesimo Anno,* to the U.S. economy (Byrnes, 1991: 29). Speaking for the nation's Protestant denominations, the Federal Council of Churches, in a 1932 statement entitled "Revised Social Ideals," formally amended the group's 1908 "Social Creed." The organization now advocated a wide array of liberal goals, including social planning and social control of credit, social security legislation, reduction in hours of labor, the right of workers to engage in collective bargaining, and the abolition of child labor. Implicit in the 1932 statement was an acceptance of expanded federal authority and the "positive state."

Despite this basic similarity in regard to the Depression, the two religious communities differed in their reactions to the New Deal. America's mainline Protestant bodies, represented at the national level by the Federal Council of Churches, were supportive of the New Deal and its underlying philosophy. Thus, Franklin D. Roosevelt, while campaigning for president in October 1932, declared in a Detroit speech that he was "as radical as the Federal Council," and a year later, speaking as the nation's president at the Federal Council's twenty-fifth anniversary celebration in New York, FDR equated the ideals of the church and the government. Protestant intellectuals identified with the FCC wrote books ardently defending the New Deal, which included two by Benson Y. Landis, *The Third American Revolution* (1933) and *Must the Nation Plan?* (1934), and one by F. Ernest Johnson, *Economics and the Good Life* (1934). The Catholic Church and the Catholic bishops, on the other hand, were not totally integrated into the New Deal. The Detroit radio priest Father Charles Coughlin offered an alternative Catholic position in anti-New Deal diatribes, especially after 1934, and the New Deal was subjected to withering editorial attack in the nation's leading Catholic publication, the *Brooklyn Tablet.* (These two Catholic voices differed chiefly in that whereas Coughlin accused FDR of being a Communist, the *Tablet* forbore applying that label.) The Catholic hierarchy, as leaders of an immigrant church, centered their political activity at the local level, and the bishops were hostile to any permanent extension of national power (Byrnes, 1991: 29). Yet such reservations from official and semi-official Catholic sources did not typically call into question expanded government per se but only expansion at the federal level—a point to be kept in mind in the discussion to follow.

The Great Depression in New York and Detroit

The Depression affected communities of all sizes, but most seriously the nation's large cities. In both Detroit and New York it was estimated that at the depth of the Depression a third of the workforce was unemployed. In New York, over 800,000 were being aided by public or private charity by 1932, and 1 million by 1934. By 1932, the city's soup kitchens and municipal lodging houses for the homeless were crowded beyond capacity, with lodgings and meals to indigent individuals serving into the hundreds of thousands, even the millions. As the crisis deepened, the lines of harassed and hungry New Yorkers became increasingly familiar sights. In New York State as a whole, the number of factory wage earners dropped from 1.1 million in 1929 to 733,000 in 1933, while wages over the same period shrank by more than half (Schneider and Deutsch, 1969: 294–96). In Detroit, the picture was the same. The Depression in Detroit was accompanied by layoffs, drastic reductions in the length of the workweek, and hyper-deflation. The burden placed on the city by welfare expenditures rose astronomically; while in late 1929 city officials estimated that the relief load would not exceed 3,500 families, by January of the following year 12,500 families were receiving assistance, and by the end of 1931 that figure had increased over ten times. The very high rate of tax delinquency forced the city to borrow in order to meet immediate expenses, and by 1932 the municipality was spending 40 percent of its budget for debt service. The Depression reached its most devastating point during the early weeks of 1933 when one-third of the Detroit workforce was jobless, and evidences of despair were everywhere apparent (Glazer, 1965: 97–98).

The general public's initial response to the Depression in both cities was to deal with the emergency through private charity. In New York, two of the city's oldest philanthropic societies, the Association for Improving the Conditions of the Poor and the Charity Organization Society, both essentially Protestant groups, were the first to accept the challenge to provide jobs for the unemployed. After first attempting to act independently, in September 1930 the two joined hands to create the Emergency Unemployment Committee, generally known as the "Prosser Committee" after its chairman, Seward Prosser, the chairman of Bankers Trust Company. This effort eventually raised some $8.5 million with assistance from both Catholic Charities and the Jewish Social Services Association, suggesting that its efforts were not perceived as exclusively sectarian Protestant. The Committee formed a private agency known as the Emergency Work Bureau that distributed the funds on a city-wide basis (Blumberg, 1979: 19).

In Detroit, the board members of the Detroit Council of Churches were typical of the city's social notables in reacting initially by organizing a job-seeking effort aimed at their own constituency. In March 1930, the Council's board addressed a resolution to the city's ministers pleading "for help in securing odd jobs—such as work about the house, on the lawn, in the garage, etc.—for the great army of worthy unemployed in our city." (DCC board minutes, 1930, Walter Reuther Archives, Wayne State University). The response to this appeal, in the words of the DCC president, Paul H. King, was "pathetically insignificant." Determined to secure a more positive local-church commitment, King in April 1930 wrote local ministers in the most strenuous terms: "We beg you to lay this matter on the hearts of your people and to urge them to advise the Office of the Council of Churches *in writing* concerning any work which they can offer to the unemployed . . . Please make this appeal personal and individual" (King to ministers, April 4, 1930, Reuther Archives). Yet in the end this and all other private efforts were little more than palliative. As the Depression deepened it became recognized that government alone possessed resources on a scale commensurate with the need. Thus, demands upon government became ever more frequent and urgent.

In October 1930, the mayor of New York, James J. Walker, created the Mayor's Official Committee for the Relief of the Unemployed and Needy, and in its eight months of existence this group raised $1.6 million, chiefly from contributions by city employees and from private donations. Most of the relief was furnished in-kind, and the New York City Police Department was given chief responsibility for its distribution, with police precincts serving as relief stations.

In 1931, when the Prosser Committee's funds were exhausted sooner than expected, New York City responded to urgent demands that it establish a municipal work-relief program under the authority granted to cities through state legislation enacted in 1919. With the establishment in April 1931 of the New York work relief program, the city's resources for the first time were committed in a major way; the New York Board of Aldermen authorized an appropriation of $8 million for this purpose (Schneider and Deutsch, 1969: 298–301).

In Detroit, a similar effort was launched. Detroit was one of the few American cities at this time with a strong tradition of public relief, and in this crisis citizens turned to the city in large numbers. An emergency agency, the Mayor's Unemployment Committee (MUC) was established in 1930, and it soon earned a favorable record for accomplishment, especially since it was occasionally in a position to take action where the city's Department of Public Welfare was unable to do so (Fine, 1975: 292). Still, the primary responsibility for confronting the Depression crisis remained vested in the Detroit Department of Public Welfare. Detroit's welfare-related municipal spending soared from 1.1 percent of the city budget in the pre-Depression years of 1924–25 to 3.5 percent in 1930, and finally to 9.5 percent in 1938–39 (annual budget, City of Detroit, selected years).

Yet in both Detroit and New York, the city-based relief quickly broke down in the face of an overwhelming demand coupled with a shrinking municipal tax base. Despite the efforts of public officials and the support of local notables, the situation remained extremely serious. In Detroit, the Department of Public Welfare was unable to make adequate provision for even the most desperate families. A 1931 study of families dropped from the city's welfare rolls found that only 25 percent were living on earned income. "The poor were helping the poor," Mayor Frank Murphy lamented, but their resources were limited (Tentler, 1990: 313). In New York, the relief effort undertaken by the municipal government in the 1930–32 period was equally inadequate. Basing her findings on a 1931 survey of the local New York situation, a social worker, Lillian Brandt, wrote a report that included such phrases as "relief not adequate," "widespread deficiencies of diet," "accumulation of lowered vitality and diseased conditions," "living conditions even less favorable to health and a wholesome family life," "disastrous effects on mental health and moral attitudes," and "a wholesale pauperizing process" (quoted in Schneider and Deutsch, 1969: 301–2).

With the resources of state governments no less overwhelmed, the nation's cities, New York and Detroit included, had no choice other than to appeal for help from Washington. President Herbert Hoover feared that federal relief would undermine the "spirit of responsibility" of state and local government and charitable organizations while also impairing the character of recipients. Detroit's Mayor Frank Murphy did everything in his power to combat such thinking. In early 1931 he appealed for federal unemployment insurance and old-age pensions as a means by which Washington could aid the cities, and a few weeks later voiced his support of a petition to the president for a special session of Congress to provide federal relief (Fine, 1975: 343–44). The Hoover administration was unpersuaded by the appeals for federal aid, but in January 1932 the president did reluctantly approve direct federal relief for the unemployed through a newly created Reconstruction Finance Corporation (RFC). Such funds came with strings attached, including the fact that they could not be given to unemployed persons who were not in institutions.

The advent of the New Deal in March 1933, with its program of "Relief, Recovery, and Reform," finally brought the federal government squarely to the center. Not only was federal welfare spending now significantly increased, but the earlier restrictions were removed and eligibility for relief was expanded to include rent, clothing, fuel, and medical care costs. Fiorello La Guardia, who had been elected mayor of New York in November 1933 after a decade of service in the U.S. House of Representatives, accepted an invitation from Harry Hopkins, one of President Roosevelt's most trusted lieutenants, to help plan the new Civil Works Administration. Within days of his election as mayor, and weeks before taking office, La Guardia was helping design the most significant program of urban assistance in U.S. history. In his visit to Washington late that November, the mayor-elect was also greeted by another close associate of the president, Harold Ickes, the director of the Public Works Administration, who was then beginning to make large-scale public works allocations. La Guardia succeeded in securing for New York City an ample allotment from Washington's massive federal relief program (Kessler, 1989: 294). Detroit mayor Frank Murphy would almost certainly have acted in similar fashion, except that FDR, within days of his assuming the presidency, appointed Murphy—a strong FDR supporter during the 1932 presidential campaign—to the post of governor general of the Philippines, thus abruptly ending Murphy's mayoral career.

Catholic Responses to the Great Depression

As the dispensers of federal aid and the focus of urgent demands from the general public, municipal government in both New York and Detroit became increasingly linked to both the social service departments of citywide church federations and to the chanceries and charity departments of Catholic dioceses. The leading Catholic bodies in the two cities also responded to the needs of their constituents created by the economic crisis.

New York

There is no in-depth published account devoted to the Archdiocese of New York in the Depression, but Monsignor Florence Cahalan's brief account offers some useful insight. In regard to the Depression, Cahalan makes three things clear: first, Catholic Charities was hard hit by the Depression, with ever fewer contributors available to help fund an ever-increasing demand; second, the Depression emergency forced Patrick Cardinal Hayes to make "a permanent change in his fund-raising procedure" with the formation in 1933 of a Special Gifts Committee that tightened and centralized the fund-raising process; and third, the cardinal and other archdiocesan officials devoted considerable time and action to interacting with government, especially state government, to cope with the emergency (Cahalan, 1983: 253). In 1931, New York became the first state to help local government units meet their welfare commitment through the provision of grants of money—a development that impacted the work of Hayes's Special Gifts Committee. Cardinal Hayes chose Al Smith—a leading Catholic layman and former governor of the state—to head the committee. There were richer New York Catholics than Smith, and if wealth alone had been the cardinal's main concern, he might well have selected otherwise. (One thinks, for example, of Joseph P. Kennedy—a multimillionaire New York Catholic real estate magnate, later to become better known as the father of President John F. Kennedy.) Yet Hayes chose Smith, presumably on the basis of the latter's close connections to the New York political establishment and national prominence as the 1928 Democratic nominee for U.S. president—the first Catholic to be nominated by a major party. Smith was a leading contender to be nominated by the Democrats again in 1932.

Brooklyn

As earlier noted, New York Catholicism is bifurcated between the Archdiocese of New York and the Diocese of Brooklyn. A church historian, John K. Sharp (1954), has provided a useful history of the latter ecclesiastical body, including treatment of the Great Depression and New Deal eras, and the section to follow summarizes his findings.

By 1930, Brooklyn's Catholic population comprised 35 percent of the borough's total, surpassing the Protestant population (32 percent) and the Jewish (31 percent). (In 1900, Brooklyn Protestants had outnumbered Catholics by an almost two-to-one margin.) The Diocese of Brooklyn was unique on the basis of its very crowded population—denser per square mile than any other diocese in the United States save one. Throughout the first three decades of the twentieth century, the diocese maintained a number of charity institutions to which, in most cases, state aid was provided. Yet from the late nineteenth century onward, diocesan leaders voiced repeated complaints that the public aid provided was far short of their actual costs. For example, in 1911 the state paid $165,000 to the Catholic Orphan Asylum Society when the ordinary expenses of the society were almost double that figure. Evidently, in the pre-Depression era, relations between the diocese and public officials, while fairly extensive, were neither especially cordial nor mutually supportive.

At the time of the 1929 stock market crash, the Catholic bishop of Brooklyn, the Very Reverend Thomas E. Molloy, was forty-five years old. As the magnitude of the Depression emergency became clear in the weeks and months to follow, Molloy acted quickly. In 1930 he reorganized the Bureau of Diocesan Charities into a more highly professional Diocesan Commission on Catholic Charities with clearly defined functional divisions. A younger priest, Monsignor J. Jerome Reddy, was appointed as its executive secretary. The following year, the bishop acted to enlarge the number of active conferences of the Society of St. Vincent de Paul while also organizing a lay committee to more adequately finance the diocese's growing charities budget.

Significant for present purposes is the fact that these and other administrative changes were quickly followed by expanded diocesan linkages with agencies of the city and state government. The Catholic Charities Commission of the Brooklyn Diocese now enlarged its ties with the local and state courts and with other public welfare agencies, while also making advantageous use of the newly enacted state social welfare legislation. The Commission's Division of Family Welfare began 1930 by assuming much of the work previously performed by the St. Vincent de Paul Society, including expanded casework in the local courts. Following the enactment in 1931 of the State Emergency Aid Act, the diocesan family welfare division secured public funding for families in their homes. Additional state legislation in 1933 enabled the welfare division to provide allowances for dependent mothers. The Brooklyn Diocese organized Catholic Big Brothers in 1933, and that unit was soon deeply enmeshed in providing assistance to juvenile delinquents assigned them by the courts. Finally, as the city and state governments erected new courts, diocesan organizations stepped forward to serve as points of referral of cases involving children and adolescents (Sharp, 1954: 226–39).

These increases in governmental contacts were accompanied by an apparent warming in the diocesan-city relationship. Patrick Scanlon, the editor of the nation's largest Catholic publication, the *Brooklyn Tablet,* which operated under the aegis although not the actual direction of the Brooklyn diocese, voiced his opposition to the Roosevelt New Deal, which he warned would lead eventually to a "Prussian Junker state." Yet in making this case, Scanlon upheld the authority vested in state (and by implication municipal) government, since the states "could be held to a stricter accountability to the wishes of the people . . . " (McNamara, 1994: 23). The fact that New York was governed by a succession of Catholic mayors from 1914 to 1934—John Puroy Mitchell, John Hylan, James J. Walker, and John O'Brien—probably contributed to this trend toward expanded Catholic Church–urban government relations. (The city had never had a Catholic mayor before 1914.)

Another significant Depression-era development in New York was the ending of any genuine claim to power on the part of the city's "native American" Protestants. (In this context, "native American"—or occasionally "Yankee" or "old stock"—is a commonly used term to denote Protestants of wealth, old-family business and social prominence, as opposed to African Americans and nonelite whites.) Of the seventeen mayors elected since the formation of the Greater City until the present, seven have been Protestant, two Jewish, and the other eight Catholic. New York has had but three Protestant mayors since 1914 (La Guardia, Lindsay, and Dinkins). However, as Theodore Lowi reveals in an insightful discussion, from the formation of the Greater City in 1897 through the 1920s, native American Protestants and Irish together comprised between 60 and 70 percent of all mayoral cabinet appointments while all other ethnic categories combined never yielded over 15 or 20 percent of the top appointments (Lowi, 1964). Many old stock Americans in the pre-Depression era continued to serve as party leaders or functionaries, and they contributed heavily to the treasuries of both parties—this despite the fact that Protestants were a steadily declining fraction of the city's population.

This era ended in the early 1930s. Beginning with James J. Walker and through the end of the 1950s, every New York mayor save one (La Guardia) appointed mostly Catholics to his mayoral cabinet, usually by a wide margin over Protestants (Lowi, 1964: 35). While there is nothing to suggest that

Church leaders were parties to these partisan political calculations, one can reasonably infer that Church interests indirectly benefitted from them. The Church has been a major player in the New York political arena from the 1930s to the present.

Detroit

As was true in New York, the Catholic Archdiocese of Detroit was deeply affected by the Great Depression, but here the political implications were rather different. As was typical across the country, the resources of the archdiocese, and also of individual parishes, were quickly overwhelmed by a tide of destitute, mostly working-class, individuals. Reports flowed in to Catholic parishes of alarming destitution and despair among the faithful. The pastor of Our Lady of Help parish reported, for example, "Of the 286 families who are represented in our school, 150 are in the bread line" (quoted in Tentler, 1990: 315). As the Depression deepened, Detroit Catholic leaders became alarmed that increasingly desperate individuals might be drawn to extremist movements.

The archdiocese's initial response to the Depression consisted in appeals to affluent Catholics to be unstinting in their charity. Those in a position to give were asked to contribute generously to parish-based relief efforts as well as to the Community Fund Drive, fourteen of whose beneficiaries were citywide Catholic agencies. Catholic leaders were generally accepting of the conventional wisdom that the emergency would swiftly run its course. Thus, at the March 1930 quarterly meeting of the Society of St. Vincent de Paul, the executive secretary, James Fitzgerald, assured his listeners that the bottom of the economic crisis had been reached and that better times were near. In such depressions, he went on, the Society "thrives," and its "real spirit of charity" becomes manifest (*Michigan Catholic,* March 13, 1930).

Such optimism in the face of adversity was soon to vanish, however. Early in 1933, in the closing weeks of the Hoover administration, a local priest wrote despairingly to Archbishop Michael Gallagher, "In 1931 we were told that we were at bottom . . . [yet now] we find ourselves a great deal lower than ever, and whether we are at the bottom or not God alone knows. Homes in towns and country continue to be lost and evictions are becoming more and more numerous. . . . Our people are drained dry; yes, bled white" (quoted in Tentler, 1990: 315). Gallagher appealed to Washington for federal bank deposit insurance and for "public works on a vast scale," but he did so with little hope that the Hoover administration, now in its twilight, would listen. While the inauguration of Franklin D. Roosevelt in March 1933 brought a dramatic increase in federal relief, it would be months before such aid would reach Detroit in substantial amounts, and even at that point the city's relief effort would remain heavily dependent upon local resources.

By mid-1930 the full magnitude and prolonged character of the nation's economic crisis had become apparent, and Bishop Gallagher and other Catholic leaders fashioned a response intended to alleviate the widespread distress among the faithful. It consisted partly in reenergizing the existing array of lay-led Catholic charities, of which the largest and most visible were the previously mentioned League of Catholic Women, formed in 1915, and the Society of St. Vincent de Paul, whose Detroit presence dates from the 1880s. Both these groups now greatly expanded their relief efforts. Yet such groups' long-standing autonomy and resistance to chancery oversight inhibited their developing a unified Catholic strategy. Bishop Gallagher was therefore obliged to act through the chancery directly, establishing under direct archdiocesan auspices, for example, a soup kitchen (the "Catholic Free Kitchen") at 540 Monroe Street. This facility served more than five hundred individuals at its first meal. Collaboration among the various Catholic agencies scarcely extended beyond the bishop's annual appeals, as promulgated in a full-page advertisement in the *Michigan Catholic,* which pled for clergy and laity participation in the city's Community Fund.

Yet as the Depression deepened, all such purely church efforts were forced to confront a mounting, often unbearable, financial burden. Parishes that could not pay their teachers or meet interest payments on their mortgages were in no position to pay any but nominal taxes to the chancery. In the 1920s Gallagher had encouraged parishes to build on a generous scale in order to accommodate future population growth, and the parishes had borrowed extensively. That policy now came back to haunt him as church bankruptcies soared. The collapse of Detroit banks in 1933 brought matters to a crisis, for the archdiocese had its funds frozen in insolvent institutions. By 1935 the archdiocese was effectively bankrupt and was desperate to find a banker prepared to refinance the entire diocesan debt. The situation did not improve with time. In January 1937, when Bishop Gallagher died, the Detroit Archdiocese was in financial chaos (Tentler, 1990: 316–19).

This somber picture underscored the importance of a second, and for present purposes more arresting, aspect of the Catholic response to the Depression emergency. It consisted in the close, even symbiotic, relationship that developed between Catholic charity organizations and the city of Detroit—

a development facilitated when Frank Murphy became mayor in a special election held in 1930. Detroit Catholics for the most part took great pride in Murphy, who helped symbolize their group's coming of age. He had burst upon the local political scene in 1923 in a successful campaign for election as a Detroit recorders court judge, one that had pitted him and three allies, all of them immigrants and lower-class in background, against an entrenched group of four sitting judges, all middle-class, "good government" Protestants who enjoyed the backing of the Detroit Citizens' League. Among the latter, one was the above-mentioned Pliny Marsh. Not surprisingly, perhaps, the Detroit Council of Churches threw its weight into the fray behind the Citizens' League–backed candidates (Fine, 1975: 110). The 1923 election was an instance of what Banfield and Wilson refer to in a classic study (1963) as the "two cultures" of municipal politics—the "good government" culture, which stresses the virtues of honesty, efficiency, impartiality, and strict enforcement of laws against vice, and the "immigrant ethos," which is more tolerant of vice and is less concerned with good government in the middle-class sense.

Anti-Catholicism figured in the 1923 election as it did in the subsequent 1930 mayoral campaign. The special election that brought Murphy to the mayor's office resulted from a corruption scandal involving his predecessor, Charles Bowles, who had been elected to office in 1929. Undeterred by the scandal or the subsequent recall, Bowles announced his mayoral candidacy in the special election, and proclaimed his Protestantism in hopes of securing a political edge. That tactic failed, and Murphy was elected by a comfortable margin.

Murphy's appeal to Detroit Catholics went beyond his immigrant origins and Catholic roots. He stressed in his speeches that his political views were rooted in Catholic theology, especially in papal encyclicals, which he viewed as providing "moral signposts." The encyclical *Rerum Novarum,* with its admonition that government should be placed at the service of humanity, impressed him greatly. Murphy took this as the basis for his fight for social justice through social action, for the redistribution of purchasing power, and for the removal of the basic causes of destitution and dependency (Fine, 1975: 254). Detroit had seen previous Catholic mayors, but none so steeped as he in Catholic thought or as organically connected to Catholic and other immigrant voters.

Murphy's assumption of office on September 23, 1930, was, therefore, an occasion for celebration among members of the local Catholic hierarchy and lay-led Catholic organizations alike. Under a headline, "Detroit Tackles Great Task," the *Michigan Catholic* editorialized: "Every one interested in the progress of Detroit and the welfare of all its people will rejoice at the splendid cooperation given Mayor Murphy's committee on unemployment and the energy with which it is tackling this critical problem . . . Detroit is doing what can be done to alleviate the situation, and it is fortunate in having a social-minded mayor" (*TMC,* October 2, 1930: 4). Early the following December, Bishop Gallagher, in a letter addressed to all pastors in the city, referred to the mayor in terms that bordered on the reverential: "His honor, the mayor of Detroit, has issued a proclamation urging the people of our city to send their used clothing of every description to his relief committee or the clothes bureau of the Society of St. Vincent de Paul in order to meet the growing demand for assistance" (*TMC,* December 18, 1930: 1). And after Murphy had served a year in office, Gallagher told a mutual friend, the radio preacher Father Charles Coughlin, that Murphy had been "a godsend to Detroit . . . and to the Catholic church during these troubled times." The bishop held unswervingly to this view until his death six years later (Fine, 1975: 454–55).

There is no indication that in seeking to alleviate Detroit's economic crisis Mayor Murphy discriminated against other religious faiths. Still, the Murphy administration was assiduous in maintaining contact with Catholic leaders and in addressing their needs and concerns. In December 1932, the mayor named the Rev. Edward Hickey, a faculty member at Detroit's Sacred Heart Seminary, to the post of chairman of the Mayor's Unemployment Committee. (Hickey was the third person to hold this office; the earlier two had been G. Hall Roosevelt, a cousin of New York governor Franklin D. Roosevelt and a close Murphy associate, and the Rev. Frank D. Adams, a Universalist minister.) Furthermore, the director of the city's Department of Public Welfare, John F. Ballenger, a Catholic, was a frequent attendee of the quarterly meetings of the Society of St. Vincent de Paul, where he addressed the delegates on the progress of the city's family relief and on related concerns.

While the principle of church-state separation obviously prevented the city and Wayne County from directly aiding churches or church-affiliated organizations, no constitutional barrier existed to prevent city and county aid going directly to individuals, many of them served by Catholic charities. Such aid benefitted such organizations indirectly, as it relieved some of the demand for their services. With assistance from the Murphy administration, programs of this type now expanded. In late 1932, the executive secretary of the Society of St. Vincent de Paul announced that the society had distributed 142 tons of flour, and that plans were in place to continue the distribution of farm produce through the society's central office. All such efforts were predicated on cooperation from Detroit's Department of Public Welfare. For example, it was announced at the St. Vincent de Paul Society's December 1993 meeting that material relief had been furnished to more than 4,700 families, or over 25,000 individuals, with about 50 percent of the funding from "special grants obtained from the federal government." Furthermore, the Society's child-care department in the same year had disbursed $208,000, of which about half was derived from Detroit Juvenile Court and from Wayne County (*TMC,* December 14, 1933: 1–2).

The Depression emergency exposed numerous gaps and inconsistencies in Catholic social service. An overlapping of roles among Detroit's Catholic charities, and related waste and duplication of effort, became a source of concern for Archbishop (later Cardinal) Edward Mooney, who succeeded Gallagher following the latter's death in January 1937. Mooney looked upon centralized control of Catholic charitable work as essential toward insuring that such work was done efficiently and in a manner responsive to emergent social problems. He was convinced of the need for clerical as opposed to lay control of Catholic enterprises; priests represented the church in a way not open to the laity. Thus, during the Mooney years, Catholic charities and Catholic education alike were brought firmly under chancery supervision. In addition, Mooney moved to strengthen chancery control over an already well-disciplined corps of priests. Every priest in the diocese was visited by a chancery representative in 1940, and again in 1943 and 1954, to insure proper compliance with its directives and expectations (Tentler, 1990: 350–52).

It is highly plausible that Cardinal Mooney's insistence on diocesan centralization reflected an awareness on his part of the increased importance of government and of the desirability that church representatives be in a position to deal with government from a position of authority. Even though not as close to the Detroit mayors of his era as Bishop Gallagher had been in his, Mooney had observed firsthand the Roosevelt presidency and drew from it certain conclusions that in his mind were relevant to the Detroit case. Mooney's experience in the nation's capital predated his appointment as bishop. From 1936 to 1939 he served as chairman of the Administrative Board of the National Catholic Welfare Conference (NCWC), and he would remain a board member throughout the 1940s. Along with two others, Cincinnati's John McNichols and Chicago's Samuel Stritch, Mooney was a dominant figure in the NCWC, and it was he especially who exerted influence over his fellow American bishops on public policy issues during the war years and immediate postwar era (Tentler, 1990: 352–53). A man in his position would have understood that a widely disparate set of Detroit Catholic organizations, whose separateness might have been justified in earlier and simpler times, was no longer adequate to the Church's interests in an era of positive government and economic turbulence. Unity of command could help alleviate that deficiency while promoting the Church's long-term interests. It would be an enduring legacy of his tenure in office.

Summarizing the Depression-era experience of all three Catholic dioceses—New York, Brooklyn, and Detroit—one can say that city and state leaders, on the one hand, and Catholic Church leaders, on the other, were made aware as never before of their interlocked interests and policy concerns. Whatever the reservations of Catholic leaders regarding the Roosevelt New Deal and the emergence of "positive" government nationally did not apply at the local level, where a parallel expansion in state and municipal government was also occurring, facilitated by federal dollars. In the two cities under discussion, Catholic leaders evidently found the state-local expansion congenial to their policy views and compatible with their ecclesiastical and organizational interests.

Protestant Responses

The picture outlined above of Catholic diocesan Depression-related responses in Brooklyn, New York, and Detroit was paralleled only in part by their Protestant citywide counterparts. In both New York and Detroit the Protestant response to that emergency differed from the Catholic in certain fundamental ways.

New York

In 1935, the Greater New York Federation of Churches, with some 1,100 member churches, was by far the largest Protestant federation of its kind in the metropolis. (Two other smaller federations also existed, the Brooklyn Church and Mission Society and the Queens Federation of Churches, the former older than the GNYFC and independent, and the latter, formed in 1930, a GNYFC offshoot body still at that time dependent on the parent group's patronage.) Yet the GNYFC's size did not shield it from serious trouble in this time of economic emergency; the national downturn severely affected the group's finances. Out of a total budget of slightly under $50,000 for the year ending January 15, 1936, the group reported a net loss of $5,300. It was further reported that the preceding year, 1934, had seen a loss of just under

$10,000 and that "accumulated deficits" for the years previous to 1934 stood at $17,500 (*1935 Annual Report,* GNYFC, July 1936: 16). Clearly, the federation was staggered by its Depression-related financial vicissitudes. The annual report makes clear that the church federation by 1935 was regularly in contact with an array of city and state agencies, but that its own diminished resources presented difficulties in fully exploiting those official contacts. Two sentences in the report are revealing: "Quite naturally the Federation becomes the gate of approach to the churches on the part of various [groups and official agencies]. . . . Unfortunately, because of the limitation of human ability, the response of the Federation has *too often been most inadequate*" (*1935 Annual Report:* 3).

Protestantism's Social Welfare Impasse

The church federation's problems were not limited to inadequacies of funding and staffing, nor to its related inability adequately to fulfill its mission—all of which could be considered temporary and likely to improve with the return of general prosperity. Problems of a more deep-seated nature were also present. As presented in a probing discussion by Leonard Stidley (1944), the federation's leaders for some years had been involved in an effort to bring coherence and unity to Protestant social work in the metropolis. This problem had its roots in events dating back to the decade previous, which require brief recapitulation at this point.

In 1921, Protestant leaders involved in the social welfare field launched a new organization: the Federation of Institutions Caring for Protestant Children. This agency was the outgrowth of a meeting called the previous September by the New York City commissioner of welfare, Bird S. Coler, and held in his office. The meeting was attended by Coler and the representatives of New York's Protestant agencies then in receipt of monies from the city and state. The commissioner suggested that the participants agree to the establishment of a child-care advisory committee to be comprised of representatives of the three major faiths, and pointed out to them that New York's Jewish and Roman Catholic children's agencies were already grouped into coordinating bodies—the former into the Jewish Philanthropic Societies of New York (formed in 1916) and the latter into the Catholic Charities of the Archdiocese of New York (formed earlier that year, 1920). The existence of these agencies was proving its value from a public policy standpoint. For example, Jewish and Catholic representation on various social welfare advisory committees could now be easily arranged. Yet in the case of Protestants, there was no single agency to call upon. Coler therefore proposed, and the agency representatives finally agreed, that the above-named Protestant coordinating body be formed. In 1925, the fledgling agency was renamed the "Federation of Agencies Caring for Protestants," and in 1931—in the midst of the Depression—it became the "Federation of Protestant Welfare Agencies" (FPWA), a name that would persist.

As welfare work became more formalized and professionalized under FPWA auspices, pressure mounted for it to mesh operations with the Greater New York Federation of Churches (the larger of the two) and the Brooklyn Church and Mission Society (the smaller). Despite repeated attempts throughout the 1920s, those efforts came to naught: social workers were distrustful of the clergy people who predominated in the church federations, and the clergy were often unprepared to accept what the social workers were trying to do. Disputes over power and authority within a merged organization added fuel to the controversy. Thus New York Protestant leaders entered the Depression era still at loggerheads with government agencies in the vital area of social service.

As the Depression deepened, all three Protestant federations (FPWA, GNYFC, and the Brooklyn Church and Mission Society) increased their involvement in efforts to combat economic hardship among their clients and constituents, and that, in turn, further highlighted the interorganizational malaise. The Greater New York Federation of Churches had established, in 1927, a social service department. Now, with the onset of the Depression, that unit was upgraded and renamed "Protestant Social Service" and its mission expanded beyond the child welfare area. The wider Protestant public became increasingly confused and frustrated by the resulting intergroup rivalry. For example, the minutes of a Federation of Protestant Welfare Agencies board meeting held in 1936 record that: "The Federation of Churches reaches into the social welfare field and often issues statements upon social questions. This has resulted in overlapping and confusion in the public mind as to where the real leadership of Protestant social service lies . . . " (quoted in Stidley, 1944: 53).

Concern over this duplication of agency effort and overlapping of agency missions soon came to the attention of New York city officials. Once again, as in 1920, the city demanded fuller Protestant cooperation, with city officials pointing out the artificiality of any sharp distinction between church work and sectarian social work. Nowhere was this view more strongly expressed than by Mayor Fiorello La Guardia following his assumption of office in 1934. As

Flanagan remarks: "As the Federation of Protestant Welfare Agencies developed, the Mayor of the City of New York turned now to the Federation of Agencies, now to the Federation of Churches, and, being an Episcopalian, now to Bishop [William] Manning, meanwhile complaining about the lack of unity among the Protestant groups" (Flanagan, 1948: 132). In the wake of this mayoral intervention, some Protestants protested La Guardia's reliance on Manning, the Episcopal bishop of New York and a high church Anglican, as the city's Protestant spokesman. To this the mayor shot back, denouncing the lack of any authorized Protestant central body (Flanagan, 1948: 73). The mayor wished to see the churches positively involved in meeting the Depression crisis, but he was frustrated by the intra-Protestant structural barriers.

Finally, in the face of the continuing pressure, the leaders of the various federations acquiesced in the logic of the situation. In 1936, the Protestant church federations agreed to relinquish their social welfare work to the FPWA in exchange for securing representation on the FPWA's board of directors. While this move was nominally a quid pro quo, it involved greater political gains for the FPWA, which henceforth would serve as Protestantism's official agency for dealings with city and state welfare departments (Stidley, 1944: 53). This apparent FPWA success stemmed in part from its superior financial resources. Whereas the federation of agencies survived the Depression in good financial shape, aided by the continuing the support of well-to-do business and professional people and a nearly $1 million bequest conferred on it in 1929 from the estate of Henry Baldwin, the church federations suffered severely, as pointed out above in the case of the GNYFC. Moreover, both the greater New York and the Brooklyn federations were beset by recurrent internal tensions. Their left-leaning and socially activist directors—Searle and the Rev. J. Henry Carpenter, respectively—encountered recurrent complaints from conservatively inclined board members over their alleged "socialist" and "communist" tendencies (Flanagan, 1948).

The 1936 interorganizational agreement resolved certain problems but left others unattended, and with a view toward resolving them discussions soon resumed among the various federation leaders that would continue well into the 1940s. Their results are discussed later. For present purposes, the point to be emphasized is that the Greater New York Federation of Churches proved unable to capitalize on the Depression-related expansion of city and state social welfare programs in the manner, for example, of New York Catholicism. The GNYFC's fraught relations with the FPWA were partly responsible for that, but there were other factors as well.

The GNYFC might have survived the 1930s in better shape had it been successful in establishing satisfactory relations with New York politicians and lawmakers. Yet on the basis of fragmentary evidence, it appears that such relations were anything but good. As was generally the case throughout the non-southern United States, the partisan leanings of New York Protestants were decidedly Republican. That leaning was well known, and to an extent accepted by the mostly Democratic New York political elite. Its existence did not wholly prevent Protestant leaders from wielding a measure of political influence, especially during the La Guardia years. Still, it could not have been helpful to the GNYFC's political standing to have it reported in the *New York Times* at the height of the 1932 presidential race—one in which New York's Democratic governor, Franklin Roosevelt, was pitted against the incumbent president, Herbert Hoover—that the GNYFC had taken a straw poll at one of its meetings, and that out of 206 votes cast Hoover had received 177, the Socialist candidate, Norman Thomas, 25, and FDR but 3. The remaining single vote was cast for an "unknown" (*New York Times,* November 1, 1932: 14). While this poll obviously did not formally commit the organization, local politicians could logically conclude that the poll participants, presumably a cross-section of the GNYFC constituency, were prepared to abandon their home-state governor, and a devout Episcopalian, in favor of an outsider.

It could not have been politically helpful, either, that in the early Depression period the GNYFC reiterated its long-standing support for strict enforcement of New York State's "dry" laws (*New York Times,* February 4, 1930: 14)—at a time when public support for the dry position was waning and leading politicians, FDR included, were increasingly supportive of Prohibition's repeal. The GNYFC must have paid a political price for its continued advocacy of the "noble experiment," which the American electorate in growing numbers now considered burdensome and ultimately unwise.

Detroit

Differing views are possible, but one can make a strong case that the Depression-era behavior of the Detroit Council of Churches more closely parallels the New York Catholic pattern than it did the Protestant Greater New York Federation of Churches. Admittedly, the DCC resembled the GNYFC in certain respects: a general reputation as Republican in its partisan leanings (this despite Detroit's nonpartisan form of government), strong, consistent support for national Prohibition and the "dry" laws, a drastic decline in revenues during the Depression period—from a pre-Depression high of $42,300 in 1929 to a low of $16,738 in 1933 (archives, Christian Communication Council of Metropolitan Detroit Churches). Still, the record gives no indication that the Detroit church federation experienced anything approaching the internal disruptions and factional strife that marked its New York City counterpart. Despite the revenue decline, the DCC managed to maintain its membership base, which throughout the 1930s varied between seventeen and eighteen Protestant communions—the same range as in the late 1920s—and its complement of full-time staff varied between eight and nine individuals, no different from the pre-Depression year 1929 when the number was nine. Local churches making an annual contribution to the federation remained steady at around four hundred; while the dollar amounts sagged, the number of contributing churches did not. And unlike New York, the Detroit church federation had no outside Protestant welfare federation to contend with, and evidently was under no pressure from public officials to build bridges with other social service organizations in the community. Finally, the DCC seems to have avoided any "political" expressions that might have caused it public embarrassment.

Detroit's nonpartisan system of government, which stood in marked contrast to New York's partisan regime, was evidently a factor in the former's more successful weathering of the Depression emergency. The consolidation of nonpartisan government in Detroit following the adoption of the 1918 city charter significantly impacted Detroit interest groups of all kinds. In the case of the Detroit Council of Churches, it served to moderate the perceived need for a Protestant status group in the city, one aiming to uphold the Protestant banner against other forces in the community, both sectarian and otherwise. Admittedly, in its early years of existence, the DCC had cast itself in a status-group role, as is suggested by the following statement that appeared in its annual reports for the years 1920–23: "The Council has been the agency through which united Protestantism has functioned in all the ways which pertain to the good of the city and the progress of the Kingdom. The Council is the visible expression to the people of Detroit of the spirit of unity which prevails among our denominations" (DCC annual reports, Reuther Archives). In the same vein, the council's first executive director, the Rev. Morton C. Pearson, declared that "these years [1919–24] have witnessed for the first time the power and commanding influence of united Protestantism in the life of this rapidly growing metropolitan community" (quoted in Lennox, 1969: 5).

Beginning in the late 1920s, however, this Protestant emphasis mostly disappears from DCC reports and publications. While remaining Protestant in composition, the group appears to abandon its earlier sectarian edge. Detroit's nonpartisan system of government probably contributed to that apparent change in group self-definition. In contrast to partisan government, which inclines politicians to engage in ticket balancing as a means of placating various ethnic, religious, and minority-group interests, a nonpartisan, at-large system of elections tends to subordinate particularistic concerns to broader, more inclusive themes. For example, a keen observer of the Detroit political scene, Maurice Ramsay, remarks in a 1944 dissertation: "There is no evidence that the British-Canadian group, numerically the largest group of foreign-born in the city, have ever attempted to influence the mayor, nor have the Catholics, who are the dominant religious group" (Ramsay, 1944: 83). "British-Canadian" immigrants, it should be noted, would consist predominantly of Protestants.

The Detroit Council of Churches might well have persisted in a status-group role had its constituency perceived a significant Catholic threat in the city, or if local officials had pressed them, as officials pressed their New York counterparts, for a more unified "Protestant presence" in municipal affairs. Neither of these conditions applied. Ramsay points out that the events of the 1920–29 period should have developed the Catholic political bloc had it been latent. The activities of anti-Catholic groups like the Wayne County Civic Association and the Ku Klux Klan to secure passage of a state constitutional amendment outlawing parochial schools supplied sufficient reason for that kind of Catholic action. Yet "there is nothing to indicate any organized effort either to placate Catholics on the [City] Council, or to create a Catholic block among councilmen" (Ramsay, 1944: 99). The Depression era saw a significant rise in the number of Catholics on the city council: from a low point of two in 1922 to four (among nine to ten members) throughout most of the 1930s. Yet that change resulted, not from any overt campaign to increase Catholic representation in city government, but rather from the rise of the Democratic Party, in which Catholics were especially well represented, in county, state, and national politics; after 1930, the city became consistently and decisively Democratic in state and national politics. Moreover, despite the rise of Catholic representation on the city council, Protestants throughout the 1930s continued to predominate on that body—outnumbering Catholics in every year, unusually by a margin of five to four. In short, nonpartisan government had the indirect effect of maintaining a strong Protestant presence in Detroit and Wayne County government, long after the point that Protestants had ceased to be a majority of the city's population.

It is an interesting question why Detroit Catholics were not more reactive to the wave of anti-Catholicism that marked this period, including the possible formation of Catholic defense groups intended to ward off the perceived threat and to return the situation to relative normalcy. Part of the explanation was internal to the Catholic community. As Jo Ellen Vinyard points out in an insightful analysis, individual Catholics had long taken leading roles in Detroit high society. The Irish, in particular, were prominent charter members of some of Detroit's more prestigious clubs and civic associations, formed toward the close of the nineteenth century with wealth rather than religion or nationality counting as the important attribute (Vinyard, 1976: 299). Also, the Detroit Archdiocese during the episcopate of Archbishop John Foley (1888–1914) was steadfast in its support of the assimilation of immigrant Catholics. Foley, alarmed by what he considered to be unfounded suspicions on the part of many Protestants toward Catholicism, proclaimed the necessity of religious liberty and religious neutrality in politics. Anxious to reach out beyond Catholicism to the larger community, the archbishop was the first Catholic bishop or archbishop to play a conspicuous role in the city's civic life (Tentler, 1990: 124–25). Presumably, a Catholic self-defense strategy would not have accorded well with that larger objective.

In addition, the city's non-Catholic voluntary organizations and civic elites also contributed something to a general absence of overt sectarian strife. The Detroit Council of Churches and its ally, the Detroit Citizens League, divorced themselves from overt association with anti-Catholicism, and while generally favoring Protestant candidates over Catholics for elective office, they did so without rancor and in language suggestive of civic betterment, not of sectarian advancement. As pointed out in the previous chapter, the Citizens League was successful in attracting voters of diverse ethnic origins, Catholics included, to League-approved policies and candidates. For its part, the DCC mostly withdrew from its initial status-group role in favor of a broader form of Christian ecumenism.

Pattern Persistence through Time

In rounding out this picture, I now return to the question raised at the outset, namely whether the pattern of fairly close church-state relations initiated under the emergency conditions of the '30s persisted into the wartime and post-war era to follow, or whether instead the earlier pre-Depression pattern essentially reemerged, with little by way of long-term change. The evidence summarized below validates the former of these possibilities.

As early as the mid-1930s, the sociologist H. Paul Douglass observed that government was beginning to play an increasing role in shaping American religious faith, with the social service role, until now the domain of churches, increasingly passing over to the state. In the course of this change, Douglass observed, relations between urban churches and local and state governments were becoming more subtle, more complex, and more wide-ranging (Douglass, 1930: 200). Documentary sources from the post-Depression era suggest that the development noted by Douglass was deep and long-lasting in its impact. While data pertinent to this point is not available for all the citywide church bodies covered in this study, what information is available suggests persistence of close church-state interactions more so than otherwise.

In the case of the Detroit Council of Churches, the group's 1944 *Annual Report* documented an extensive array of DCC-government relations—city hospital chaplaincies, juvenile court linkages, the directorship by DCC staff member Edward M. Smith of the city's War Emergency Commission, and other departmental programs the detailing of which space forbids. So pervasive had such linkages become, indeed, that the *Report*'s authors at one point felt obliged to strike a slightly defensive tone: "Suffice it to note that, while the Detroit Council of Churches has made its influence increasingly felt in public affairs in [numerous areas], there has been no ignoring of the primary responsibility of the Christian church in reaching men and women with ever more effective challenge to discipleship with Jesus Christ in loyalty to the plan and purpose of Almighty God" (Detroit Council of Churches, 1944: 3). In short, the church federation gave reassurance that it had not lost sight of its mission.

One gains a better sense of the magnitude of this change from a comparison of the DCC's budgetary priorities in the last pre-Depression year, 1929, with the early and mid-1940s. At the earlier point, the DCC's departments of Social Service, Women's Work, and Hospital Service—the units that logically would be those most governmentally involved—accounted for 18.4 percent of total disbursements ($7,800 out of $42,500), whereas in a typical post-Depression year, 1943, a comparable set of public policy and welfare-related departments (social service, public affairs, hospital chaplaincy, public schools' bible teaching, and war chaplaincy) together accounted for fully 34.7 percent of all disbursements ($15,500 out of $44,700).

With regard to the New York Archdiocese, it is noteworthy that a modern director of Catholic Charities, Monsignor James Murray, remarked in an interview, "For the most part, it was in the '30s that the government became the major, or primary, funding source [for our programs]" (Murray, interview, 1996). There is, unfortunately, no published account as to how this shift may have affected relations between the archdiocese and government—city, state, and national. Yet the effect was likely parallel to that outlined for the Catholic Diocese of Brooklyn by John K. Sharp. His findings demonstrate that the very dense pattern of Catholic Church–city and state government relations in the borough, dating from the 1930s, persisted into the decades to follow (Sharp, 1954).

Finally, with respect to Detroit Catholicism, Tentler observes that the Church, under the guidance of "an increasingly powerful Chancery," in the late 1930s and '40s greatly expanded its involvement in city and state political affairs. In 1942, Michigan's five Catholic bishops jointly agreed to sponsor what amounted to a Catholic lobbyist in Lansing. Two years later the bishops established the Michigan Catholic Welfare Committee, which was expected to monitor state legislative developments and to recommend needed action. This coincided with the continued wartime and postwar growth of professionalism of Catholic charities in the archdiocese (Tentler, 1990: 350–51; 488). In all likelihood, this brought Charities' personnel into increasing contact with their professional peers in city and state welfare agencies.

Conclusion

The information presented supports four conclusions of relevance to the larger themes of this study. Firstly, at the local and state levels the Depression-related welfare programs established in the 1930s did not, with ending of the economic emergency, pass out of existence or shrink to insignificance, but instead laid a basis for expanded cooperation between government agencies and sectarian welfare institutions that, in one form or another, would prove enduring. Clearly, urban residents accepted the premise that the states and municipalities are obliged to play a large, ongoing role in the social welfare field, and that churches and sectarian welfare agencies had a part to play in that process.

Secondly, in the 1930s New York and Detroit diverged ever more widely in terms of the local pattern of relations between churches and sectarian welfare institutions on the one hand, and city and state governments on the other. Consistent with the well-documented contrast in political behavior between "reform" and "machine" cities, ethnic politics remained at the forefront in New York but, in the aftermath of the adoption of the 1918 city charter, and despite occasional sectarian flare-ups, was fairly muted in Detroit. Thus even a deeply committed Catholic like Mayor Frank Murphy refused to play the sectarian card. There is no evidence that he gave any special consideration to Catholic, as opposed to Protestant, civic leaders. In New York, on the other hand, with machine politics tending to push ethno-religious considerations to the fore, the shift in the balance of political power from Protestant to Catholic that began in the late 1910s, and that accelerated after 1930, impacted church leaders directly. It explains, in part, the obvious frustration felt by GNYFC leaders in their dealings with outside organizations, city agencies included.

Thirdly, the Catholic Church and Catholic voluntary organizations in the two cities reacted differently to the Depression and the New Deal as compared to their Protestant counterparts. Despite a generalized Protestant endorsement of the New Deal at the national level, especially among Federal Council of Churches activists, such acceptance did not always apply locally, where traditional principles of liberalism and voluntarism held sway and where acceptance of the newly enacted welfare legislation was more cautious. For their part, Catholic leaders regarded the Depression as an opportunity to apply Catholic social teachings on an unprecedented scale, an attitude that underlay their generally supportive attitude toward expanded local and state government at the time. The Catholic Church was ideologically prepared for the advent of local-level positive government to a degree not paralleled in the Protestant case.

Finally, the concept of "disturbance" is relevant to explaining the apparent behavioral changes among certain of the religious groups discussed. Most significantly, it helps illuminate the behavior of the Greater New York Federation of Churches as that group identified certain threats in its wider environment and sought to develop appropriate responses. They included a tendency to become, among other functions, a Protestant status group. Although still only incipient through the 1930s, such a role would become more concrete in the decades to follow—as detailed in the next chapter.

3

Churches, Civil Rights, and the Great Society

New York and Detroit, their churches included, were deeply affected by the events of the late 1950s and 1960s, including especially the Civil Rights movement and the related Kennedy-Johnson administration's New Frontier and Great Society programs. The Civil Rights movement is generally dated from the 1955 Montgomery bus boycott. This was followed by violence surrounding the 1957 integration of Central High School in Little Rock, which ultimately required the dispatch of National Guard troops under orders from President Eisenhower. In the early and middle 1960s, the march for civil rights for blacks surged across the country, exemplified by the Freedom Rides and demonstrations in Birmingham and Selma, Alabama. At a certain point, northern cities such as Chicago also became the site of civil rights demonstrations. Crucial to the movement's strategy was the federal government, whose involvement was regarded as essential given that blacks could otherwise be intimidated and oppressed by white-dominated local and state governments. Such federal involvement included newly enacted federal legislation, beginning with the fairly weak Civil Rights Act of 1957 and culminating with the much-stronger Civil Rights Act of 1964 and Voting Rights Act of 1965.

Detroit and New York were also impacted at this time by a large-scale expansion in federal domestic spending. Officials in the two cities lobbied Washington for assistance with a fair degree of success. The two cities were first and second, respectively, in the amount of federal aid received in that decade (Sugrue, 1996: 264). The question becomes, therefore, to what extent did the civil rights revolution and the related expansions in federal social programs and grants in aid to cities impact relations between churches and municipal governments in the two cities?

Changes in Local Political Scenes

New York

New York was similar to other large American cities in the 1960s in terms of political changes related to heightened expectations among its racial minorities and the enlargement of community action programs financed, in part, with federal dollars. The policy initiatives coming out of Washington, while momentous from one perspective, never appeared adequate to black and Hispanic Americans, so miserably oppressed for so long. Rising minority-group expectations were now coupled with growing frustration over public program inadequacies and the slow pace of policy change (McNickle, 1993: 193).

New York City managed to avoid a major riot in these years but only narrowly. Its Bedford-Stuyvesant and Harlem neighborhoods saw six days of rioting in July 1964 following the shooting of a black youth by a white police officer, and early in 1965 the *New York Herald Tribune* ran a series entitled "City in Crisis" detailing the accumulation of problems in the city for which no solutions were in sight (McNickle, 1993: 194). New York's success in avoiding a major riot on the scale of Detroit, Los Angeles, Newark, and several other cities was attributable in part to Mayor John Lindsay, who assumed office in 1966 and proceeded to walk the city's black neighborhoods on a nightly summertime basis listening to local residents and helping to calm the situation; the new mayor had an almost magical effect on young blacks. Lindsay won black approval, too, for his establishment of a civilian-controlled police review board—this, despite the strong objections of the NYPD rank-and-file, and the review board's eventual abolition in a citywide referendum. Also involved was the exceptionally skillful use of police riot control and intelligence techniques under Mayor Lindsay's police chief inspector, Sanford Garelik (McNickle, 1993: 216).

If wider national developments were one explanation for the transformation of New York politics in the 1960s, another was a series of developments unique to the city itself. The city entered a new political era after the November 1961 city election in which Mayor Robert Wagner sought reelection for a third term. As Chris McNickle points out in a perceptive discussion, in fifteen of the sixteen city elections between 1909 and 1961 the Democrats had adhered to a standard formula: the nomination for mayor of a Democratic politician of Irish-Catholic descent, sensitive to Jewish concerns about discrimination, honest (or at least perceived to be so), and liberal in social outlook. The success of this strategy depended upon persuading Jewish voters in large numbers to support the (Irish-led) Democratic ticket, and to give Italians, the third spoke in the Democratic wheel, an important place in the ticket-balancing equation (McNickle, 1993: 319–20). Toward the end of this five-decade-long period, however, this strategy was increasingly viewed as problematic given the political emergence of "new" ethnic groups, blacks and Puerto Ricans especially, which strained the traditional arrangements. It was tough to offer something to everyone. Wagner succeeded in his 1961 reelection bid, but the city's politics would never be quite the same again. His success resulted in part from a new constellation of political forces that included, in part, the destruction of Tammany Hall and dismissal of the long-time Tammany boss Carmine DeSapio. Yet if Wagner now cast himself as a "new Democrat," he was also emblematic of the old—Catholic, perceived as Irish even if not technically so, and unshakably honest, even though adroit at playing the political game.

The political formula that began to break down in 1961 was definitely a thing of the past by the early 1970s. Jews demanded, and ultimately achieved, dominance over the party, not merely their traditional role in shaping party policy, and blacks for the first time were accorded some role in the distribution of political rewards, even if not fully commensurate with their long record of Democratic support at the polling booth. African American politicians achieved an increasing number of racial firsts in city and state politics. In 1962, the state Democratic Party nominated Edward Dudley to challenge the GOP incumbent, Louis Lefkowitz, for the office of attorney general—the first black ever chosen by that party for a statewide office. And the Harlem politician J. Raymond Jones was named in 1964 to replace Edward Costykian as the New York County Democratic leader. For a time it appeared that the city would see a new governing coalition built upon Jewish and black votes and based upon a shared experience of bigotry, but events intervened to drive Jews and blacks apart and to prevent any such enduring alliance. Still, the old order was now displaced, seemingly for good, and from this point forward there would be a new mayoral style and governance strategy. Given the declining role of party, New York mayoral leadership came to depend increasingly on an ability to command the mass media and to speak directly to the voting public (Eichenthal, 1990: 63–64).

Detroit

The Detroit scene was no less fundamentally affected than New York by the events of the 1960s. In the city election of 1961, a political unknown, Jerome

Cavanagh, defeated Detroit's incumbent mayor, Louis Miriani, in a reelection bid despite the former's almost total lack of endorsements by the city's political, social, and business elites. Cavanagh, a liberal Catholic in the mold of John F. Kennedy, effectively ended the era of conservative, subtly anti-black dominance at city hall. That era began in 1939 with the mayoralty of Edward Jeffries, who assumed office following the resignation of his predecessor, Richard Reading, in a bribe-taking scandal. Although initially sympathetic to black demands for city jobs, Jeffries turned to the right on race issues after the Detroit riot of 1943 and would remain so for the remainder of his time in office ending in 1948. Thus, from 1943 through 1961, racial conservatives—Jeffries, Eugene I. Van Antwerp, Albert E. Cobo, and Louis Miriani—dominated the mayor's office.

Cavanagh broke with that tradition and sought to rebuild interracial trust and improve black opportunity. That strategy was implicit in Cavanagh's 1963 support for a strong Detroit open housing law, a measure supported by most liberals but strenuously opposed by conservatively inclined neighborhood associations (Sugrue, 1996: 226). As was true of several other mayoral proposals of the time, open housing was finally defeated by the Detroit city council. Cavanagh's liberalism extended to federal civil rights initiatives and New Frontier/Great Society programs, all of which he embraced. In addition, he was a reformer in the Frank Murphy and Hazen Pingree tradition, fighting against corruption and inefficiency in city government and trying to develop mechanisms for citizen participation. He put the city on a sound financial footing by pushing for a city income tax on both residents and nonresidents employed in the city (Conot, 1974: 450–52).

Mayor Cavanagh was elected to a second term in 1965, but it would be his last hurrah. His 1966 bid for Michigan's vacant U.S. Senate seat drew him into a primary fight with Michigan's popular ex-governor G. Mennen Williams, who received the endorsement of organized labor. The primary contest split the state Democratic Party, and Cavanagh ended up losing not only the party nomination but a good deal of his earlier political luster. He also underestimated of the depth of black despair and rage in Detroit. In seeking to cope with urban unrest, he was neither as lucky nor as skillful as his New York City counterpart, John Lindsay, and whether fairly or unfairly, local residents generally held him responsible for the 1967 Detroit riot, the most costly of several urban revolts around this time in American cities. The riot caused much loss of life and property destruction, and it effectively ended Cavanagh's political career.

The Civil Rights era extended beyond Detroit mayoral politics to encompass the community as a whole. Community activists engaged in rising protests against racial discrimination in housing and the workplace. The civil rights leader Martin Luther King Jr. visited Detroit at least once yearly throughout the 1960s to participate in the heavily attended noon Lenten service at Central Methodist Church. In his 1963 visit, King also led nearly 250,000 blacks on a protest march through the city. His last visit came in 1968, just days before his assassination in Memphis. This black militancy met with intensified opposition from "white Detroit," strongly opposed to both civil rights and open housing. In 1965, twenty-five crosses burned throughout the city, and the newly formed Homeowners Rights Organization initiated a campaign to abolish the Detroit Commission on Community Relations. The votes of anti–civil rights whites contributed to the defeat of Michigan's liberal former governor G. Mennen Williams in his November 1966 U.S. Senate bid. Thomas Sugrue argues convincingly that Detroit's racial turmoil of the 1960s was not a product of the liberal social programs of that era but was the culmination of past racial injustices and ghetto isolation, now deeply implanted and festering. Sugrue contends that federal programs launched in the 1930s and '40s that continued into the 1950s and '60s—especially ones administered by the Federal Housing Administration, the Federal Home Loan Bank Board, and the Department of Defense—were a major, if unacknowledged, factor in the charged racial atmosphere and the ultimate 1967 debacle (Sugrue, 1996).

Detroit Protestant Churches in the Civil Rights Era

Detroit's city church federation was deeply affected by the civil rights ferment, and it responded in many ways both tangible and symbolic. The DCC, which in 1962 renamed itself the *Metropolitan* Detroit Council of Churches (MDCC) in acknowledgment of a membership base that now extended beyond the central city, was proactive in confronting the city's racial situation and in affirming commitment to the civil rights cause. The group's house organ, *Detroit Church Newscaster* and documents on file in the Walter Reuther Archives at Wayne State University evidence the fact that no year passed without some expression of MDCC commitment on civil rights. The council participated, for example, in various three-faith appeals for racial integration and open occupancy housing and in 1967 spearheaded the formation of an "Interfaith Council on Racial Justice." The church federation was the chief sponsor of the above-mentioned annual Detroit visitations by Martin Luther King Jr., and its Public Affairs Department, directed by the Rev. H. C. McKinney Jr., was in frequent contact with the Detroit Police Department in efforts to resolve tensions between the department and the city's minority community. The council was a font of position papers, policy statements, and pronouncements on racial justice. Finally, its representatives repeatedly appeared before the Detroit city council on behalf of ordinances related to open housing, fair neighborhood practices, and similar matters. Such commitment is arresting considering that the group was not, as such, a civil rights organization and lacked any significant African American membership.

For reasons not wholly clear, however, the organization showed little apparent interest in, or response to, the expansions occurring at this time in government-sponsored community action and social service programs. While its views on social issues obviously paralleled those of the liberals who occupied the mayor's office (Cavanagh after 1961) and the state governorship (G. Mennen Williams, George Romney, and John Swainson), its newsletters and internal documents suggest that the group was little involved with government in any regular, ongoing way. During the 1960s, no governmental official addressed an MDCC annual meeting or a meeting of one of its associated organizations (for example, the Detroit Pastors Association or the Council of Church Women). The annual report of the executive director, Merrill Lenox, seldom mentions government or politics, and never in a pointed way. While the reports of the MDCC Department of Public Affairs contain occasional references to government agencies—the Detroit Police Department, the Michigan Liquor Control Commission, the Detroit Commission on Human Relations—such references relate only to the agencies' policies and practices, and give no indication of stable, ongoing relationships with the city or state. MDCC contracts with government agencies for the provision of services to local residents were few and of little apparent significance. For example, in the spring of 1967 the Council of Churches, though a Summer Opportunity Action Program, received city authorization for a youth jobs program at forty-four city playgrounds across the city. Yet a close observer, Sidney Fine, suggests that this effort did not amount to much, remarking, "Since the total sum disbursed by the program was $2,760, it is doubtful that anything substantial was achieved" (Fine, 1989: 145). It appears, in other words, that the council at this time had no "elite accommodation" with city agencies, notwithstanding its role as an interest group actively involved in petitioning government on various issues.

One gains further insight into the nature of MDCC-city relations in these years from an account published in the *Detroit Church Newscaster* in the immediate aftermath of the 1967 Detroit riot. The account is a verbatim text of a meeting held in the council's offices between council officials and Mayor Jerome Cavanagh. The interview began with Cavanagh affirming that he has "had the opportunity to work closely with [G. Merrill Lenox] and the members of Council of Churches, both church groups and individual clergymen," and that "we have moved a long way in a couple of years."

While these opening pleasantries could be taken as suggestive of a warm, stable relationship, the mayor's further comments suggest that this was not the case. At one point, Cavanagh remarked that the MDCC "has been fortunate in that it has developed a technique and the ability of making its will known, at least, to the governmental leadership." But he then proceeded to chide the council, pointing out that it has "moved slowly [on low income housing], more slowly than the [Catholic] Archdiocese in Detroit." Even though well-intentioned, the MDCC, he continued, had not succeeded in getting its message out:

> There is a lack of knowledge frequently on the part of too many people, including a tremendous number within the Council of Churches, that don't really recognize some of the policies and the leadership that's been developed and what some of the policies they have been formulating are, at the present time. *I find that Protestant churches out in the community, of which I speak, are really in the dark as to what some of the leadership of the Council of Churches might be doing on a given social project.*

Toward the close of the interview, Cavanagh challenged the MDCC directly:

> I cannot expect, nor should the Council of Churches . . . necessarily agree with me and my judgements . . . , but one thing of which I am at times mildly critical and other times feel even more keenly about . . . is the approach they sometimes use, and that is to communicate with the Mayor, and the leadership of government, through the press. I have had occasion where I've picked up the newspaper and read a story, sometimes a very critical story, and *that was the first occasion that I knew of the Council of Churches' position on the matter. . . . I do think they ought to give government a chance to respond first before trial by press.* (*Church Newscaster,* September 1967: 1 and 5; emphasis added)

Other evidence tends to confirm the mayor's belief that the council was often unable to influence "the Protestant churches . . . in the community" or to communicate its social concerns effectively to its local-church constituency. In the words of one observer, Thomas Sugrue, "Many members of Protestant

Churches paid little heed to the exhortations of the Detroit Council of Churches, particularly those that challenged conventional racial wisdom" (Sugrue, 1996: 192). It was a problem that Council of Churches officers and staff evidently were well aware of. For example, a 1958 Public Affairs Department internal memorandum observes that "unless we can develop organizational clarity on a functional basis, we will continue to waste our limited resources and . . . continue to leave a leadership vacuum. . . ." It went on to point out that "access to responsible denominational leadership familiar with the denominational legislation relating to social issues and public affairs is presently tenuous." Another internal document remarks that "the tie between existing denominational committees and the [DCC] Public Affairs Department is weak" ("Toward Organizational Clarity in Public Affairs" [PAD Position Paper], and Minutes of PAD Meeting of June 25, 1958," MDCC file, Reuther Archives).

In 1964, the church federation's revenue reached an all-time peak of $221,500, an amount adequate to support a full-time staff of fifteen. After that, revenues commenced an inexorable slide—slowly at first but accelerating in the wake of the 1967 riot. By 1970, it was a mere $121,000, which in "real" inflation-adjusted terms, was less than half that of 1964. The MDCC was now forced to slash staff, drastically pare back programs, and draw down its available reserve funds.

Several factors underlay this reversal of fortunes. They included, among other things, declining mainline Protestant church membership nationally, lessened support for the basic concept of councils of churches, and white flight to the Detroit suburbs, where local church support for collaborative efforts such as the MDCC had never been as strong as it was in the central city. An additional factor was also probably involved. The MDCC might have coped more successfully with its troubles had it been more responsive and proactive in relating to government agencies and public officials. A closer linkage with the Cavanagh administration in particular might have benefitted the organization by enhancing its legitimacy in the eyes of constituents and supporters and by enhancing its revenue base.

Despite the MDCC's troubles in certain areas, the group was highly successful in one respect, namely in managing to avoid serious criticism or estrangement from Detroit's African American community. Indeed, there are indications that black leaders generally approved of its strong civil rights commitment. The group was not made a target of ridicule from black militants such as that directed in the late 1960s against the National Council of

Churches of Christ (Pratt, 1972: chapter 10), or that was focused on the Detroit federation's New York City counterpart.

The Civil Rights Era and New York Protestantism

The Civil Rights era deeply impacted the Protestant Council of the City of New York (renamed in 1969 "The Council of Churches of the City of New York," or CCCNY). Such impact was partly a result of major shifts in the city's population. The post–World War II era witnessed an out-migration of middle-class whites from the city: over 400,000 in the 1940s, 1.2 million in the 1950s and another 500,000 in the 1960s. At the same time, an equivalent number of black and Latino migrants moved in. The newly arrived African Americans were overwhelmingly Protestant; in a city whose black population numbered 1.7 million at the beginning of the 1960s, only about 40,000 were Catholic (Gartrell, 1959).

Population shifts were, however, only one of the background factors involved in the events of the 1960s. Several long-planned structural alterations in the city's Protestant church and social welfare organizations, including a major merger, now finally reached fruition. As pointed out in the previous chapter, New York Protestantism was in some disarray in the Depression era, with critics both inside and outside the churches voicing concern over the overlapping of effort and absence of coherence and vision in social service projects. Seeking to resolve this impasse, Protestant leaders in 1941 launched a renewed effort aimed at merging the city's Protestant church and social-welfare institutions. Representatives of several institutions participated in these discussions: the three church federations (Greater New York, Brooklyn, and Queens), the Federation of Protestant Welfare Agencies, and two smaller, more specialized agencies (the Federation of Daily Vacation Bible Schools and the Interdenominational Committee on Released Time). They achieved agreement on a joint statement that included, as one of its main themes, unity of purpose in social education and action.

A report by the consultant Tamblyn and Brown, Incorporated, identified this field as one to which a merged organization should commit itself. The firm's recent survey of parties involved in the merger discussions had discovered widespread support for such a thrust. The *Survey* placed government relations and a perceived need for improved Protestant representation in local affairs at center stage. It stated:

> The crux of the need for greater coordination was presented by several as consisting in the absence of any Protestant body qualified to deal with any city wide policy. . . . The Protestant church as a whole is seriously handicapped in bringing to bear on government and other bodies in New York the weight of its judgement and influence because of the lack of a representative Protestant group. (Tamblyn and Brown, 1941: 32, 36)

And in an implied reference to Fiorello La Guardia, the *Survey* observes, "The Mayor of New York cannot today turn to any single group and obtain from it the promise of Protestant cooperation in the solution of any problem, or the opinion of Protestant people in the city" (ibid.: 36).

Finally, in addition to the obvious advantages of improved fund-raising capacity and the elimination of wasteful overlapping and duplication, the *Survey* insisted that a merged organization would be expressive of Protestantism's latent political power:

> Such unity would not only make for greater efficiency, but would be a demonstration of the strength which actually exists. It would serve to hearten those who may be discouraged by their own efforts and would answer to some extent the critics of the church. It would enable Protestant groups to take their proper place with other social groups in the city, and would *enable Protestantism to be heard more effectively in public matters.* (ibid: 78; emphasis added)

The *Survey* appears to have had a substantial impact, given that essentially all of its recommendations, including the social action element, were ultimately adopted as part of the proposed merger.

The Protestant Council, consisting of an assembly of over one hundred Protestant leaders, held its inaugural meeting in April 1943, and in October of that year the new church and social welfare organization was legally incorporated under the laws of New York State. The Federation of Daily Vacation Bible Schools and the Interdenominational Committee on Released Time merged into the PC, and the subsequent merger of the other four bodies—the three church federations and the FPWA—was widely anticipated. The Federation of Protestant Welfare Agencies provided seed money for the new federation, including the payment of the executive director's salary and office space.

These early unity hopes were never fully realized, however. The Federation of Protestant Welfare Agencies, in particular, remained a holdout as was, for a time, the Queens Federation of Churches. (The latter did not become integrated into the church council until much later, in the early 1980s.) While it is unnecessary to burden this discussion with an enumeration of everything involved in this abortive attempt to combine groups, one factor does seem worthy of emphasis. When plans for a Protestant Council were initially developed, Fiorello La Guardia—a Republican, anti-machine reformer, lifelong Episcopalian, and favorably disposed toward religious leaders of all stripes—was the sitting mayor. He was then at the height of his popularity, having just been reelected to a third four-year term by a comfortable margin in the November 1941 city elections. Yet by 1944 and early 1945, the city's political climate had changed profoundly. In the words of Wallace Sayre and Herbert Kaufman: "When La Guardia's zest and energies flagged in his third term [1942–46] . . . the mayoralty was isolated and overshadowed. La Guardia could not adjust his style and methods to the new environment" (Sayre and Kaufman, 1960: 692). The mayor's political stature declined as his third term progressed, and "By the time politicians began contemplating the 1945 mayoralty campaign, La Guardia's fortunes had reached bottom" (McNickle, 1993: 53). He was now a sick man, and would die of cancer in just two years' time in 1947. Obviously, he was no longer in a position, as he might have been earlier, to influence the city's opinion climate toward furtherance of Protestant unity aims.

Moreover, La Guardia's successor, William O'Dwyer, who was inaugurated in 1946 and served until 1950, was as indifferent to Protestant concerns and aspirations as La Guardia had been supportive. O'Dwyer was Irish, devoutly Catholic, and strongly identified with the city's Tammany Democratic machine. Given this abrupt change in city administration, it is highly plausible that the new church council's early financial and organizational vicissitudes stemmed in part from this wider political development. Social education and action was an apparent casualty of the PC's fraught organizational life in the early years. The group's Human Relations Commission existed for only three years (1947–50) before being disbanded. And the PC's executive director from the late 1940s to the early '50s, the Rev. Clifford Petitt, was loath to involve himself in any manner in city affairs. Given the council's strained finances and general organizational fragility at this time, such avoidance on his part was perhaps prudent. Still, it is arresting that an informant could later remark of him that "Mr. Petitt shied away from politics; he shied away like the plague. He was called to the [Protestant] Council primarily for his fund-raising abilities, and that was his chief concern in office. His emphasis was always on Christian Education and other non-controversial matters" (Dan Potter, interview, 1961). Thus in the years immediately preceding the Civil Rights era, the PC did not significantly participate in the city's governmental process, and its founders' early hopes that the federation would serve as the moral and social conscience for the city went mostly unrealized.

It is difficult to fix a precise date for the Protestant Council's transition from an early state of organizational fragility—beset by financial woes and forced to compete with the stronger, better-funded Federation of Protestant Welfare Agencies—to one of organizational health and autonomy. Bearing in mind some inevitable uncertainty, it would appear that the turning point came over a two-year span, 1952–53. The former of these two years was significant for Protestant Council government relations in the following four ways:

1. The Rev. Dr. Dan Potter joined the PC staff in the newly created post of associate executive director. His initial role was to provide staff support for six PC operating units, including the new Department of Christian Social Relations, successor to the Human Relations Commission.
2. The church federation signed a renewable contract with the City Youth Board providing for the initiation and oversight of a church-based anti-delinquency program.
3. The U.S. Supreme Court, in the case of *Zorach v. Clausen* (343 US 306), gave constitutional sanction to the New York Released Time law, under which public school children could receive religious instruction at nearby churches and synagogues during designated school hours. This decision directly affected the PC, which had earlier endorsed the act and now became the released-time nerve center for the city's Protestant churches.
4. The PC contracted with the city to provide for the employment of a Protestant worker at the Domestic Relations Court.

The year 1953 also marked a watershed, since an event occurred then that would later prove significant for the PC, namely the mayoral victory in the November 1953 city election of Robert Wagner Jr. While he was Catholic like his predecessors, Paul O'Dwyer and Vincent I. Impellitteri, Wagner would prove to be more inclusive than either of those men during his three terms in office (1954–66).

The Protestant Council's growing resource base enabled it to develop an expanded bureaucratic capacity and to increase its access to New York City officials. This is exemplified by its Department of Church Planning and Research, established in 1954. This unit was charged with (1) analyzing sociological factors affecting parish life; (2) cooperating with religious leaders, both in the neighborhoods and citywide, in developing appropriate coping strategies for city churches; and (3) identifying the religious identifications of New York City residents—Protestant, Catholic, and Jewish—among other functions. Government relations were one of the Church Planning and Research department's chief preoccupations, and in that it soon proved quite successful. For example, its expertise in the fields of church comity and neighborhood planning helped foster PC acceptance among city agencies, including especially the Housing Authority and the Mayor's Committee on Slum Clearance. The department's work also helped the PC to stabilize its internal affairs. Church Planning and Research's published reports were frequently commended by local denominational leaders and ministers, and were also frequently quoted as authoritative by the *New York Times* and other news sources.

The PC's Department of Christian Education likewise earned a reputation for professionalism, and its executives gained recognition by the City Youth Board and the New York Board of Education. It would appear, therefore, that various sectors of city government granted Protestant Council representatives "elite accommodation" in their operations. This concept, developed by the political scientist Robert Presthus, denotes a stage beyond mere political access in which interest group representatives and government officials are involved with one another in a mutually respectful, ongoing manner in confronting shared public policy concerns (Presthus, 1974).

Notwithstanding its increased financial strength and local-church acceptance, the church federation remained fairly obscure for a decade or more following its inception in 1943. Its stands on local and state issues, while routinely conveyed to the appropriate public officials and lawmakers, and occasionally referenced in the *New York Times* and elsewhere, made little apparent impression on the wider community. Sometime in the middle 1950s, however, that situation began to change. Dan Potter was elevated to the post of executive director in 1955, replacing the retiring Clifford Petitt, and he moved quickly to enhance the church federation's governmental presence. Within a few months the PC would expand its pronouncements on social and public policy concerns and increase outreach toward the press. By the mid-1960s, the church group was among the most widely publicized interest groups of any kind in the city (Pratt, 1970).

Further enhancing the council's resource base and level of interaction with parish churches throughout the city was its sponsorship of the 1957 New York

Billy Graham crusade—an event aptly described in a newspaper account as "the longest and biggest evangelistic crusade in modern times" (*New York Times,* September 3, 1957: 29). The crusade occurred over a sixteen-week period, May–September 1957. Figures provided by the Graham organization and not disputed by outsiders showed that Billy Graham had preached the Bible to nearly 2 million people, many of them repeat attendees. This included an attendance of 100,000 at a Yankee Stadium rally held on July 20. In addition to handling the local arrangements, the PC served as the point of contact between the Graham organization and New York's 1,700 Protestant churches.

"Decision for Christ" cards were signed by some 55,000 crusade attenders. The church federation gathered these up, sorted them by borough and neighborhood, and delivered them to area churches for follow-up. This brought the organization for the first time into large-scale, direct contact with city parishes and congregations. Such contacts dismayed, even infuriated, some local denominational officials, who resented the perceived intrusion on their turf. In the years to follow that negative image would grow, and eventually become a major contributor to strained relations between council officials and denominational executives. For the moment, however, the crusade appeared as an unalloyed benefit.

A final development of significance to the church federation in the pre–Civil Rights era was the establishment in 1958 of the Mayor's Committee of Religious Leaders (MCRL). Mayor Robert Wagner established this agency in part on the advice of the City Youth Board, which had recently entered into contracts with several religious groups, the PC included. Youth Board executives urged the mayor to consider the value of convening, on an ongoing basis, a panel of "religious advisors." In accepting this recommendation, however, the mayor chose not to target youth matters alone, but to expand the scope so as to encompass any and all matters of concern to religious groups. PC director Dan Potter helped to spearhead the establishment of the MCRL. (His curriculum vitae, released around the time of his departure from the council in 1981, lists him as the MCRL's "founder and co-chairman.") In conversations with Mayor Wagner, Potter pressed the advisory committee concept, and following the committee's creation, he was second to none in his level of commitment to it. The existence of MCRL served the interests of the PC in at least several ways: legitimation of the church federation in the eyes of constituents and supporters, dissemination to the wider public of PC positions, and facilitation of the group's campaign to combat Protestantism's perceived disadvantage in the larger urban community. While the various MCRL co-chairs were all typically devoted in their service, the PC stood out in terms of its level of commitment. As Potter later expressed it, "From the point of view of the Protestant Council, the Committee was an arm of broader influence and a source of greater power" (personal communication).

The designation "Mayor's" in the committee's name was taken seriously, as it signified the linkage to city hall without which the religious leaders' influence would have been greatly diminished. All three of the mayors who held office during its existence—Robert Wagner, John Lindsay, and Abraham Beame—met at least once with the committee at the mayor's official residence, Gracie Mansion, and in some cases several times. On the occasions when the mayor was present, each faith community would be represented by fifteen or twenty individuals. The mayor would speak for about fifteen minutes, and the group as a whole then would discuss the issues at hand. It was a rule that the press would not be present. The committee held many press conferences, invariably well attended, and, in addition, MCRL representatives appeared regularly on a local TV station, WPIX, which had a weekly program devoted to religious issues.

The MCRL was frequently a source of influence over public policy development, both small- and mid-scale. An example of its "small policy" influence concerned the city's long-standing practice of having three prayers delivered at official gatherings—an invocation, a "middle prayer," and a benediction. Not infrequently these had proved overlong and disruptive. The committee discussed the practice and finally decided that a single prayer would suffice on such occasions. An example of MCRL-influenced "mid-scale" policy concerned the thorny issue of chaplaincies. (City chaplains in some cases serve clients in institutions, for example, those in city hospitals and prisons, and in others city employees, for example, police officers and firefighters.) Every facet of the chaplain position was fraught: the number required, their appointment, job descriptions, supervision, and accountability. MCRL discussed all this, and eventually recommended a revised statement of chaplaincy policy, which the mayor subsequently accepted and ordered implemented. In short, while MCRL was never a very dramatic or highly visible influence on city government, it did impact a number of public policy concerns.

Civil Rights and Threats to PC Internal Cohesion

"The problem of cohesion," remarks David B. Truman, "is a crucial one for the political interest group. Other factors bear on its capacity to assert its claims successfully upon other groups and institutions in society, but the degree of unity in the group is probably most fundamental in determining the measure of success it will enjoy" (Truman, 1951: 79). In the case of the PC/CCCNY, the maintenance of internal cohesion posed few if any problems during its early, fledgling years. Other problems at the time—financial, interorganizational—were indeed present, but internally, at least, the group was fairly harmonious. All of that was to change in the wake of the civil rights revolutions and the rise of black nationalism. Now the problem of cohesion presented itself in a serious way.

By the early 1960s, the New York church federation had evolved from its fairly simple beginnings into a complex organization. From a small group of leaders, mostly male clergymen but including also some lay members, male and female, all mainline Protestants and mostly carryovers from the old Manhattan- and Bronx-based Greater New York Federation of Churches, the leadership now consisted of representatives from four of New York's five boroughs (Queens being the exception)—black, Latino, and white; mainline and evangelical; Protestant and Eastern Orthodox—by no means all liberal and mainline as had once been the case. On the basis of its four borough divisions and thirty-plus denominational members, the council now represented some 1,700 widely diverse city churches. While this increased diversity involved potential long-term dangers from the standpoint of group cohesion, it was not immediately perceived as such. As of 1965 the council had reached a pinnacle in terms of financial strength, citywide visibility, and generalized Protestant acceptance. That year was the last of Robert Wagner Jr.'s long tenure as mayor, and the council had gained strength from the fact that Dan Potter and Wagner had developed a warm, fraternal relationship. The PC director also was on friendly terms with Cardinal Spellman, who for another year would remain directly in charge of the New York Archdiocese.

This period also witnessed a second important development from a PC standpoint, even though its implications from the civil rights angle would not become apparent for some time. In 1958, New York's Interchurch Center was formally opened at 475 Riverside Drive in Manhattan, in a parade ceremony led by President Dwight Eisenhower. This building opened a new chapter in relations between the PC and its denominational constituency. For the first time, denominational offices could be clustered in close proximity to one another rather than scattered about the city as had heretofore been the case. Moreover, the several denominational headquarters were now adjacent to offices of the Protestant Council, which also relocated to the center at about this time. In all, five denominational judicatories—the American Baptist, the

United Methodist, the United Presbyterian, the Reformed Church in America, and United Church of Christ—elected to relocate their headquarters in this manner. This had the side effect of bringing the five into close physical proximity to the Cathedral of St. John the Divine, headquarters of the highly prestigious Protestant Episcopal Diocese of New York. (Both the cathedral and the Interchurch Center are in Manhattan's Morningside Heights, about a half mile distant from one another.) By the 1960s some of the denominational directorships were held by African Americans.

While these six mainline Protestant denominations were only a fraction of the more than thirty denominations represented in the church federation, their superior staffing and larger financial resources had long given them a disproportionate influence. The other council-affiliated Protestant and Eastern Orthodox bodies, while more numerous, often found it difficult to sustain interdenominational linkages. This applied especially to the several among them that maintained no office in the city or its immediate environs. Hence, with impetus provided by the church federation's enhanced visibility and power, and with the means for collaboration provided by their new location, the six Protestant judicatories were in a position, beginning around 1958, to assert themselves in church federation affairs as never before. The question was, how would that increased leverage be wielded?

The answer to this question was shaped in part by the revolution in civil rights, which impacted the New York City church federation as much as any event in the group's post–World War II history. With the Civil Rights movement gaining momentum, the council identified itself closely with Martin Luther King. "The Sixties were Dr. King's time," Dan Potter later affirmed. "Civil rights took major national attention, and we worked with King. We were with him in Selma and in Birmingham, and following his death we were invited to his funeral." When the U.S. Senate was debating the Kennedy civil rights bill in 1963, a delegation of some two hundred Protestant clergy from the New York area, including Dan Potter and others from the Protestant Council plus elected officials and staff personnel from the National Council of Churches, flew to Washington at the behest of President Kennedy and his brother, Attorney General Robert Kennedy, to lend their support to congressional enactment of the pending civil rights bill. The group met with the attorney general in a room at the White House and reached a consensus on the problem at hand and the necessary steps required to pass the bill.

The momentum for civil rights was reflected in various internal changes. The PC's citywide staff consisted almost entirely of whites up through the middle 1960s at which point a large contingent of African Americans were named to staff positions. In addition, the city church federation responded to the Civil Rights movement by making various organizational adjustments, by promoting enhanced outreach toward other faiths, and by lending its support, both tangible and symbolic, to the civil rights cause in the nation's capital and in communities throughout the South.

Notwithstanding such efforts, however, the CCCNY was adversely affected by the rise of civil rights militancy around this time. The prevailing mood was captured in this description given by Dan Potter to an interviewer:

> A lot of my last decade as executive director [1971–81] was spent dealing with the new level of tension within the Protestant community, especially along racial lines. We ended up with black presidents of our borough divisions, black chairs of various committees, an increasingly black staff, and a newly appointed associate director, also black. It was a difficult time. There was a feeling among denominational executives that I should not presume to be the spokesman for Protestantism, and that I should not appear as such on local TV. And that feeling was coming from the various denominational offices and black leaders alike. Toward the end, we could scarcely have a major event or meeting but that some militant would not burst in and demand to be heard. I remember one such person who held forth for fifteen or twenty minutes, and our Board Chairman, Cleveland Dodge, after hearing all the cursing and vituperation began to fear for his safety.

While a variety of factors entered into this atmosphere of tension and animosity, one of them was clearly the council's annual Family of Man dinner, which became a lightning rod for protesters of all types.

A word of background on this event is in order. In 1961, the Protestant Council established an entity known as "The Society for the Family of Man." The "Family of Man" label derived from a highly regarded photographic exhibit of that name held a few years earlier at New York's Museum of Modern Art. On the basis of an agreement with the museum, the publishing firm of Simon and Schuster had assembled the exhibit photographs into a book, *The Family of Man,* edited by the distinguished American photographer Edward Steichen (Steichen, 1955). This soon became an industry classic, selling in the hundreds of thousands throughout North America and beyond. Seeking to build on that success, someone suggested that a mechanism be established to give formal recognition to individuals of diverse national and racial/ethnic backgrounds and the PC become the instrument for furtherance of that objective.

Whereas the exhibition at the museum had portrayed persons of all stations in life, the humble and the exalted alike, the Society for the Family of Man took a different tack, recognizing persons of outstanding achievement: statesmen, heads of government, and others of eminence. Essential to this strategy was securing acceptances from those chosen to be honored. In so doing, the Society exploited New York's status as a world city and site of the UN world headquarters. The society's main event became the annual "Family of Man Dinner," to which major corporations were invited to send representatives at a large per-plate cost. Many corporations were prepared to cooperate and to pay the price.

In its nearly two decades of existence, the society honored many highly esteemed persons, all of them invited to attend the banquet and to deliver an address. At the first banquet in 1961, President John F. Kennedy was honored. In the years to follow, the honorees included, among others, U.S. presidents Lyndon B. Johnson, Richard Nixon, Gerald Ford, and Jimmy Carter; Israel's Yitzhak Rabin; Egypt's Anwar Sadat; and South Africa's Desmond Tutu. In the early years, at least, all this recognition was to the church federation's decided advantage. The society's banquets garnered (1) publicity, almost entirely favorable, (2) prestige accruing from the council's close association with persons of prominence, and (3) revenue, with proceeds from the banquet contributing to the federation's financial base.

Within two or three years of its inception, however, the annual banquet began to attract trouble—only minor at first, but more serious with the passage of time. Beginning around 1965 several black clergymen, supported by some whites, began to demand that the Protestant Council give more attention to the betterment of New York's poor and minority groups. They brushed aside assurances from council leaders that the organization was already strongly committed to the cause of racial uplift and betterment. The Family of Man banquet was an easy venue for the promotion of such demands. One or two picketers showed up to lodge a protest at the first banquet in 1961 honoring JFK. A larger group of protesters rallied outside the 1966 dinner honoring President Lyndon Johnson, and a still larger and more vocal group protested the honor conferred on President Richard Nixon at the 1969 banquet.

Eventually race protest and antiwar activism combined forces to confront the council. One especially outspoken and colorful protester was the Rev. Robert M. Kinlock, a firebrand preacher well known for his appearances at construction sites throughout the city to protest the lack of minority hiring in the building trades. On one occasion, an angry Kinlock appeared at a Family of Man banquet wearing a banner across his chest like a beauty contest winner emblazoned with "Commission for the Elimination of Racism." With the help of collaborators, he later staged a sit-in the at the PC's headquarters at 475 Riverside Drive in Manhattan, where again he wore the banner. (The commission mentioned on the banner referred to an early effort by the council of churches to deal with the growing racial tensions in its ranks.) In 1975, still another protest demonstration occurred outside the annual banquet. Demonstrators now accused the federation of fostering a wicked dependency on large corporations and of pursing policies detrimental to the minority poor. Dan Potter, in particular, was targeted (*New York Times,* November 13, 1975). None of these issues proved amenable to any easy resolution and, as detailed in the chapter to follow, criticism of Potter on race and poverty issues would become a factor in his eventual dismissal from his council post.

In response to the rising tide of race protest, the council in 1971 appointed a black clergyman, the Rev. Franklin Graham, to the newly created post of program director. Graham's appointment was intended to moderate the one-man (white) dominance of Dan Potter. In that sense it was fairly successful, since for the remaining years of Potter's tenure he would never again be the group's sole voice; administratively, council leadership henceforth would be shared between Potter and Graham (*New York Times,* November 13, 1975).

It would be wrong to suggest that the council's growing internal discord was entirely attributable to racial concerns and protests. Another factor was Potter's leadership style, viewed as controversial in some quarters. During discussions in May 1971 over whether or not to reappoint Potter to another term as executive director, one of the council's more influential member bodies, the United Church of Christ, announced its intention to withhold its financial support, and even to quit the organization, if its concerns over the director's alleged "ineffectiveness" and failure "to really represent the . . . black Protestant majority of its constituents" were not adequately dealt with. For its part, the Episcopal Church, while not threatening to quit, withheld its council support pending the conclusions of discussions scheduled for that fall where the option of establishing "alternative agencies" to the council would be on the agenda (*New York Times,* July 11, 1976). As the voice of united denominationalism, the Committee of Denominational Executives (CODE) was flexing its muscles on matters of central concern to the council, including its policies and leadership.

In addition to racial tension, there was anti-Vietnam War protest. In a humiliating embarrassment, the church federation in 1971 was forced to revoke a Family of Man award that had been extended to, and accepted by, the comedian Bob Hope. Critics of this invitation considered Hope unacceptable given his high-profile support for the U.S. war effort. Indeed, criticisms leveled at the Family of Man invitations to U.S. presidents Lyndon Johnson and Richard Nixon were in large part war-related. A final source of controversy was over the council's 1963 World's Fair exhibit. The Protestant-Orthodox Center at the fair was successful in the sense that it was visited by more than 3 million fair attendees, and the film shown at the center, "Parable," proved highly popular both there and at subsequent showings elsewhere. As an investment, however, the center turned out badly, resulting in a debt of over $400,000 and requiring five years for the council to pay off. Critics were appalled.

The response of Protestantism to the Great Society/New Frontier era differed significantly in the two cities. Whereas the Detroit Council of Churches was perceived as positively identified with the Civil Rights movement, its New York City counterpart, while favorably disposed toward civil rights, was less successful in persuading its constituency of its racial justice commitment. In the end it was subjected to an embarrassing tide of black protest arising from both within and outside its ranks. In terms of organizational maintenance and revenues, however, the two organizations had different success rates. Whereas the Detroit council experienced an alarming resource shrinkage beginning around 1965, its New York counterpart managed to weather that period in sound financial shape. (As detailed in a later chapter, the New York group maintained annual revenues of some $2 million until 1980.)

In accounting for this contrast, it is plausible that differences in the extent of governmental contact—ongoing and fairly close in the case of New York, episodic and fairly distant in that of Detroit—were involved in the different outcomes for the church organizations. While the relations between the New York group and government involved little by way of tangible benefits (for example, lucrative contracts for services), they remained symbolically important. The links helped the group to maintain its legitimacy and perceived importance in the eyes of constituents and supporters, and to fend off, at least temporarily, the tide of black anger and frustration. The New York federation benefitted from sources of support beyond its formal constituency, particularly the Family of Man banquet and the Billy Graham crusade. Government helped enhance these organizational assets. For example, the Family of Man banquet was successful in part because of the support given it by public officials, including those who agreed to be honored and others who were content to be part of the audience. Absent the support of city and state political elites, the banquet format probably would not have gotten off the ground. Detroit's MDCC, on the other hand, was almost entirely dependent on its own internally generated resources, and when those resources began to plummet in the late 1960s the group had little to fall back upon.

Civil Rights, the Great Society, and Catholicism

Big-city Catholic dioceses were substantially impacted by the social turmoil and related government initiatives of the 1960s. The programs of the Kennedy-Johnson administration helped transform American urban politics, including the pattern of relations between local governments and city-based nongovernmental organizations of all kinds. The Economic Opportunity Act, centerpiece of the Lyndon Johnson War on Poverty, essentially bypassed the states in favor of large-city mayors and other urban officials, and that, in turn, impacted faith-based social welfare agencies, most especially Catholic. Local Catholic dioceses, confronted with mounting demands for social services and a possibility for increased government funding, were under considerable pressure to assert themselves politically. New York and Detroit were illustrative of that wider national pattern, and detailed attention to their behavior thus offers a potentially fruitful perspective on the Catholic response at this point in American urban history.

In addition to treating the wider political setting, the discussion to follow considers two other changes that impacted the two Catholic archdioceses at this time, namely the Civil Rights movement and developments internal to the Church. In regard to the latter, as becomes clear, a religious institution long accustomed to one mode of self-definition and understanding now shifted in order to embrace a new self-definition and a fresh understanding.

Vatican II, Civil Rights, and Expanded U.S. Programs

The Second Vatican Council, held in Rome from 1961 to 1965, was arguably the single most transformative event in twentieth-century American Catholicism. The magnitude of the change becomes clear on the basis of several council-adopted statements. In *Pastoral Constitution on the Church in the Modern World,* Vatican II revolutionized the Church's traditional standoffish, defensive stance toward the wider world, based in part on a deep-seated fear of secularism, and replaced it with one of outreach and acceptance of mutually respectful dialogue with non-Catholics. Moreover, in a reversal of policy especially relevant to the American situation, the council adopted the *Declaration on Human Freedom,* which involved the abandonment of the traditional Church view that religious freedom is not an inherent right of the individual but is a matter of discretion by national governments. Instead, the statement proclaimed, "The human person has the right to religious freedom." This document bore the strong imprint of the council's American delegation, which lobbied for it strenuously based on an acceptance of the U.S. Constitution. This new statement of policy paved the way for expanded cooperation between Catholics and other Americans, and for a new Catholic approach to American government (Byrnes, 1991: 39–40).

The changes introduced by Vatican II were not limited, however, to alterations in Church doctrine and teaching. The meeting also marked a turning point in terms of power relations among the American bishops. On the one hand, New York's Francis Cardinal Spellman, for twenty-five years a strong and often dominant hand in shaping policies of both the Catholic Church and American government, found his brand of social conservatism no longer widely accepted among his fellow bishops and cardinals. When Spellman voiced opposition to the changes under discussion at Vatican II—regarding, for example, conscientious objection and the right of individuals to reject violence—he was not uncommonly voted down. The New York Cardinal-Archbishop was now finding himself out of step with the mood of change embodied by Pope John XXIII (Cooney, 1984: 282). On the other hand, the assembly conferred increased stature on Detroit's John Cardinal Dearden, considered a leading progressive. Dearden's ascendancy was implicit in the council's adoption of the *Decree on the Bishops' Pastoral Office in the Church,* which implicitly recognized the growing importance of social problems and the role of government in addressing such problems, and that explicitly recommended that Church statements on public policy issues be made "in the name of all the bishops." As Byrnes points out, this document clearly foreshadowed the formation in November 1966 of the [U.S.] National Council of Catholic Bishops (NCCB), which replaced the old National Catholic Welfare Conference. Dearden, it should be noted, was elected the NCCB's first president, and under his guidance it quickly became the mechanism for broadened Catholic involvement on national issues and increased unity among the bishops as compared to its predecessor. Dearden's progressive principles shaped the new group's essential outlook during its formative years (Byrnes, 1991: 51–52).

If changes internal to the Church were one major factor in the changing shape of American Catholicism in the 1960s, two other factors emanated from the outside. The first of them was the Civil Rights movement. Civil rights, and its cousin the farm workers' movement, had a deep impact, helping to define "a new Catholicism." Large numbers of Catholic laypeople and clergy, including some bishops, involved themselves in social justice—a novel thing for Catholicism. It was no less novel for Catholic priests to be found on the front lines in protest demonstrations (Dolan, 1985: 446–47).

Second, there was a newly enacted set of U.S. government programs. Their existence challenged the American bishops to an unprecedented degree, especially since their congressional sponsors clearly intended the programs to be permanent and not just temporary as was typically true of their New Deal counterparts in the 1930s. Confronted with this wave of new federal initiatives, many of them directly affecting the Church, the American bishops initially found themselves ill-equipped. Their eventual decision to form the NCCB was, in part, a response to the unstable public policy environment of the time. As Byrnes remarks, "The American bishops of the 1960s and 1970s were practical men who understood their social and political circumstances. . . . [T]hey recognized that a cohesive organization was probably essential for meaningful participation on [the national] level" (Byrnes, 1991: 51). The Catholic archdioceses of New York and Detroit were both well positioned to benefit from such national-level Church developments.

Archdiocesan Policies: New York

Francis Cardinal Spellman's response to the events of the 1960s, as they impacted the New York Archdiocese, was essentially one of grudging acceptance combined with thinly veiled displeasure. The cardinal was not hostile to blacks, but their lack of political power and inability to help him on his various moral crusades—against the "Communist threat," against morally objectionable movies and plays, against public displays of nudity, and so on—caused him to regard their concerns with indifference. When his deputy, Bishop McGuire, bought him a lifetime membership in the National Association for the Advancement of Colored People (NAACP), Spellman complained that the money was "wasted." On one occasion, he was locked into attending a New York NAACP dinner, and those in attendance gave the cardinal a standing ovation. This astonished the cardinal; he knew he "had done nothing to deserve it" (Cooney, 1984: 283).

John Cooney offers an illuminating portrait of Spellman's response to the Civil Rights movement. There were no black bishops in New York during Spellman's lifetime and few black priests. In the mid-1960s, with civil rights momentum building and with numerous other church leaders, Catholic and non-Catholic, declaring their support for Martin Luther King and his protest demonstrations across the South, some New York Catholics looked toward Spellman for encouragement. Such persons were dismayed, however. When the cardinal did finally act, it was only after a delegation of nuns and priests had met with him and bluntly demanded that he step in. He capitulated by providing funds for a New York delegation of priests and nuns to attend the civil rights protests in Selma, Alabama. In doing so, the cardinal reiterated the limits to his civil rights acceptance, and made no secret of his suspicions of the movement's adherents, whom he believed subversive (Cooney, 1984: 283–84).

Paralleling the Cardinal's standoffishness on civil rights was his suspicion of newly enacted social legislation. The election of John F. Kennedy as president in 1960 created a serious possibility for the enactment of federal aid to education, following many years of legislative deadlock. Spellman did not wait for Kennedy to be inaugurated before denouncing in the strongest terms a proposal for federal aid prepared by advisers to the president-elect, on the grounds that it failed to provide for nonpublic, especially Catholic, education (Glazer and Moynihan, 1963: 280). While the exact extent of the New York Archdiocese's involvement in the Johnson War on Poverty is unknown, it was likely minimal given the estrangement that developed between the cardinal and Mayor John Lindsay following the latter's election in November 1965. While the archdiocese, often referred to as "the Powerhouse," had remained highly influential in city affairs through the 1950s, its influence began to wane during Mayor Robert Wagner's third term, 1962–66, and it all but ceased during Lindsay's administration. At Lindsay's 1966 inauguration ceremony, the cardinal was not on the dias—his first such absence since taking office a quarter century previous. Moreover, subsequent to Lindsay's taking office, the cardinal was cut off from access to city hall, and, in another break with tradition, was disregarded in the filling of city offices (Cooney, 1984: 301–2). In short, the incentives implicit in the Johnson War on Poverty, as mediated through the city bureaucracy, had little apparent affect on the Archdiocese of New York.

Archdiocesan Policies: Detroit

If the Catholic Church in New York under Cardinal Spellman marked one end of a continuum of responses to the Civil Rights/Great Society era, the

Detroit Archdiocese, under John Cardinal Dearden, defined the other. With respect to race, the Archdiocese was preeminent in the joint resolve of Detroit religious leaders—Catholic, Protestant, and Jewish—to support public authorities in the quest for greater racial understanding and equity. The Archbishop's Committee on Human Relations was organized in 1960 and became fully operative two years later when James T. Sheehan became its executive secretary. The committee, through its Project Commitment, sought to combat racial prejudice and promote parish acceptance of black migration to changing neighborhoods. Moreover, in launching Project Equality in May 1965, the archdiocese, like the city, resolved to limit its purchases to equal opportunity employers. Chosen to head this initiative was a former executive of the National Catholic Welfare Conference, Thomas H. Gibbons (*Michigan Catholic,* May 13, 1965; Fine, 1989: 22–23).

The same basic attitude characterized the archdiocese's response to Detroit's antipoverty effort. In December 1964 the Mayor's Committee for Human Resource Development (MCHRD) designated the archdiocese as one of two "delegate agencies" for the city's antipoverty effort (the other being the Detroit Board of Education), thereby insuring a major role for the Catholic Church in the overall program. To oversee the Catholic effort, Cardinal Dearden appointed one of his brighter, more energetic lieutenants, Father [later Auxiliary Bishop] Thomas J. Gumbleton. The Church's antipoverty program had several dimensions: job counseling for college-bound high school students, job placement for low-income families, and various noncurricular education programs. Ninety percent of the cost came from the federal government, and the archdiocese contributed the other 10 percent (*Michigan Catholic,* January 14 and 28, 1965). At its peak in mid-1965, 46 Detroit inner city parishes and more than 450 inner-city teaching nuns were involved in the archdiocesan poverty effort (*Michigan Catholic,* August 5, 1965).

Neither the Johnson administration's War on Poverty nor the Civil Rights movement, as a coherent force, survived the 1970s, the former being terminated by the Nixon administration (1969–74) and the latter fading from the scene under the impact of events like the Martin Luther King assassination, the rising intensity of the Vietnam War, and the urban riots of the middle and late '60s. Yet one should not assume that the closer Catholic Church–municipal government relationship that developed in the '60s vanished with the return of quieter times. The Detroit Archdiocese's anti-poverty effort, for example, contributed to Father Thomas J. Gumbleton's rise from relative obscurity as a parish priest to a level of civic prominence rivaling that of Cardinal Dearden.

The two archdioceses' obvious response to the developments of 1960s testifies to the fact that the incentives implicit in expanding government programs, federal and municipal, had the potential to influence Church behavior. Their impact could be heightened in cases where local government officials were prepared to cooperate with the Catholic hierarchy. When they were, as was true in Detroit during the Cavanagh years, the effect could be fairly dramatic; where the relationship was cool and distant, as in Cardinal Spellman's New York during the Lindsay years, the behavioral changes were minimal. In other words, for the newly available public incentives to have any real significance from a church standpoint, it was necessary that the local bishop (or archbishop) be both proactive and responsive.

The apparent reluctance of the New York Archdiocese to respond more positively to the Civil Rights/Great Society era could well have stemmed in part from a judgement arrived at regarding the wider external setting. New York's Catholic population remained stable between 1964 and 1975 at around 2.9 million, and Catholics maintained themselves as the city's largest religious group (*New York Times,* August 14, 1975). While Cardinal Spellman's remoteness from Mayor Lindsay and the city's civil rights movement may have been awkward at times, the cardinal and his advisors quite possibly judged the consequences as unlikely to be serious, and readily correctable by Spellman's successors assuming correction was called for. The city's rising Hispanic and declining white populations—by 1975, Hispanics constituted half of all New York Catholics—while constituting an obvious challenge, were not, presumably, seen as seriously destabilizing events. The number of Catholic households in Detroit, Hamtramck, and Highland Park dropped from 103,380 in 1976 to 48,804 in 1988, and much of this was the result of whites moving to surrounding suburbs such as Southfield, Birmingham, and Harper Woods. Cardinal Edmund Szoka, in his initial announcement in September 1988, called for the closing of 43 Catholic churches, about a third of these were in the city of Detroit; his goal was to address the flight of mainly white parishioners to the suburbs that started following the 1967 urban insurrection (*Detroit Free Press,* September 29, 1988). Eventually thirty inner city Detroit churches that served about 80,000 Catholics were closed in 1990 (*Detroit Free Press,* January 8, 1990). The Detroit Archdiocese, confronted by a far greater change in the size and composition of its central-city Catholic population, may have been under greater pressure to fashion a more aggressive and expansive public policy response.

4

New York Protestantism and Appointments to City Offices

As brought out in the previous chapter, in the late 1950s and '60s New York's Protestant Council became keenly interested in city politics and government, partly in response to events at the national level and partly in the wake of developments unique to the city. Whereas the earlier discussion emphasized the development of *formal* linkages between the church federation and municipal government—the Youth Board contract, the mayor's religious leaders committee, and so on—there was also another, more *informal,* aspect to the evolving church-state relationship. It consisted of the federation's campaign to overcome a perceived bias against Protestants in the appointment of individuals to fill city offices, and to insure that in the filling of such posts Protestant candidates were accorded full and fair consideration.

The Protestant Council's effort was representative of the ambiguities and dilemmas that any voluntary organization is likely to face when it commits itself to a campaign more related to high-stakes partisan politics than to the public policy concerns characteristic of interest groups. The following case study, therefore, illustrates an aspect of group politics not limited to the church-state relations field but broadly relevant to pressure group behavior generally. The discussion also illuminates the early growth of race consciousness on the part of the council, a traditionally "white" church organization with little prior interest in racial issues. Such consciousness, even though at this point but weakly developed and poorly articulated, would gain enhanced importance for the PC in the years to follow.

Background

As the Protestant Council became increasingly involved with New York City government in the 1950s, its leaders were made aware of a pattern of political appointment that involved, from their standpoint, an apparent bias against Protestants in appointments to high-level city offices. Acting on that perception, PC leaders initiated a campaign to combat the perceived bias. The campaign was rationalized chiefly on two grounds. First, they believed that Protestantism has an ongoing role to play in areas of public policy deemed important from the standpoint of Christian ethics and morality. Those areas included, in particular, social welfare, public chaplaincies, the administration of justice, and public education at all levels (elementary, secondary, and higher). Second, the council desired to be of service to those in its constituency for whom a major city appointment was regarded as a prize, the securing of which would benefit (so it was argued) not just themselves and Protestantism but also the wider urban community. In a larger sense, the council's involvement in the appointments area reflected a resolve on its part to reassert Protestantism's traditional influence in the New York metropolitan community. In so doing, the group proposed, in effect, to transcend the function usually defined by the term "interest group" (that is, concerned with promoting certain public policy objectives) and to affirm, also, a "status group" role (that is, concerned with promoting the aspirations of one particular population in competition with others).

The council's campaign in the policy-making arena paralleled those of other interest groups—a general pattern that two analysts of New York government, Wallace Sayre and Herbert Kaufman, allude to as follows: "One way for a group to be fairly sure the governmental decisions in which it is interested will coincide with its own preferences is to help pick the men who make them . . . the group instrumental in installing a man in office may then have a claim upon him that makes him responsive to its wishes" (Sayre and Kaufman, 1960: 489). Council activity in this area gained added legitimacy from the fact that Jewish and Catholic leaders were active on behalf of candidates for city appointments from their particular faiths (Sayre and Kaufman, 1960: 490).

Impediments to Influence

The council's efforts to influence nominations confronted serious obstacles, and it was unclear at the outset that the group had much hope of success. The obstacles included the screening process that precedes the making of city appointments, which is fairly secretive; the political calculations and deal-making occur behind closed doors where outside scrutiny is typically not possible. Having arrived at their decisions, the mayor and other elected officials invariably portray their choices as entirely merit-based, and challenges to their actions are not readily accepted nor warmly received. Groups and individuals who choose to protest against the nominees do so at their peril. Such critics may end up having their existing access to city hall seriously eroded if not terminated altogether.

Furthermore, a group's political resources—which in the council's case included excellent access to the city's print and electronic media—may prove of only limited value with respect to appointments, marked as they are by low visibility and high barriers to outside scrutiny. Thus the group may find itself required to devote time, money, and other scarce resources to developing a capacity specific to appointments that may have little spill-over benefit to other areas of its operations. The Protestant Council nevertheless decided that it had little choice other than to make the necessary investment.

Data Requirements

Early in its campaign, the Protestant Council endeavored to determine the religious composition of the city's appointive political elite. A regular member of the staff, the Rev. Walter Offutt, was designated as its civic affairs specialist and instructed to identify to the extent possible the religious affiliations of existing municipal officeholders. Offutt was to pay particular attention to various "exempt" positions in the municipal service: city line agencies, especially the Department of Welfare, city boards and commissions, and municipal judgeships. In fulfilling his assignment, Offutt made use of standard reference and biographical sources while also availing himself of less routine, "inside dopester" information. In the latter connection, he obtained the cooperation of an aging Greenwich Village political veteran who agreed to examine the list of sitting municipal judges and sort them out according to religion: Protestant, Catholic, and Jewish. Yet despite Offutt's best efforts, the results were often less than satisfactory. The Department of Christian Social Relations (DCSR) minutes at one point record, for example, that "Mr. Offutt expressed much concern over his inability to secure the necessary information on the faith of holders of non-exempt positions in the City's civil service" (DCSR minutes, January 22, 1959).

Dilemmas

Aside from the above-mentioned technical difficulties, the appointments campaign also posed certain conceptual problems. In pressing for a more "equitable proportion" of Protestants in appointive office, the council had to decide the extent to which it was prepared to endorse the candidacy of one individual at the expense of others in situations where all the aspirants were politically ambitious and all Protestant. Difficulties also arose over the DCSR's desire to keep secret the content of its recommendations lest those not recommended turn angrily against the council, with potentially damaging organizational consequences. Finally, how much weight, if any, should the council assign to a candidate's degree of Protestant involvement and commitment, as opposed to one's objectively defined merit? This conundrum became acute in those cases, by no means rare, where the individual in question lobbied the council in behalf of his own candidacy.

One such person, whom the council hesitated to endorse for other reasons, was an active churchman:

> The candidate attends a Protestant church, works with Protestant agencies, speaks for Protestant organizations, and, publicly, admits his Protestantism. . . . It is impossible to state what arguments he advanced with other groups in the city, but to the [Protestant Council] he presented his Protestantism as a shining reason for his selection. He attempted to use his faith for political advancement. (Barr, 1960)

Council leaders were acutely conscious of these dilemmas. As Dan Potter pointed out around that time in an interview: "Our nominating of candidates has backfired almost more than it has succeeded. Some persons have a tremendous drive for a particular spot. They try to get a big snowball going. Sometimes the pressure on us is so great that we have to go along. One man [we supported] is now in a high City office who I didn't feel was qualified" (interview, January 1961). Clearly, Potter and the other council activists shared a concern with how to effectively campaign for appointments without endangering group internal consensus.

Differing Approaches

With respect to the principle that positive steps were called for in seeking to redress New York's pervasive religious imbalances, the council leadership at this time was in substantial agreement. Yet consensus at an abstract level left room for disagreement regarding the application of principle to real-world circumstances. Three differing applications finally emerged, which can be termed, for the sake of convenience, the "civic-educational," the "moderate-activist," and the "militant-activist."

The Civic-Educational Approach

The Honorable Robert M. Marsh, a charter member of the council's board of directors, the chair of its Department of Christian Social Relations from its inception in 1953 until 1956, and a former municipal judge, was the council's leading proponent of the "educationalist" stance. Wishing to deflect the problem to elsewhere in the organization and thus minimize its potential for discord, Judge Marsh stressed the obligations of the local church and the need for Protestants to enter politics at the district level and from there work their way up the political ladder. It was not for the PC to seek redress for any imbalances stemming from a lack of individuals' partisan-political involvement and commitment. In a lengthy 1955 resolution submitted for consideration by his fellow DCSR committee members, Marsh expounded on this view:

> Recent surveys into the religious affiliations of the occupants of public office in the City of New York reveal the number of Protestants in such positions in comparison with the number of Roman Catholics and Jews is far less than the proportion of Protestant citizens in the population as a whole. . . .
>
> *Resolved* that Protestant citizens of New York, both men and women, be urged to *give more attention to their Christian obligation to bear their full share of the burden* of providing the best possible government for the City, State and Nation by personal participation therein;
>
> *Further Resolved* that local ministers serving congregations and parishes be urged to *emphasize this obligation in their teaching and preaching and to encourage full political and civic activity* on the part of the individual members of their churches. (DCSR minutes, November 7, 1955; emphasis added)

The committee minutes make it clear that this position was intended, in part, as a counter to the possibility that the council might embrace a more activist, potentially embarrassing, position. The minutes record that Judge Marsh's action "was prompted in part by a recent decision of the executive committee [of the PC board of directors] that it should be the policy of the Council not to endorse candidates for public office" (DCSR minutes, November 7, 1955). The judge himself, in all likelihood, was the one chiefly responsible for that board action, given his long board service and reputation for political sagacity. Endorsement of the board's action by the Department on Christian Social Relations was presumably aimed at enhancing the legitimacy of that position.

Judge Marsh was not alone in these views. Over the period 1953 to 1955 the council's house organ published several articles which argued one or another facet of the civic-education position. In a 1953 piece, Arthur Swift, a professor at New York's Union Theological Seminary, urged that "some participation is obviously both a Christian duty and a Christian obligation. Every Christian should be *intelligently informed* on all matters affecting local government, including policies, budgets, and general welfare" (*Protestant Church Life,* March 28, 1953). Several months later, the Rev. Norris Tibbetts, a longtime council board member, urged in the same publication that it was a *responsibility of the local church* to establish committees on Christian social relations, where "social situations can be confronted in the light of Christian principles" (*Protestant Church Life,* January 30 and February 6, 1954).

The Moderate-Activist Approach

Judge Marsh stepped down as chair of the Department of Christian Social Relations in February 1956, and for several months thereafter the committee, and the council as a whole, continued to adhere to the "civic-educational" strategy. While not closing their eyes to the evidence of perceived Protestant under-representation, the favored approach remained one of urging fellow religionists to become more active in partisan politics and thereby to enhance their attractiveness as candidates for city vacancies.

By early 1957, however, with Marsh now gone from the scene, a fresh approach made itself felt. The entering wedge, evidently, was the situation reported to exist in the New York City Department of Welfare. Concern over this agency was one of long standing in the council. In 1948, the Human Relations Commission (forerunner of the Department of Christian Social Relations) had reported that the Welfare Department was "a Roman Catholic lobby" (HRC minutes, January 15, 1948). Now the situation gained heightened visibility as a result of pressure placed on the Protestant Council by the St. George Association, the voice of ecumenical Protestantism among New York City municipal employees. At a meeting of the council's board of directors in early 1957, it was reported that:

> The St. George Association expressed its anxiety about the present situation in the Department of Welfare where the top staff consists of 12 Roman

> Catholics, 8 Jews, and [only] 2 Protestants. A meeting [by the Protestant Council] with the Mayor is scheduled for this week. The Council and the Federation of Protestant Welfare Agencies have agreed on a candidate for one vacancy. (Board of directors' minutes, January 24, 1957)

The meeting with the mayor evidently did not succeed in allaying the council's anxieties, since in the months to come both the board of directors and the DCSR repeatedly discussed the matter of Protestant under-representation. By late 1957, the situation had evidently come to a head, with some now calling for a new approach:

> The lack of Protestant representation in judicial office was discussed. At the present time there is no Protestant on the Supreme Court in the metropolitan area. How can this lack be overcome? It was suggested that some Protestants who would like to be active in the Democratic Party find it difficult to do so with the condition of the party as it is. Someone responded that despite bad conditions one cannot be resigned to them by withdrawing from activity. *It may be that we must revise the whole Protestant philosophy of politics.* What is the place of a political party according to Protestant thought? It was suggested the this problem of Protestant representation in public office might be given special study by a special committee of the department. (DCSR minutes, January 24, 1957; emphasis added)

On the basis of unrelenting St. George Association pressure (DCSR minutes, April 7, 1958), coupled with its own self-generated concern, the council now began to exploit its access to Mayor Robert Wagner and to other high officials in a systematic campaign to achieve redress of what it perceived as a wide pattern of appointment inequities. In this, the New York City Department of Welfare was never far from the center of attention:

> Mr. [Paul] Rischell [executive secretary, Department of Christian Social Relations] reported that a conference with Mayor Wagner was held on January 3 [1958] to discuss the subject of Protestant representation in public office. . . . The figures presented indicated that . . . in the Welfare Department, there is only one Protestant on the executive staff and no Protestants among those 6 persons who make policy for the Department. (DCSR minutes, January 13, 1958)

Among the several council leaders involved in this effort, none played a larger or more visible role than its newly appointed executive director, Dan Potter. Potter was promoted to the top post in 1955, having served for the previous three years as executive secretary (or director) of several PC departments,

Christian Social Relations included. That experience had placed him at the center of the council's expanding array of government relations and made him aware of the scope and nuances of the appointments process. In addition, he was relatively young—still in his thirties—and accustomed to dealing one-on-one with local officials, a skill honed both during his time at the council and earlier as a church federation executive in both Attleboro, Massachusetts, and Washington, D.C.

In their meetings with the mayor and other city officials, the council's representatives—Potter, Paul Rischell, and Orrin Judd, the chair of the Department of Christian Social Relations—were assertive, but also cordial and respectful. "Moderation" seems an apt term to characterize their political style. This was partly a matter of personality and temperament; Potter, for example, is naturally quiet and soft-spoken. Yet it was also a matter of strategic choice, reflecting a judgement as to what was likely to produce the best results under the circumstances.

The Militant-Activist Approach

A contrasting, more militant view regarding the appropriate Protestant response to this situation also arose in the 1950s, but it did not so quickly find a clear organizational niche. It was premised on a recognition that the representatives of New York's other two major faiths actively promoted candidates based on religious affiliation, and that Protestantism's low representation in government was at least partially attributable to its reluctance to do likewise.

The decision of the board of directors "that it should be the policy of the Protestant Council not to endorse candidates for public office" prompted a reaction from some who saw the issue differently. Shortly after the resolution was passed, Marsh received a letter from one of the council's "elder statesmen," Charles C. Tuttle, a leading New York attorney and one-time GOP nominee for state governor. Tuttle asked permission to attend the DCSR's next regular meeting to submit a resolution for its consideration. Marsh granted this request. The Tuttle resolution began by noting that "in nominating candidates to public office, political parties frequently seem to pursue the practice of selection and exclusion according to sectarian adherence, rather than according to merit." It concluded as follows: "RESOLVED. That the Protestant Council of the City of New York hereby make emphatic protest against such practice . . . [and that] merit, character and qualification alone should be the basis of political selection (DCSR minutes, December 5, 1955).

It is unclear whether Tuttle intended this as a rebuttal to the position earlier proposed by Marsh—there being no necessary inconsistency between the two. In any event, the response to Tuttle's resolution on the part of the DCSR committee members suggested the existence of widely varying opinions, some of them contradictory to Tuttle's and more militant. In the discussion that followed, the members voiced three distinct positions on the question of Protestants in public office. Tuttle continued to stress that the council should "get the best persons into office, regardless of religion." Marsh argued in favor of a "long-range view of obtaining proper Protestant responsibility." Both these positions were by now fairly familiar in the organization. But a third faction held that what all this amounted to was clear "discrimination" against Protestant candidates, a situation calling for the most strenuous possible response. The minutes do not indicate who in particular took this stance or how widely it was supported, but it was clear that it was not supported by either Marsh or Tuttle (DCSR minutes, December 5, 1955).

The members decided not to adopt the Tuttle resolution but instead to request that Tuttle, Marsh, and Orrin Judd (soon to replace Marsh as the DCSR chair) seek to arrive at a compromise position. At the next monthly meeting, the members were told that the three men had met and that whatever council action might be required in this area should be conducted "without publicity" (DCSR minutes, January 9, 1956). In short, the substantive issue remained unresolved.

After three years during which the council continued its adherence to a moderate-activist stance, resistance to that position finally crystallized, with a new, and decidedly more militant, mood now making itself felt. In 1958, the board of directors voted that when the situation so required, council representatives could, with board approval, make specific individual endorsements (board of directors' minutes, April 24, 1958). At around this same time certain members of the Department of Christian Social Relations began to protest against the Dan Potter style, one that in their view did not always result in the appointment of the best-qualified Protestant candidate. These critics maintained that Potter and Paul Rischell had allowed themselves to be outmaneuvered by the mayor and other party officials, and had not fought hard enough for the principle of Protestant proportionality. The leading exponent of this view on the committee, Rev. Robert Stone, pastor of Adams-Parkhurst Presbyterian Church in Manhattan, charged that Potter and Rischell "tended to make their contacts merely a social gathering. They liked to go down and shake the Mayor's hand. They'll never get what they deserve because they're too interested in 'socials.' The very Protestants who get up in the world did not have Protestant Council support" (interview, spring 1961).

In addition to Stone, the other leading advocate of the militant position on the Christian Social Relations Committee was Rev. Pasquale Zaccara, who was active in both the Federation of Protestant Welfare Agencies and the St. George Association. On May 4, 1958, Stone seized the initiative by convening at his church a widely publicized "Conference on Christian Social Ethics and the City's Politics." Those in attendance almost filled the Adams-Parkhurst sanctuary. (It bears mentioning in this context that the "Parkhurst" in this church's name memorializes Rev. Charles H. Parkhurst, whose political role in the 1890s was discussed in the opening chapter.) Dan Potter, Paul Rischell, and Arthur Atha, the newly elected chair of the Christian Social Relations Committee, were all present at the meeting, but it was not one that any of them would later look back on with much pleasure or satisfaction. As Rischell later remarked in an interview: "I went to the Stone meeting. It was a meeting called to embarrass the Protestant Council. Dr. Potter had already been active on the appointments issue, but it was charged that the Big Names weren't getting anywhere" (interview, May 1961). At the meeting, Stone made clear his objectives: (1) maximizing Protestant political representation in the short run, (2) developing a climate of responsibility for Protestant governmental participation in the long run, and (3) achieving "balanced representation" in city government.

Growth of Race Consciousness

At the committee's next monthly meeting, held the day after the assembly at Stone's church, Chairman Atha won approval for the establishment, under DCSR auspices, of a "Committee on Protestant Responsibility in Political Life." Stone was named chair and was granted wide discretion in the selection of members to serve. In terms of composition, the committee represented a clear break with past PC practice. To a far greater extent that was true of the council as a whole at this point, CPRPL was comprised of African Americans, with four of its ten members (Walter Offutt, H. R. Hughes, Edler Hawkins, and Anna Arnold Hedgeman) being black. The written record is ambiguous as to the extent of CPRPL's commitment to a race agenda. What is clear is that earlier that same year the PC had named Rev. Gardiner Taylor as its first African American president, and that beginning in 1955 it had named five African Americans to its board of directors (Taylor and four others). This constituted a major shift for a traditionally white organization whose board in the decade previous had had but one black board member, O. Clay Maxwell. Evidently, CPRPL was responsive to that changed outlook, and black community activists may well have assumed that the PC was now open toward increased racial involvement. The committee members, black and white, were all personal friends of Stone's, and three of its four black members were newcomers to the federation with no prior PC involvement. The fact that all ten members were registered Democrats, in an organization widely identified as Republican-oriented, further testifies to its liberal, civil rights cast.

Drawing a Sharp Line

CPRPL's statements and actions soon made clear the wide gulf that separated it from the council's more established figures. In June 1958, at its first joint meeting with the parent body, the Christian Social Relations Committee, Chairman Stone outlined his conception of the new group's authority: "We shall have responsibility to develop relationships with the political parties in securing appointments and nominations. All officers and executives on the citywide level, and all potential candidates will work through this committee exclusively in so far as they work through the Council" (DCSR minutes, June 2, 1958).

Paul Rischell, who was Potter's successor as DCSR executive, wrote to Stone around this time with a gently worded reminder of the limits of the latter's authority: "I would hope that the Committee would not promote individuals for particular officers, but would be more general and promote the idea of an equal distribution of Protestants, Catholics, and Jews in public office. At an *ad hoc* meeting held a couple of months ago to discuss this very question, it was suggested that such a committee should not be a pressure group" (letter in DCSR files, June 19, 1958).

Stone's reply to this was cordial, but he took issue with Rischell on a key point: "You must define pressure group in a different way from me for it seems to me that we inevitably are such. . . . You must be thinking of pressure group in a different sense" (undated letter, DCSR files).

Yet the written record provides little hint of the sharp disagreement that arose within the church federation. As Rischell later remarked in an interview:

> I felt that Stone might dilute Dan Potter's efforts. Potter's prestige and that of the Advisory Committee he headed carried more weight than any group

> Stone might get together. All the work that Potter had done might be dissipated. One of my contentions was that this would be too explosive in the Council. [One candidate for appointment] called me up and called me all kinds of names. He said he had supported the Council, but that the Council had passed him over. (interview, May 1961)

Rev. Stone was undeterred by such concerns and was disdainful of the argument that open advocacy of candidates could threaten the council's patterns of internal accountability and authority. Thus his committee set forth a wide agenda, which included reinvigoration of Walter Offutt's research into religious backgrounds, a publicity campaign to inform the PC constituency of the committee's existence, screening potential candidates for public office, informing the mayor and New York party leaders of the committee's choices, and cooperation with other interest groups—the League of Women Voters, the Citizens Union, the St. George Association—with a view toward placing "political responsibility" information into members' hands. With respect to one of these functions, publicizing the committee's existence, little effort was required given that the council's interest in this area was already well known, and the group for some time had been the object of a stream of communications from people seeking the council's imprimatur. These communications were seldom marked by any great self-denial or modesty. The following, from 1958, is typical:

> Judge Kopfs advises me that the city court vacancy caused by his retirement ought to be filled by a Protestant and that continuing pressure should be brought on Sharkey to accomplish this. He believes that I am the logical qualified candidate and that my name should be hammered into Sharkey's thinking by the Council at both levels. Also the governor should be informed since he might request this of Sharkey. (DCSR files, March 1958)

In one area only, the possibility of recommending candidates for citywide *elective* office, did CPRPL hold back. This idea was discussed but never acted upon (CPRPL minutes, October 16, 1958).

Some Political Realities

Before discussing further the church federation's political behavior, it is useful to explore the wider political setting. In the post–World War II era, the Democratic Party dominated New York politics. While Republicans did occasionally receive high-level city and state appointments, such appointments were the exception, and typically occurred only when it suited the interests of the city's dominant Democratic machine. Thus many otherwise qualified Protestant candidates for appointive posts were effectively disqualified on the basis of their GOP affiliation. This presented the council with a difficult choice: should it demand that the Democratic chieftains essentially ignore party in the selection process, thereby opening things up for Protestant Republicans, but with little likelihood that the chieftains would agree, or should it instead avoid any mention of party and insist only that Protestants be given fair consideration? The latter stance would shrink the Protestant availability pool to the fairly small number of white Democrats plus a somewhat larger number of qualified blacks. Whichever the choice, some council constituents would be left dissatisfied.

Other difficulties related to the perceived "availability" of Protestant candidates for public service, whether Democrat or Republican. White Protestants, for their part, were typically less active in city politics than was the case for Catholics and Jews of similar age, education, and social standing. The Protestant ethic has long emphasized the virtues associated with corporate capitalism and business as compared to those related to partisan politics and government service. Should the council insist that Protestants be given consideration even in cases where a given candidate had not worked his/her way up the partisan political ladder? Availability concerns also applied to African Americans. The black community in the 1950s was characterized by a generalized apathy and lack of firm grounding in city politics. Such apathy reflected decades of racial hostility and prejudice on the part of whites, and a prevailing low level of black income, education, and political sophistication. African Americans were difficult, therefore, to organize for political ends and slow to enter the urban political mainstream. In light of this, should Protestant Council representatives insist that the usual criteria for availability be relaxed in the case of blacks? CPRPL essentially answered in the affirmative, since in its eyes the availability criterion was inherently racially biased and thus unworthy of being applied to people of color. It is less clear that the same position was taken by the council's moderate activists, who were disinclined to make race an issue in their conversations at city hall.

In proposing, therefore, to challenge the existing rewards-allocation system in city government, the Protestant Council found it necessary to mount a campaign of some cost, intensity, and finesse while at the same time delicately weighing the potential payoffs of such interventions against the risks, both to the council and to New York Protestantism. Elites within the church federation were divided over the relative merits of a moderate versus a militant stance, and differing public policy outcomes would likely occur depending on which of the two was chosen.

Experience with Moderate Activism

While its origins traced back to earlier years, the council's embrace of the moderate activist approach dates from 1955, and it would last well into the 1960s. Overall, this effort can be considered a modest success. A 1960 announcement prepared for distribution to Protestant Council supporters reports, "In 1955 there were only five Protestant judges out of 208 in our metropolitan area. With patient and determined work in this area we now have 13 Protestant judges" (mimeographed statement, DCSR files, October 1960). Furthermore, council protests resulted in a Protestant appointment to the position of Deputy Commissioner of Welfare. Noteworthy is the fact that the council's limited achievement in promoting candidates did not come at the expense of its existing access to the mayor and other high-level city officials. A bond of sorts had already developed between Mayor Wagner and Dan Potter, and it continued to develop after 1955. The two men had some important things in common. Both were white, male, and of similar age and temperament. While Wagner was himself a Roman Catholic, his wife was a Presbyterian. Potter was an ordained Presbyterian clergyman. When the mayor in 1958 established the Mayor's Committee of Religious Leaders (MCRL), he named Potter as its Protestant representative. There seems little reason, then, to doubt the accuracy of Potter's recollection of an incident that occurred during this period: "In most cases the Mayor hasn't had to ask us for suggestions on vacancies, since the Council usually puts in nominations on its own initiative. But I do recall that at the end of one meeting that we both attended the Mayor came over to me and asked how the Council would react to the appointment of Newbold Morris to a City judgeship. 'Will you check up and let me know,' he said" (interview, spring 1961).

While, as indicated above, council leaders devoted a good deal of time and energy to municipal judgeship and Welfare Department appointments, one gains a fuller understanding of its political action from another area of public policy, the choice for city school superintendent. New York's religious interest groups normally became politically aroused whenever the school superintendency falls vacant, and competition among them in this arena was very likely. As Sayre and Kaufman point out: "The Mayor, the party leaders, and most of the interest groups have become accustomed to their roles as marginal participants in the choice of a Superintendent. Only the religious interest groups appear to have a more direct access, relying upon their status as established by the equal tripartite division of the members of the Board among the three major religious faiths" (Sayre and Kaufman, 1960: 236).

The superintendency became vacant only infrequently, with but seven individuals having occupied the post from the formation of the Greater City in 1897 until 1960 (Sayre and Kaufman, 1960: 235). One vacancy occurred in 1958 with the retirement of Superintendent William Jansen, and the Protestant Council was immediately alert to the situation. In deciding on its position regarding a replacement for Jansen, PC leaders confronted a problem. There was but one serious Protestant candidate, John J. Theobald, and his Protestant credentials were deemed to be suspect. Although Theobald had been raised as a Protestant and as a child had attended a Protestant church, he was married to a Catholic and both his children attended Catholic parochial schools. A rumor circulated in Protestant circles, later proved unfounded, to the effect that he was taking instruction to become a Catholic. Ordinarily, all this would likely have precluded his being supported by the council. Yet for the church federation not to support Theobald would mean that the position almost certainly would go to the other leading candidate, a Catholic. As Dan Potter later remarked: "Theobald could get it with our support, but any other Protestant we might support probably wouldn't have a chance. If we did not go along with it, then our Protestants on the Board might have been forced to accept the Catholic candidate. The Protestants have had this position for some time and there was a feeling that it should not go to a Catholic" (interview, spring 1961). In the end, Theobald got the council's support—support that was immediately conveyed to the three Protestant members of the board of education. Furthermore, in the belief that Mayor Wagner was keenly interested, given that Theobald was then serving as deputy mayor in the Wagner administration, Potter made it a point to inform the mayor of the council's position. In the end, for whatever reasons, Theobald was the person selected to be the new superintendent.

Experience with Militancy

While the moderate position on appointments enjoyed a secure place in the church federation's structure, and resulted in no apparent diminution in council access at city hall, those identified with the militant position had a less satisfactory experience. CPRPL, the embodiment of the militant position, met a total of nine times between June 1958 and September the following year. Rev. Stone resigned as chair early in 1960. Thus, the committee remained active for just over a year. Their political success was marginal: of the six committee-endorsed candidates, only one was later appointed (CPRPL report, DCSR files, May 1959).

The committee's problems were partially external. As noted above, Stone had anticipated that the committee would "have responsibility to develop relationships with the political parties in securing appointments and nominations." Yet the chairman's efforts to arrange appointments with the mayor and others in official positions fell on deaf ears:

> We asked for an appointment with Judson Morehouse [Republican State Chairman], but got put off. Representative [Charles] Buckley [Democratic leader in the Bronx] simply refused to see us. He would not talk politics with Protestants. I hardly think they felt we were pressuring them, because we were always willing to settle for their men, but they were not always very helpful. We did get through to [Carmine] DeSapio [the New York County Democratic leader]. (interview, February 1961)

The committee minutes record somberly that "The chairman [Stone] sent a letter to the Mayor regarding appointments and no reply was received" (CPRPL minutes, November 14, 1958, DCSR files).

Such frustrations with external groups were matched by internal ones. As noted above, Stone had expected, "All officers and executives on the city-wide level . . . will work through this committee exclusively. . . ." That expectation, too, went unfulfilled. An event that occurred after the committee had been functioning for about a year illustrates the point. Early in 1959, the council learned that Judge John W. Hill, a Protestant, was soon to resign as presiding judge of the Domestic Relations Court. Since this position traditionally had been held by Protestants, the council resolved that Hill's replacement also should be of the same faith. Four sitting judges, all Protestants (Dudley, Thurston, Hannah, and Waltemede) contended for the council's endorsement. (Three other contenders, all Roman Catholics, were not considered.) The council's selection process was complicated by the fact that one of the four choices, the Honorable Richard W. Hannah, was a leader of the council's Brooklyn Division while a second, the Honorable Wilfred Waltemede, was a member of its citywide board of directors. CPRPL met to consider the four contenders and, making no effort to win consensus internally, agreed to endorse Dudley, a Democrat, and Thurston, a Republican.

Those endorsements were conveyed for approval to the parent body, the Committee on Christian Social Relations, at a meeting held later that month. The minutes record that the submission aroused "extended discussion lasting over two hours." One can imagine that some members were bewildered and angry. A compromise of sorts was finally reached: a delegation would arrange to meet with the mayor and, while mentioning all four Protestants, would confidentially indicate to him that Dudley and Thurston were actually the preferred choices.

To carry out this mandate, a delegation of five was chosen: Orrin Judd, Pasquale Zaccara, and Robert Stone (from the committee), and two noncommittee members: Dan Potter and Charles Tuttle. These five forgathered at the mayor's official residence to agree among themselves on exactly what was to be said. Since a formal report on the meeting would later be submitted to the council's board of directors, where both Hannah and Waltemede would likely be in attendance, a certain circumspection was obviously required. At this point a dispute broke out. Stone interpreted his mandate to mean that, although Hannah and Waltemede should be mentioned to the mayor in a perfunctory way, he should be left in no doubt that neither man was really considered to be qualified for the presiding judgeship. Tuttle objected strenuously to that strategy. He could not participate in any delegation that intended to suggest that Hannah and Waltemede, whom he had known for years as fellow members of the New York bar, were unqualified. Endorsing the four while indicating a preference for the two was one thing, and he could accept that. But to suggest that two were qualified but the others were not was unacceptable. He would leave if the latter was the intention. In this, Potter supported Tuttle. After these preliminary fireworks, the actual conference with the mayor was an anticlimax. The delegation voiced approval for the four Protestants, but in a manner that indicated who were the real choices. The mayor indicated that he understood.

The results of this meeting left Stone angry and frustrated. That evening he phoned Potter and delivered a tirade concerning the latter's alleged sellout to Tuttle. He regarded the incident as a severe blow to his, and the CPRPL's, prestige. The committee held just one more meeting before deciding to disband.

Conclusion

These events illustrate the situation that is likely to arise when an interest group seeks to designate some of its supports, but not others, for outside offices and preferments. The council's achievements on the public appointments front, while not large, were probably the most that could be reasonably expected given the circumstances. The greater success of the moderate-activist, as compared to the militant, approach is explainable in terms of the moderates' greater identification with the PC, including the church group's sustainability and internal consensus requirements. The moderates' accommodating style, one that the militants found highly irritating, can be regarded as a logical response to the existing cross-pressures within the church federation and the limited patience of public officials for citizen protests that exceed a certain limit. A more aggressive style could have heightened internal tensions and animosities while at the same time antagonizing the target politicians.

For its part, the CPRPL faced a variety of handicaps which proved its undoing. Two of them applied to the council as a whole: an inability to offer political money or other tangible inducements to politicians, and a lack of stable support among constituent churches for council-sponsored political action. Another handicap applied to the committee itself: a failure to secure full compliance from the council's leadership for its actions, and its naive assumption that it could move forward even in the absence of such legitimation. While Rev. Stone claimed an exclusive prerogative in selecting people to support for appointments, the council's board of directors evidently had no intention of granting him that. CPRPL's early demise is instructive, though not perhaps wholly surprising. All New York City interest groups, not just church federations, are at a disadvantage when they seek to approach political party leaders (Sayre and Kaufman, 1960: 494).

In a larger sense, the organizational dilemmas discussed in this chapter serve to underscore the difficulties that any interest group is likely to encounter in assuming a candidate-screening function with respect to public office. This function is one that leaders of political party organizations fulfill routinely. Their machines typically have well-oiled techniques for placating members when, as is inevitably the case, certain of them must be denied in their quest for party preferment. Party leaders are accustomed to taking steps aimed at insuring that any party activists passed over in this setting are not left entirely empty-handed. Side payments, preferments of various kinds, and promises of support for a future candidacy all can be offered in some combination as palliatives. Such techniques are essential toward insuring the machine's stability and survival. Interest groups, on the other hand, typically lack such tools of adjustment and recompense. Their leaders are for the most part unschooled in this branch of the art of politics.

5

The Urban Church in a Conservative Political Era

Beginning in the 1970s, and continuing into the '80s, newspaper readers in the two cities under discussion learned that the citywide church structures serving their communities were undergoing profound changes. In regard to Protestantism, the mainly Protestant councils of churches in Detroit and New York—only recently large, robust, and stable—were now reported to be shrinking, with related organizational instability. It was even suggested that these groups' very survival was in jeopardy, so great were their burdens and so slender their available resources. In regard to Catholicism, the archdioceses serving the two cities faced no such imminent threats to survival—their jurisdictions extended far into the surrounding suburbs where large, fairly affluent Catholic populations provided them a stable base of support. Yet the two archdioceses still confronted major problems and difficult choices.

While population movement from central city to suburb contributed to the stresses besetting these citywide church structures, other factors were also involved, not the least among them being a change in the relations between those structures and state and local governments. The discussion to follow explores this topic, in doing so maintaining the earlier emphasis on the complex, interdependent relationship between church and state in the two cities, one with roots in the past but that continues to evolve.

The Demographic Element

Given the importance of demography in the developments treated below, it is useful to begin by noting the timing and scope of late-twentieth-century demographic changes in the two cities. In New York, blacks reached 20 percent of the city population by 1970, and by 1990, 22 percent—in the process becoming the city's largest identifiable minority. (Hispanics were a close second.) This population shift was highly significant from the standpoint of the ethnic makeup of New York's Protestant churches. Whereas as recently as 1960 black churchgoers comprised only about half of the city's Protestant church population of roughly 1.75 million, fifteen years later their number would far surpass their white brethren. Estimates developed by the Council of Churches of the City of New York revealed that as of 1975, the city's Protestant population, having recently increased to 2.4 million, was now 80 percent black. (The other 20 percent consisted about equally of whites and Hispanics, each numbering around 100,000.) In the words of a local journalist, the black church now represented "the heart of [New York's] Protestant strength" (*New York Times,* August 18, 1975). Detroit witnessed the same change in even more dramatic form. In only twenty years, the city's population went from majority white to overwhelmingly black—more specifically, from 29 percent black in 1960, to 63 percent in 1980. By 1990 the city was 77 percent black. Detroit's African American population was not of any one religious persuasion. Variety, not uniformity, marked its religious pattern, with Catholics and Muslims both well represented at roughly 100,000 each. Still, the city's black citizenry was chiefly Protestant, and more particularly, by over 50 percent, Baptist. White Protestant and white Catholic church members, who until recently had jointly comprised a clear majority of congregational membership, now became numerically insignificant.

The above changes deeply impacted citywide church structures. In New York, the council of churches by 1975 had come to be regarded as "little more than a weak umbrella agency" (*New York Times,* August 18, 1975); a little over a decade later the same group was seen as having experienced a "precipitous decline" and was now viewed as "an outsider, not a major player." In a period of black protest and generalized black intolerance of traditional ecumenical groups, a contemporary account noted that "The Council's voice has barely been heard" (*New York Times,* March 6, 1988). There was a widespread consensus that Protestantism's troubles stemmed from "the new demographics," involving the exodus of one million whites from New York and their replacement by one million blacks. In the same vein, the religion editor of one of Detroit's two metropolitan dailies in a 1994 article alluded to "the fading influence" of that city's council of churches, which the writer explained in terms of Detroit's new population makeup, coupled with "the nationwide trend away from old-style ecumenical councils of Christian clergy" (*Detroit Free Press,* January 21, 1994).

The same set of circumstances applied to Catholicism. In accounting for the 1989 large-scale forced closing of Detroit Catholic parishes, a press account quoted the city's auxiliary bishop to the effect that "there are just too many Detroit Catholic parishes for too few members" (*Detroit News,* March 24, 1985). Likewise, in his church-closure announcement of September 29, 1988, Cardinal Szoka mentioned a number of contributory factors—the slow progress in evangelizing blacks, aging structures in need of repair, and a nationwide shortage of priests—but went on to identify as the driving force "white flight during the past several decades" (*Detroit News,* October 1, 1988). In short, there can be no escaping the importance of urban migration as a key element in the malaise of the more established church organizations in the two cities.

Urban-Related National Developments

America's cities are, of course, significantly linked to national politics, and it is therefore useful to consider that larger picture as a means of better understanding the setting in which local church leaders and city officials now interacted. The twenty-year period from 1975 to 1994 was marked by a political shift to the right in the nation's politics. That applied especially to GOP presidents Gerald Ford, Ronald Reagan, and George Bush, all of whom were generally to the right of their post–New Deal Republican predecessors, and also the two Democratic presidents of the period, Jimmy Carter and Bill Clinton, who were both "New Democrats" to the right of their pre-1970 Democratic counterparts. While New York and Detroit both persisted in their accustomed "liberal" molds—even the most conservative of the group, New York's Mayor Rudolph Giuliani, was to the left of his GOP counterparts elsewhere in his own state and in the nation—they did so in an atmosphere more at odds than before with the prevailing mood in the nation's capital.

An early harbinger of that strain was the federal government's response to New York City's looming budget problems of the early 1970s. By 1975, the city's troubles had reached crisis proportions, with bankers refusing to extend the city further credit and the city's finances in turmoil. Appeals to Washington for assistance were initially rebuffed by President Ford, which resulted in a now-famous *New York Daily News* headline, "Ford to New York: Drop Dead." Finally, in November 1975, the president relented. The White House supported legislation that extended up to $2.3 billion per year in FY 1976, 1977, and 1978 in short-term loans to the city (Shefter, 1992: 134).

This financial assistance occurred in the wake of an extraordinary church lobbying effort directed at the president and others in the Ford administration.

It was spearheaded by leaders of the New York Archdiocese and the Diocese of Brooklyn, with the backing of the city's Federation of Protestant Welfare Agencies, Board of Rabbis, and Council of Churches. For some time preceding the crisis, representatives of these organizations had been meeting on a monthly basis to determine where cuts in the city's social service budget should be made in order to least hurt the people. Following a three-faith joint press conference held at the Rectory of New York's St. Patrick's Cathedral, officials of the New York Archdiocese and Brooklyn Diocese traveled to Albany where they met with their counterparts elsewhere in the state whose dioceses jointly comprised the New York Catholic Conference. With the endorsement provided by that body, a delegation of New York Catholic leaders then proceeded to Washington where they got the National Conference of Catholic Bishops to buy into their fiscal bailout plan. It had been only a week since a city delegation consisting of Mayor Abraham Beame and other notables had met with President Ford to plead their case for federal support, but without success. Yet with pressure mounting from additional sources, the Catholic Church most notably, the president shifted ground. While his basic outlook remained unchanged—cities should take responsibility for their own fiscal health without Washington's involvement—he relented sufficiently to provide New York with the loans it was seeking (interview, Msgr. James Murray, Catholic Charities of the Archdiocese of New York, 1996).

New York officials felt under pressure to offset declining federal funding, and they did so by increasing the city tax burden. The general fund budget rose from $11.1 billion in FY 1975 to $31.6 billion in FY 1995, and spending on "public welfare and social services" also surged, from $2.6 billion in FY 1975 to $7.3 billion in FY 1995 (budget, City of New York).

While Detroit was initially more successful than New York City in its dealings with Washington, that advantage would fade with time. Mayor Coleman Young, employing an "executive centered coalition" strategy, early on succeeded in wresting substantial federal resources for his city. Between FY 1975 and FY 1978, Detroit realized a remarkable 62 percent increase in federal support, with federal and state aid combining to produce fully 41 percent of city revenues (Anton, 1983: 17). But the mayor's strategy contained a major weakness: it was highly personal and fragile, with the mayor himself directly holding most of his political coalitions together. In 1983, a close student of Detroit municipal affairs, Thomas Anton, observed that the Young machine was vulnerable to any diminishment of funding from Lansing and Washington (Anton, 1983: 49). Subsequent events would lend credence to this view. As compared to the favorable treatment given him by the Carter administration, Young's influence in the nation's capital diminished in the Reagan years, 1981–89. Moreover, by the early 1990s his own ill health (emphysema) and advancing age further sapped his administration's influence in the nation's capital.

It is not surprising, therefore, that in the later years of the Young era the city found itself increasingly dependent on its own tax base to meet its obligations. In a fifteen-year period beginning in 1979, the city's "appropriated budget—tax levy allocations" nearly doubled, from $725 million in FY 1979–80 to $1,397 million in FY 1994–95, while its health and social services budget grew even more rapidly. The Hospitals and Public Health budget, for example, increased four-fold from $21.6 million in FY 1979–80 to FY $84.5 million in 1994–95 (budget, City of Detroit).

There were clear limits, however, in the extent to which Detroit and New York taxpayers could compensate, out of their own pockets, for the marked decline in urban-related federal outlays, especially in light of middle-class exodus to the suburbs and the related loss of taxpaying business. As a result, faith-based social services programs in the inner city experienced a loss in revenue, as did many welfare-oriented inner city churches—traditionally a mainstay in city church federations.

A major tenet of conservative ideology is the devolution of power away from Washington to both state government and nonprofit private providers. Consistent with that view, the Reagan administration lent rhetorical support to the return of religion to the public sphere and to the revitalization of "third party government" whereby voluntary agencies, faith-based included, would provide needed social services, as opposed to their provision largely, if not exclusively, by government. Such support represented a significant departure from the ideology dominant in the New Deal and post–New Deal liberal era, the 1930s through the first term of the Nixon administration (1969–73), which placed government at the center of assistance programs (Nathan, 1975). The new ideology undergirded a Reagan-era "channeling of millions of public dollars to faith-based and other nonprofits . . . [and a related] enormous growth in the quantity and range of activities undertaken by religious organizations" (Meredith Ramsay, 1998: 601).

While this policy shift was potentially beneficial to religiously based social welfare agencies, it ended up being overwhelmed by another, much more powerful trend, namely the basic shift in federal spending priorities away from social services. The Reagan administration's initial budget proposals for the years 1982 through 1985 would have reduced by $33 billion—about 20 percent—the funding for private welfare institutions. Moreover, for certain types of welfare agencies, the administration's proposed cuts far exceeded the 20 percent figure.

For example, its FY 1985 estimate for nonprofit social services projected a drastic 64 percent cut as compared to that proposed in the Carter administration's last year. Congress ultimately approved only a portion of these proposed cutbacks, thus reducing somewhat the severity of the change. Still, federal support to nonprofits ended up significantly below the level for 1980. By 1986, inflation-adjusted federal support to all nonprofit organizations outside of the health field was 28 percent below the 1980 level, whereas in the social services field the decline exceeded 40 percent (Salamon, 1995).

This pattern would continue into the period following Reagan's departure from office. Excluding the two federal health programs, Medicaid and Medicare, inflation-adjusted federal spending on human services programs during the Bush administration (1989–93) was 7 percent below the 1980 amount. With but rare exceptions, moreover, state governments proved unable to compensate for the increased federal constraint, with the result that the typical private agency had no alternative other than to slash staffing and service levels (Salamon, 1995: 194, 205).

Catholic social service was especially hard hit by these developments. In the 1960s, Catholic diocesan charities in the United States had aggressively and successfully pursued the then-newly-available federal funding, to the point that their dependency on tax-derived income greatly exceeded that of their Protestant and Jewish counterparts. By the 1980s, government funds constituted fully 82 percent of Catholic charities' collective revenue of roughly $1.8 billion, and such funding underwrote an enormous expansion in their scale, quality, and scope of service. Such heavy dependency on the U.S. government rendered these Catholic agencies especially vulnerable to possible funding cutbacks. As Mary J. Oates remarks, "cuts in federal appropriations for social programs in the 1980s were immediately reflected, not only in their own agency budgets, but also in an increase in applications for help from people whom other private agencies could no longer assist." The efforts of diocesan officials to compensate for the federal funding shortfall through appeals to grassroots parishioners proved unavailing, with adverse effects for Catholic agency budget and service levels. By the early 1990s, nearly one-third of American dioceses were in financial difficulty (Oates, 1995: 170).

The Malaise of Councils of Churches

While demographic changes and the altered federal funding picture partially explain the strains experienced by church federations in the two cities under discussion, there were other roots as well. One consisted of an altered political and governmental setting.

New York

In the late 1960s, as previously noted, the Council of Churches of the City of New York for the first time in many years was beset by major internal strains. The protests staged by radical black clergy against the annual Family of Man banquets, beginning with the first such banquet in 1961, were followed by others the years to follow. By 1971, the theme of the protests had broadened to include criticism from both conservatives, who objected to the council's basic ecumenical strategy that allegedly diluted its adherence to orthodox Christian principles to the neglect of a clear "Christian message," and from liberals, who charged the council with a variety of failings: insensitivity toward minority concerns (as exemplified by the continuing presence in office of a white clergyman, Dan Potter, despite New York Protestantism's now overwhelmingly nonwhite makeup) and sexism (as exemplified by the objectionable names for the "Family of Man" banquet and "Family of Man Society") among other alleged shortcomings (*New York Times,* October 17, 1971).

Yet Dan Potter managed to survive as executive director for nearly a decade beyond 1971, largely on the basis of his continuing support from long-serving CCCNY board members, some of whom were socially prominent whites, others conservatively inclined African American pastors identified in several cases with the Council of Baptist Pastors. (The black support became more important as the charges leveled against Potter became increasingly racially tinged.) While Potter's tenure as director of the CCCNY probably would have ended fairly soon in any case, the suddenness of his actual departure could not have been anticipated.

The events that eventuated in Potter's downfall began with a September 1978 account in one of New York City's black newspapers, *The Knickerbocker News,* to the effect that the CCCNY executive director was a slumlord in Albany, the state capital. Potter was identified as the owner of several buildings in Albany's Arbor Hill neighborhood, ones acquired by him in the early 1960s on a visit to his brother, an Albany pastor. The structures were located in a neighborhood frequently cited by city agencies for building code violations. In defending himself against the this charge, Potter stated that the code violations were nothing new for the buildings: "They have had them for over 100 years. They were existent before I ever got the property, and ever since we've had them I've been working constantly on them to improve them." That defense was refuted by various local observers. An Albany rehabilitation specialist, for one, pointed out that Potter's buildings were a case of "landlord neglect, not tenant vandalism." The director of Albany's United Methodist Society, for another, insisted that Potter's "houses are some of the worst in the Albany slums." Word of all this spread quickly to New York City's black community, with state senator and reverend—elective officeholder and clergyman—Carl McCall taking the role of Potter's chief accuser. McCall's call for Potter's suspension pending further investigation was widely publicized. Moreover, the city's mostly white Protestant denominational leaders now issued a statement calling for Potter's immediate ouster (*New York Times,* November 11, 1978; February 11, 1979).

On November 1, 1978, the CCCNY responded officially to these events by appointing a nine-member investigating committee, and this body proceeded to deliberate. In January of the following year, it rendered a report affirming that "it is unclear as to whether Dan Potter is guilty of being an absentee landlord or whether he is guilty of being a poor businessman," and went on to recommend that Potter be replaced at the earliest practical moment. The board balked at suggestions that Potter be dismissed forthwith, however, and held fast to its decision to proceed deliberately despite a torrent of anti-Potter criticism that erupted following its investigation. Potter would be allowed to continue in active service until the expiration of his contract, December 1980. Still, for all practical purposes Potter's leadership ended with the January 1978 board action.

This internal firestorm coincided almost exactly with a change in administration at city hall. In the New York election of November 9th, 1977, Congressman Edward Koch defeated the incumbent mayor, Abe Beame, in a reelection bid. Koch's victory came just eight days after the CCCNY directors voted to authorize the probe of Potter, while his formal installation to the mayor's office on January 1, 1978, came the same month as the CCCNY committee vote recommending Potter's removal. While there is no obvious or necessary connection between these two sets of events, it is noteworthy that whereas the Council of Churches had enjoyed fairly good city hall access through the Abe Beame era, 1974–78, the soon-to-begin administration of Ed Koch, 1978–90, would see no repeat of that open atmosphere.

Whatever the causes, the CCCNY now found itself, for the first time in many years, essentially frozen out at city hall. This changed atmosphere probably stemmed in part from Mayor Koch's awareness of the church council's well-publicized internal troubles. Also, the new mayor was inclined to draw sharp distinctions between political supporters and nonsupporters, and minority group leaders, which included Protestants of whatever racial or ethnic stripe, were not in the "supporter" category. Whatever inclinations Koch may have had, early on, to confer with representatives of the city's three major religious bodies—the Council of Churches, the Board of Rabbis, and the Catholic Archdiocese of New York—were never great, and those inclinations would wane with time. Thus, by 1988, ten years after assuming office, the mayor was relying on particular religious leaders, Cardinal John O'Connor, for example, not the traditional "big three" organizations, for advice on church-state issues (*New York Times,* March 6, 1954). The Koch years, in short, saw the Council of Churches politically marginalized to an extent almost never paralleled in its nearly four decades of existence.

This change in city hall atmosphere probably contributed indirectly to the increased factionalism that now beset the church federation. Politically aware and ambitious CCCNY constituents, who in earlier years might have hesitated to challenge its authority given the organization's access at city hall, and to a more limited degree in Albany and Washington, now evidently felt less constrained. Critics of the council's leadership could now act out their concerns and antagonisms without fear of alienating what earlier might have appeared as a potential ally in their own governmental dealings. Precise data on this point are lacking, but there are various indications that this strategizing was the case.

In the 1980s, New York's Council of Churches reached an organizational nadir. As recently as the close of the preceding decade, the group had employed 35 persons, enjoyed an annual budget of $1 million, and claimed a reserve fund of $2.5 million. Eight years later, 1988, its payroll had shrunk to four persons, it had been evicted from its office suite in the Interchurch Center, and its debts totaled more than $300,000. Despite the appointment of an African American as executive director, Rev. Robert L. Polk, the federation proved unable to attract significant black support, and there was no "new money" forthcoming to offset loss of the "old"—a point acknowledged by Polk. A leading black clergymen in Manhattan, Rev. Calvin O. Butts, of the Abyssinian Baptist Church, now labeled the Council of Churches "impotent" and "too busy trying to survive." And a leading (white) denominational executive, Rev. Carl E. Fleminster (American Baptist), declared that "what now exists does not meet the needs of a Protestant witness in New York City." Fleminster went on to outline the steps he had recently taken to pick up some of the council's functions "if it goes under" (*New York Times,* March 6, 1988).

Further adding to the federation's woes was its continued isolation from New York Catholicism. The Second Vatican Council, held in Rome in the middle 1960s, had aroused Protestant hopes for a bridging of the city's historic Catholic/Protestant rift. In furtherance of that end, in 1969 the Protestant Council had changed its name to "Council of Churches of the City of New York" (CCCNY). This move brought the citywide organization's name more in line with that of the Queens Federation of Churches, which for the past several years, with the tacit approval of the Catholic Diocese of Brooklyn, had successfully integrated local Catholic parishes into its structure and operations without evident harm to its traditional Protestant base. But any such hopes of further collaboration came to naught. Officials of the New York Archdiocese disdained any possibility of local Catholic parishes' becoming CCCNY members, largely on the basis of Catholicism's fervent opposition to abortion and to the Supreme Court's 1973 *Roe vs. Wade* decision—positions antithetical to those espoused by most New York Protestant leaders (*New York Times,* August 18, 1975).

Robert Polk departed as the CCCNY director in 1988, and his immediate successor, Rev. Patricia Reeberg, also soon departed following a short, unhappy tenure. In the middle-1990s the Council managed to stabilize at a minimal level of operations under the leadership of a part-time director, Rev. John E. Hiemstra (Reformed Church in America). Overall, the period in question was organizationally highly stressful.

Still, this difficult period was not without its occasional bright spots, of which one in particular is deserving of close attention. For an interlude beginning in 1989, the group's fortunes marginally improved. From its earlier insolvency and indebtedness, the church federation now saw an upturn in its revenues, such that by 1992 its income totaled a not-insubstantial $262,000 (CCCNY auditor's report, 1994). This modest improvement coincided almost precisely with the mayoralty of David Dinkins, a Protestant, who was elected mayor in November 1989 and who assumed office the following January. For the first time in many years, CCCNY leaders found in the occupant of Gracie Mansion an individual aware of their collective existence and well disposed toward their principles and aims. It would difficult to overstate the new mayor's contribution to this improvement. In the words of the CCCNY president at the time, Rev. Spencer Gibbs:

> Each time a new mayor assumes office, the Council extends an invitation to him to sit down with us, and Mr. Dinkins obliged us very quickly. My sense is

> that he regarded the religious community as important. His pastor, the Rev. Fred Williams, Church of the Intercession, had been friends with Dinkins for some time. So, within weeks of his taking office the mayor met with the Council's board of directors at our regular meeting site, St. John the Divine Cathedral. It was an occasion for us and the mayor to share ideas. The mayor brought with him several of his aides, and that added weight to the occasion.

This meeting was important both symbolically and in more tangible terms. The church leaders used the occasion to air their public policy concerns, which included, among other things, a displeasure over the city's tax on fuel oil. In their eyes, this tax constituted a heavy burden on local congregations to the tune of several hundreds of thousands of dollars annually. In the aftermath of the meeting, Mayor Dinkins, after first consulting with the relevant state and federal officials, got the fuel tax abated.

Council leaders interviewed for this study dispute any suggestion that Dinkins' mayoralty and the council's improved circumstances were necessarily causally connected. They stress that other factors were involved as well. Yet these leaders share a conviction that Dinkins impacted the council favorably. One board member at the time, Archdeacon Michael Kendall of the Episcopal Diocese of New York, expresses the point in these terms:

> David Dinkins did a great deal to provide occasions for us to come together. By and large the mayor's people said that we ought to be together. That represented a dramatic change from his predecessor, Ed Koch. Under Koch, our City Hall involvement, such as it was, was crisis-driven—drugs, housing, and jobs. Dinkins provided an atmosphere that was very supportive to a more active council of churches. And there was also another element. Dinkins' [1989] mayoral candidacy stimulated an organizing effort in his behalf and against Koch, and that helped get him [Dinkins] elected. Church people were a part of that [coalition]. So, Dinkins benefitted the churches in two ways. (interview, March 1997)

Given that Dinkins, the CCCNY's president (Gibbs), and executive director (Reeberg) were all African American, one might assume that the newly favorable atmosphere was chiefly energized by feelings of racial solidarity. The parties involved, however, are also wary of that interpretation. Instead they underscore the common spiritual, or church, linkage. In the words of Gibbs (interview, June 18, 1996), "It was rather the fact that the mayor happened to be an active churchman, in contrast to his two immediate predecessors, that led us to the closer, more open relationship. Race was not the key." Whatever the causes, it would appear that council leaders benefitted from their improved relations at city hall, which served to enhance their overall reputation among constituents and marginally diminished the internal criticism directed against them.

Detroit

The above-described New York City events were roughly paralleled by developments around the same time in Detroit. The late 1970s and 1980s were arguably the most perilous in the Detroit church council's long history. When Edward Willingham assumed the directorship in 1976 following the eight-year tenure (1968–75) of his predecessor, Rev. Robert Kincheloe, the council was in financial trouble and at risk of dissolution. The organization had run deficits throughout the Kincheloe years, amounting to never less than 20 percent of total budget, and at one point (1971) fully one third. The group had managed to survive despite this by drawing on reserve funds, but by the end of the Kincheloe era those reserves were essentially exhausted. Through a determined effort on his part, Willingham succeeded in trimming the Christian Communication Council of Metropolitan Detroit Churches' (CCCMDC) deficit, thus averting a looming disaster. Critical to that achievement was the acceptance of council membership on the part of a number of local Catholic parishes, whose involvement in the church federation was tacitly approved by the chancery of the archdiocese. By renaming itself "Christian Communication Council"—a change negotiated by Willingham as a condition of his taking office—the church federation helped remove what some considered as the objectionable Protestant connotation of "Council of Churches." (It is ironic that around the same time the "council of churches" label was embraced, not abandoned, by New York Protestant leaders, and with the same object in view.) Willingham would later remark, "We would have gone under without the infusion of support from Catholic churches" (interview, 1996). The council also benefitted from a growing reputation for inclusive ecumenism, with outreach not just to Detroit Catholics, but across the Detroit River to congregations in neighboring Windsor, Ontario (several of which became members), to Detroit's African American churches (a handful of which also joined), and the Muslim community. By the 1980s, these initiatives enabled a much-scaled-back federation to meet its obligations based on a balanced budget.

Leaders of the Detroit church federation had reason to hope, early on, that the mayoralty of Coleman Young might entail an improvement in the group's relations with city hall. Upon taking office as mayor in early 1974, the new mayor displayed an openness toward the Christian Communication Council, and he and Robert Kincheloe established contact with one another. The mayor had recently become a member of Detroit's New Calvary Baptist Church, whose pastor, Rev. Charles Butler, was among his longtime friends. Yet any hopes for a mutually supportive relationship between the mayor and the Christian Communication Council did not survive Young's early months in office. Beginning 1976, a rift developed between the CCCMDC and city hall over proposals to legalize casino gambling that would not be wholly bridged during the mayor's long tenure. Detailed coverage of this dispute is reserved for the chapter to follow, but for the present purposes it bears noting that the dispute shaped relations between the mayor's office and the CCCMDC. Even though Ed Willingham was occasionally asked by the mayor's office to offer the prayer at city-sponsored gatherings—offers invariably accepted—and despite Willingham's appearance once on a dias beside Mayor Young for a discussion of city issues, the fundamental rift remained. It overshadowed all other issues, including those on which the mayor and the council of churches were of one mind—for example, on the proposal, finally adopted, to make nonresident Detroit workers subject to the city income tax.

Archdioceses and Inner Cities Transformed

In the case of Catholicism, there was never any serious threat to the continued survival of the archdioceses in either of the cities here under discussion. Yet the Church's relations with government in Detroit and New York were necessarily impacted by certain changes then under way, some internal to the Church, others relating to the wider urban community. In Detroit, the central city Catholic population plummeted, while in New York, despite a constancy in overall church membership, the Catholic population in the space of few years went from overwhelmingly white to half Latino. Financial constraints also loomed. In 1991, following decades of middle class out-migration from the city, the New York Archdiocese reported its worst financial downturn in history (Oates, 1995: 167).

It is noteworthy that in the period from 1975 to 1994, none of the individuals occupying the mayor's office in either New York or Detroit was Roman Catholic. Since before World War I this was a situation unprecedented in both cities for such a long period of time. Prior to 1975, the typical pattern was for Catholic mayors to predominate. New York's most recent era of Catholic mayoral dominance had lasted from 1945 through 1965, and encompassed the mayoralties of William O'Dwyer, Vincent R. Impellitteri, and Robert Wagner Jr. In Detroit, the post–World War II period also saw a long period of Catholic political ascendancy, as embodied in the mayoralties of Eugene I. Van Antwerp, Louis C. Miriani, Jerome P. Cavanagh, and Roman Gribbs, who left office in 1974 following his defeat by Coleman Young. These facts raise the obvious question of whether the Catholic Church's political access in city government may have depended on the presence of a Catholic in the mayor's office. Did the Church's clout wax with the inauguration of a Catholic, only to wane with the subsequent election of someone not of that faith?

One is tempted to answer this question in the affirmative. The case of New York's Francis Cardinal Spellman could be invoked in support of it. During his nearly three decades' tenure as head of the New York Archdiocese, from 1939 to 1967, and with three of the five mayors during that the time being Catholics, Spellman was undisputed as a power factor in New York politics. A keen observer of the local scene, John Cooney, reports that in the 1950s and '60s Carmine DeSapio, the boss of Tammany Hall, regarded Spellman "as one of the forces in the city that must be taken into account." The cardinal was on close personal terms with William O'Dwyer during his mayoral tenure, and in Mayor Vincent Impellitteri, Spellman "couldn't have found a more compliant personality." No less cordial were the cardinal's dealings with Robert Wagner Jr. As mayor, Wagner did favors for Spellman—for example, arranging for a gift of valuable land to Fordham University, a Catholic institution, which was adjacent to the city's Lincoln Center project. In turn the mayor was the recipient of the cardinal's beneficence—for example, intervention by the prelate to prevent city transit-worker strikes, which, had they occurred, could have seriously embarrassed the Wagner administration (Cooney, 1984: 300–301). Further support for the hypothesis that Catholism's access at city hall might be dependent on the religious affiliation of the mayoral incumbent can be found in the Church's experience in dealing with John Lindsay, a non-Catholic installed as mayor in 1966. Lindsay early on made known his unwillingness to accept Spellman's advice in connection with appointments of high-ranking city officials or judges, thus signaling a change from past years when the cardinal's advice on such matters had been routinely sought and accepted (Cooney, 1984: 301–2). Yet Lindsay is an exception to a more general pattern of fairly sustained Church political clout in city affairs whatever the mayor's personal religious affiliation. Prior to Lindsay, New York's non-Roman Catholic mayor was Fiorello La Guardia, and La Guardia maintained what an informant later described as a "close personal friendship," with Monsignor Robert Keegan, the executive director of the Catholic Charities of the New York Archdiocese.

There is likely no better illustration of the Catholic Church's capacity to sustain a large role in municipal affairs despite the presence of a non-Catholic in the mayor's office than its "privileged access" to Ed Koch, who served three mayoral terms, 1978–1990. During this time, Koch was in close contact with both John Cardinal O'Connor and the Catholic bishop of Brooklyn, Francis J. Mugavero. In his autobiography, Koch twice refers to the cardinal as a "friend," and as one whom he has requested should speak at the funeral ceremony following his death. O'Connor was among Koch's first visitors when the mayor was hospitalized following a stroke in 1987, and the cardinal rallied to his side during a controversy that erupted in 1991, shortly after Koch's leaving office. On the latter occasion, as Koch ruefully notes in his autobiography, the leaders of his own Jewish faith chose to remain silent (Koch, 1992: 222–23; 244–45). Toward the close of Koch's third term in office, the mayor and the cardinal in a friendly way took opposing sides of controversial issues in a book the two men jointly authored (O'Connor, 1989).

Mayor Koch was evidently no less acquiescent and accommodating in his dealings with Bishop Mugavero, a point nicely illustrated by an incident that occurred during Koch's first term in office. From its inception, the Brooklyn bishop had taken a keen interest in the campaign of the East Brooklyn Congregation (EBC), an association of black Protestant and Catholic churches in that neighborhood, to obtain backing for the proposed Nehemiah Project—a scheme to erect some 1,500 new homes (a number later expanded) in one of Brooklyn's most depressed, crime-ridden neighborhoods. Any possibility of support for the housing project from the City of New York initially seemed infinitesimal given the mutual animosity and enmity that existed between Koch and the EBC leadership. But the timely intervention of Mugavero changed that picture. In June 1982, Mugavero led a delegation of EBC leaders to the mayor's office, where the bishop pressed the mayor for $10 million in city benefits for Nehemiah—in the form of land condemnation, tax deferrals, and interest-free loans. The mayor, obviously discomforted and reluctant, finally voiced his approval. Yet he withheld from making his support public and was finally prodded into doing so three weeks later after a second meeting between the mayor and EBC leaders, again led by Mugavero. (The bishop, it should be noted, also intervened with New York's Governor Mario Cuomo to obtain low-interest state-subsidized loans for Nehemiah homeowners.) By

June 1984 the first of what would eventually become nearly 2,300 residents moved into the first Nehemiah home (Freedman, 1993: 336–39).

Political considerations clearly were a factor in the mayor's embrace of both O'Connor and Mugavero. In his 1977 Democratic primary campaign, as well as in the primaries of 1981 and 1985, Koch identified white Catholics, who comprised 25 percent of the city electorate, as a constituency critical to his chances. In crafting an appeal to this socially conservative group, Koch was careful to avoid dwelling on racial anxieties, an underlying factor in all three elections, lest he cause the city's white liberals, blacks, and Latinos to unite and defeat him. While there is no evidence that the Catholic Church was in any way involved in these maneuvers, the well-publicized friendship between the city's leading Catholic prelates and its chief magistrate presumably helped to cement support from this critical sector of the city's electorate (Mollenkopf, 1992: 109, 118).

Speaking of the overall relationship and not of any mayor in particular, the executive director of Catholic Charities, Monsignor James Murray, summed up the situation as follows:

> Speaking for Catholic Charities, which is the social organ for the New York Archdiocese, the relationship with government has sometimes been adversarial, but there has always been a relationship. It's not as if they're over there and we're over here and never the twain shall meet! And that goes back to the earliest days of Catholic Charities, back to 1920. (interview, 1996)

In short, while the relationship between the archdiocese and the mayor's office may be somewhat closer under a Catholic mayor as opposed to a non-Catholic, any such tendency is not especially marked, and the larger truth is that New York mayors generally find it advantageous to form and maintain strong ties with the Catholic Church.

Detroit

A similar ability to maintain a basic presence at city hall, despite sociological and other changes that might have been expected to weaken its position, applied to the Catholic Archdiocese of Detroit. In 1980, Edmund Szoka became the cardinal archbishop, replacing the recently deceased John Cardinal Dearden. Ten years thereafter Szoka departed to take up a high position at the Vatican, and he was replaced in turn by Adam Cardinal Maida. One might have assumed that relations between the chancery of the archdiocese and city hall would have deteriorated in the Dearden, Szoka, and early Maida years, given Mayor Coleman Young's well-known coolness toward Roman Catholicism. In actuality, however, there is no evidence that any such deterioration occurred and some to indicate that the church-state linkage remained strong. Two incidents occurring during the Young years lend support to that view.

The first of these involved a plan, jointly developed by the city and the General Motors Corporation and publicly announced in 1980, to clear a large tract of land on the city's near east side—termed "Poletown" for its largely Polish population—for the erection of a GM auto assembly plant. The Young administration backed the plan as a source of some 6,000 new jobs; upon completion, it would be the first new plant of its kind anywhere in Detroit proper for several decades. Upon learning of this plan to level their neighborhood, however, local residents raised strenuous objections, and rallied behind their neighborhood improvement group, the Poletown Neighborhood Council (PNC). The local Catholic parish, Immaculate Conception, was central to the community, and parish members and their priest now turned to the archdiocese in the fervent hope that it would champion their cause. Bolstering such hopes was the fact that by several indicators Immaculate Conception was a viable parish: in 62 years of existence it had never been subsidized, its edifice was fully paid for, and it possessed a $155,000 reserve fund. Cardinal Dearden, however, was unmoved by those realities and ordered the church closed. In doing so, he affirmed that the parish's dwindling membership made it uneconomical to keep it open (*Washington Post,* June 1, 1981). As is typical, the archdiocese held title to the property, and thus the cardinal's decision, once made, was final and unappealable. Clearly, the archdiocese and the city were able to show a united front on the issue.

The situation might easily have turned out differently. The Detroit Archdiocese could have caused real trouble for the Young administration had it elected to side with the local residents in opposition to the redevelopment scheme. Despite the support of two of Detroit's more powerful institutions—the city and General Motors—the success of the Poletown project was anything but assured absent archdiocesan approval. The image of neighborhood residents fighting to defend their homes and way of life proved highly attractive to the local mass media. Television stations gave the struggle prominent coverage, as did the city's two metropolitan papers, the *Detroit News* and the *Detroit Free Press.* The archdiocese would have enjoyed local support had it chosen to oppose the development project. Instead, by electing to act in concert with the city, it ended up drawing to itself a good deal of the neighborhood anger and frustration that otherwise would have been directed toward city hall.

At a very basic level the outcome of the Poletown struggle was influenced by the "reformed" character of Detroit government, which in this instance helped support the position taken by the Young administration. As Carter Wilson points out in a keen analysis, "The political climate in Detroit during the development of the Poletown project was such that direct overt support of the PNC was not politically feasible" (Carter Wilson, 1982: 208). In a more traditional "unreformed" city, the city council would have been comprised of ward representatives, and thus individual neighborhoods would have wielded substantial influence at city hall. On the other hand, under a "reformed" system of government such as Detroit's, the at-large system of city council representation has a tendency to undercut particularistic influences and to bias policy outcomes in favor of broader, citywide perspectives. Wilson's observation on this point bears emphasis, since it relates to the larger theme of this study, the observed connection between the formal structure of city politics—reformed or unreformed—and the ongoing relationship between city hall and local ecclesiastical structures—church federations and/or dioceses and archdioceses.

The Poletown project was one of two civic issues during the Young years that brought the Detroit Archdiocese dramatically to the attention of the general public. The second was the forced closing of numerous inner-city Catholic parishes—a wrenching decision that aroused dismay and anger among many inner-city Catholics and generated much press notoriety.

Early in 1986, the archdiocese's City Task Force, a body established by Edmund Cardinal Szoka to advise him on inner-city matters, determined that roughly half of the parishes in Detroit proper, as well as in the municipal enclaves of Hamtramck and Highland Park, were either nonviable or questionably viable. The task force initially proposed the closing of forty-three inner city churches, and suggested that another forty-eight be either merged with other parishes or reduced to shrines (Bridger and Maines, 1998: 327). This announcement provoked a contentious dialogue between local church leaders and archdiocesan officials, with the former protesting that the proposed closures were uncalled for and the latter insisting that there was no viable alternative. An advisory committee appointed by the cardinal heard appeals on behalf of the targeted churches, and in several instances such appeals resulted in a church's removal from closure list. Yet the debate generally failed to produce a mutually acceptable resolution, and in the final parish reorganization plan proposed by the task force and approved by the cardinal in January 1989, thirty-one inner-city parishes were slated for closure. In the words of one observer, this mass closure "was unprecedented in the long and ancient history of the Roman Catholic Church" (Fukuzawa, 1993: 1).

Mayor Young's reaction to this protracted controversy was to remain silent. Publicly, he said and did nothing. Privately, in comments to an interviewer, he indicated that he was not sorry to see the churches close. "What Cardinal Szoka did is only good sense," he remarked. "Catholics are mostly white, and they've left the city. And a lot of churches that are still here have erected racial barriers" (quoted in Chafets, 1990: 187). While this comment seems valid as an indication of Young's thinking, it may not fully convey his political reasoning.

This incident presented Mayor Young with the opportunity, had he been so inclined, to hammer the archdiocese. Consistent with his oft-declared principles, he might well have rebuked the city's Catholic leaders while also making common cause with inner-city Detroit Catholics concerned over the impending church closures. He could have pointed with alarm to the impending loss of scores of central-city jobs as churches closed and forced layoffs occurred among church staff and custodians. A few years earlier he had reacted in just that way to the Dayton-Hudson Corporation's announced plans to close the historic J. L. Hudson department store. On that occasion, the mayor did everything in his power to keep Hudson's open. Young might also have rebuked the cardinal and the archdiocese on the grounds of racial insensitivity and bias. In April 1989, twenty Catholic churches filed a grievance in civil court based on that precise argument, with their spokesperson alleging that Szoka and his advisory committee and City Task Force were "blinded by their own racism" and were guilty of "a lack of love for the city's black Catholics" (*Detroit News,* April 21, 1989). This court filing was an apparent attempt to enlarge the scope of conflict so as to involve non-Catholics as allies in the struggle. The protesters, presumably, would have been gratified to have the mayor join in their chorus. Finally, the mayor might have sided with the Detroit Catholic Pastoral Alliance, a group organized in the 1970s as a Vatican II prayer group for priests, nuns, and lay religious, who now spoke out against the cardinal's plan. The Pastoral Alliance charged that Szoka's action, if carried out, would treat parishes as analogous to branch plants of corporations, thereby abandoning the Church's historic role as minister to the poor, the weak, and the elderly—a role emphasized by Vatican II (Bridger and Maines, 1998: 328, 330).

By refusing to embrace any of these arguments, Mayor Young signaled his belief that it would be imprudent to involve himself in this issue. The archdiocese obviously preferred that the church closings be looked upon as an internal matter, of concern to Catholics only. The mayor's noninvolvement helped legitimate that position. It would appear that the mayor wished to avoid offending the archdiocese. He may well have reflected on the fact that the archdiocese had done favors for him in the past. For example, the chancery had maintained a discreet silence on an issue of great moment to the mayor, namely the proposed legalization of casino gambling. City hall must have taken satisfaction in the archdiocese's decision not to involve itself in this matter, especially since Detroit's mainly Protestant church bodies, both white and African American, had condemned the scheme as immoral and of likely harm to the community. As detailed in the chapter to follow, such criticism of the casino gambling plan was prolonged and vocal. While the archdiocese's silence on the matter was not the equivalent of assent to the mayor's view, its noninvolvement at least helped dispel the impression that the city's church leaders were unanimous in their opposition to legalized gaming. Quite possibly, Mayor Young had such helpful forbearance in mind when the archdiocese stood exposed and vulnerable in late 1988 and early 1989.

Conclusion

In the period from 1975 to 1994, the relationship between city government and the churches in the two cities under discussion, while similar in certain respects, was different in others, and it is the difference that seems especially worthy of emphasis. The two cities' contrasting political regimes—machine-based in New York, reform-based in Detroit—were associated with differing policy responses on the part of city officials toward citywide church and faith-based social service institutions.

New York's more partisan atmosphere tended to encourage its local politicians to distinguish sharply between political supporters and nonsupporters as the city sought to cope with the social service challenge. Its more "liberal" interests, which included many citywide church agencies, were directly affected by the election of conservatively inclined Mayors Ed Koch and Rudolph Giuliani, who together ruled for all but four years between 1978 and the end of the century.

In Detroit, on the other hand, the prevailing "nonpartisan" electoral system somewhat shielded social welfare interests, faith-based included, from the effects of regime changes at city hall. The Young administration maintained contact with private social service providers, religious groups included, even in cases where their leaders were independent of Young's political machine.

While the Detroit mayor was obviously closer to his perceived "friends" than to "non-friends," he tended to give some recognition to any group claiming significant central-city political support, which included citywide Catholic and Protestant church organizations. Thus, the animosity toward liberals that characterized New York's two conservative mayors, Koch and Giuliani, had no direct parallel in the Detroit setting.

The Catholic Church in both cities proved itself more successful at maintaining a consistency of city hall access as compared to the same cities' Protestant organizations. The data are insufficient to precisely identify the areas of Catholic Church municipal-policy concern, including its degree of policy influence, if any, but from all indications the Church succeeded essentially in maintaining its traditionally important role in civic affairs.

6

The Black Church in a Post-Church Federation Era

Ronald Brown

As previously pointed out, the quarter century that ended in 1994 witnessed a decline in the social space occupied by the doctrinally orthodox, historically rooted Christian denominations in a number of American cities. Social and economic changes essentially beyond its control buffeted mainline Protestantism, and the same changes impacted Catholicism as well, even though generally less severely. Citywide church federations were especially hard hit. These ecumenical bodies experienced severe jolts in many cases and not infrequently ceased to exist. While the metropolitan councils of churches serving Detroit and New York managed to survive, they did so only barely and with considerable loss in their larger metropolitan reach. These developments heavily affected relations between the orthodox Christian churches and urban governments. City officials and politicians were eventually aware of the decline in local-area church memberships and reacted accordingly.

While the above-mentioned changes were generally adverse to orthodox denominations and their citywide religious affiliations, they opened up fresh possibilities for black church organizations and clergy. Black church organizations and politically active clergy were eager to assert themselves—socially, politically, and otherwise—to cast off the last vestiges of their former second-class status in American life. By the early 1970s, politically astute black pastors realized that black nationalism had achieved mass appeal and it was competing with integration as the dominant ideology of racial liberation (see Pellar, 1995: 145; Hampton and Fayer, 1991: chaps. 21–23). Much of the mass appeal of black political nationalism may have been related to perceptions of white resistance to black demands for freedom. Traumatic events such as the Sixteenth Street Church bombing in Birmingham on September 15, 1963, Bloody Selma on March 7, 1965, and the assassinations of Medgar Evers, Malcolm X, and Martin Luther King may have increased the appeal of black nationalism as a liberation strategy (Gurin and Epps, 1975; Hampton and Fay, 1990; Peller, 1995). The resurgence of the writings and speeches of Malcolm X among students, community activists, and activist clergy was increasing the popularity of black nationalism. Also increasing in national popularity and visibility were Student Nonviolent Coordinating Committee (SNCC) leaders Stokely Carmichael and H. Rap Brown. Both of these civil rights activists tapped into black rage and discontentment by arguing that black nationalism must be part of any struggle for black liberation. Support for certain aspects of black nationalism is demonstrated in a 1968 survey of blacks in fifteen large urban cities. The data reveals that over 90 percent associated black power with having more black businesses, that blacks should shop in black-owned businesses, and that blacks should take more pride in Negro history (Campbell and Schumann, 1968: 139–44). Stokely Carmichael was given a favorable rating by almost 40 percent of the respondents and H. Rap Brown was evaluated positively by 30 percent of the respondents.

Black nationalism may have been growing in popularity among northern blacks because of the realization that white Americans were growing weary of civil rights issues. By 1968, 81 percent of respondents agreed with the statement that "law and order has broken down in the country" (Edsall and Edsall, 1992: 72). In this same year, white southern Democrats and white northern working-class Democrats shifted their usual allegiance from the Democratic Party to the Republican Party to help elect Richard Nixon to the presidency. For many white voters, restoring law and order meant repressing the political aspirations of black radicals, who they saw as a threat to the domestic security of the nation.

Thus in the early 1970s, black clergy in cities like Detroit and New York had to contend with black followers from more confrontational organizations such as the Black Panther Party, the Revolutionary Action movement, and the SNCC. Yet black clergy were in a unique social space to take advantage of the growing acceptance of black nationalism. Black scholars such as W. E. B. DuBois had claimed as early as 1903 that the black church was the first black nationalist organization in the United States because it provided a cultural space where people bound by a common oppression, history, and destiny could form a community (Sundquist, 1996: 200–206). A small number of black pastors capitalized on this sense of church community by engaging in actions whose aims were to minimize the impact of white racism and to simultaneously increase black autonomy and freedom. This point will be made shortly in our brief discussions of the political activism of pastors such as Revs. Charles A. Hill, C. L. Franklin, and Adam Clayton Powell Jr., who were all engaged in the politics of self-determination but did not label their politics as advocating black nationalism.

In the remainder of this chapter, we make several important points. First, black nationalism—or a belief that blacks should use their collective power to self-determine their political destinies—was adopted and modified to suit the political needs of politically minded clergy and church-based federations that sought to influence public policy. So citywide black church federations would keep their integrationist worldview, but the self-determination dimension of black nationalism would affect political mobilization efforts. Second, a black nationalist political worldview would create political rifts between clergy and black elected officials. This would surface in the 1984 presidential campaign of Jesse Jackson, when Coleman Young, the mayor of Detroit, did not endorse the Jackson campaign and other prominent clergy did. Third, the perception of black nationalism as a political strategy provided opportunities for countermobilization efforts by white officials, as was the case in New York City during Jackson's presidential bids and David Dinkins's 1989 mayoral candidacy. The chapter concludes by suggesting that the embrace of the self-determining dimension of black nationalism by integrationist clergy resulted in black church groups competing for political power with other interest groups that also sought to influence the political decision making of elected officials. Yet we make the point too that the efficacy of black nationalism or the politics of self-determination must be examined within the context of the black political culture and regime of a particular city.

Black Nationalism, Black Churches, and Politics in Detroit

Charles Taylor states that claims for self-determination and group autonomy usually arise among modernizing elites who believe that the dignity of the social group has been threatened (Taylor, 1997: 45). It is thus articulated as a way to transform conditions of shame and disgrace. Moreover, nationalist movements that resist attempts by dominant groups to destroy the group's dignity may attempt to transform state policy by seizing political power (Feinberg, 1997). Grace Boggs, a Chinese American self-proclaimed Marxist and community activist writes that by 1961 some activists began to think about organizing blacks as a political force so that they might seize political power at the local level (Boggs, 1998: 117). The notion that black nationalism could be a mobilizing ideology became a public issue after the historic March Down Woodward Avenue in June 1963. C. L. Franklin, pastor of New Bethel Baptist Church and a principal organizer of the march, was opposed to the growing racial militancy of Rev. Albert Cleage, pastor of the Central Congregationalist Church, who also helped to organize this event. This rift resulted in two independent conferences in November 1963. Franklin would spearhead a Negro Summit Leadership Conference, attended by national and city leaders supportive of an integrationist political strategy, and Cleage would play a key role in the Grass Roots Leadership Conference for activists calling for black self-determination.

A primary purpose of the Grassroots Leadership Conference was to encourage city residents and other black leaders to support the idea of a politically independent black movement. The inability or refusal of Detroit city officials to directly address police brutality, employment, and racial discrimination directly contributed to the idea of formulating an all-black political party. Detroit militants associated with the Grass Roots conference had created the Michigan Freedom Now Party (MFNP) in August 1963. Founders of the MFNP believed that an independent bloc of black voters could maximize its interest in a close statewide election. White candidates seeking support of this bloc might be more willing to make policy concessions, if gaining the black vote might be the difference between winning and losing an election. Ernest Smith, statewide campaign coordinator of the party, makes this very point in the January 13, 1964, edition of the *Illustrative News*, a bi-weekly paper published by the Central Congregation Church, where Rev. Cleage was pastor: "We know of course we by ourselves cannot elect a president or governor of any state directly, but by swinging our vote in one direction or the other we have great power."

The leadership of the Michigan Freedom Democratic Party sought to widen the acceptance of an independent political movement by inviting Malcolm X, a nationally renowned, respected minister from the Nation of Islam (NOI), to speak at their Grassroots Leadership Conference meeting held at King Solomon Baptist Church on Sunday November 10, 1963 (Boggs: 128; Cone 1991: 114). In his speech, "Message to the Grassroots," Malcolm X encourages blacks to accept a philosophy of black political nationalism—which meant engaging in actions that would allow them to self-determine the future of their communities. Malcolm X spoke at two other events organized by MFNP activists; on April 12, 1964, he delivered "The Ballot or the Bullet" speech, and made the point that the black separatist and black integrationist are black nationalists if they are working for black freedom. A central theme in the speeches given by Malcolm X was that the political philosophy of black nationalism could unite all black community activists, if they accepted the premise that political and economic autonomy was their stated preference.

MFNP activists hoped that the appearance and speeches of Malcolm X would increase the centrality of black nationalism among black voters, but this did not happen. The MFNP ran candidates in the 1964 general election, like most independent political parties, it did not significantly impact the voting calculus of blacks; it received less than one percent of all votes cast. Nevertheless, the presence of the political party was a clear signal that nationalists viewed engaging in electoral politics as a means to an end; to empower black Americans. The demise of the MFNP however, did little to stem the preference for an independent black political voice. In 1965, Rev. Cleage ran as an independent candidate for the City Council, known then as Common Council. He urged potential voters in a February 7 mailing to cast their ballots for candidates, who, if elected, would make police brutality, employment discrimination, and racial discrimination their first order of business (Ernest C. Smith Collection, February 7, 1965, Box 1, Reuther Archives, Wayne State University).

The July 1967 racial rebellion in Detroit was a turning point for clergy activist C. L. Franklin, who began to accept the idea that black nationalists and civil rights activists were working for the same end. This was a radical departure for Franklin, who was a strong supporter of Martin Luther King, Jr. King acknowledges Franklin's commitment to his cause in a letter, dated July 10, 1963:

> I simply want again to thank you for making my recent visit to Detroit so fruitful. Never before have I participated in a Freedom Rally and a public demonstration so profoundly meaningful and so numerically successful. You are to be commended for the significant leadership that you gave in making this venture such an overwhelming success. You proved to be superb master of a creative situation. Let me thank you again for the great financial contribution that came to the SCLC from the Freedom Rally. (Martin Luther King Jr. to C. L. Franklin, July 10, 1963, Box 1, Bentley Historical Library, University of Michigan)

The first step for Franklin was to reject the idea that the urban disturbance in July 1967 was a "race riot." In "Open Letter to White America," Franklin asserts that the events that took place in July 1967 were a rebellion caused by the dehumanizing treatment of black men that often manifested itself in limited employment, housing, and educational opportunities (C. L. Franklin, "An Open Letter to White America," 1967, Box 1, Bentley Library).

Franklin would take an even more far-reaching step by allowing the Republic of New Africa (RNA), an ultranationalist group, to have a meeting at his church on March 29, 1968. This meeting of 250 adults and numbers of children was in progress when the Detroit Police Department raided the building shortly after midnight (Thompson 2001, 75). According to the janitor of New Bethel Baptist Church, who was not a member of the RNA, a police squad car stopped suddenly in front of the church's main entrance. A police officer emerged from the car, and as soon as he reached the curb of the sidewalk, the officer fired at the church door with a rifle resembling a "pump gun." Members from the RNA then returned fire; in the explosive exchange a police officer was killed, and members of the RNA were arrested (Thompson, 2001: 75). Franklin, when asked by reporters why he allowed this separatist black nationalist group to use his church, replied that if he could be assured that the group would not have guns, it would be allowed to use the church again. Yet echoing sentiments expressed by Malcolm X in his "Ballot or the Bullet" speech, Franklin said, "their goals are the same as ours, only they approach them from a different direction" (Tilden, 1987). Convincing his congregation of the merits of his argument would start that very night with the minister of music. Shortly after arriving at the church after the shootout, Franklin has a discussion with Shelby, whom he identifies by first name only. Shelby, who was on the second floor of the church when Franklin interacts with him, sat, fanned himself, and said over and over again, "Ooh my God, ooh Lawd, who let these people have the church?" Franklin told Shelby that he was the one who allowed the RNA to use the church. He also said, "we are in the throes of a revolution, a social revolution. Some people have lost their lives in this revolution, and we have lost a little glass. I think we got off cheap" (Tilden, 1987).

David Aberbach and Jack Walker's (1970) study of black and white residents in Detroit in the fall of 1967 captures public reaction to this social revolution. This study reveals that 40 percent of blacks and 11 percent of whites had a favorable interpretation of black power. A favorable interpretation of black power meant either a belief in the sharing of power between blacks and whites or a belief in black racial unity. It is also interesting to note that non-church members had a far more favorable interpretation of black power in comparison to church members. Yet by the late 1960s, prominent black pastors could not publicly denounce black nationalism. Charles A. Hill, pastor of Hartford Memorial Baptist Church, whose commitment to the labor movement and civil rights issues led to his being called before the House Un-American Activities Committee in 1952, was labeled an "Uncle Tom" in 1966 by black militants because of his rejection of the black power slogan (Charles A. Hill Papers, 1917–1981, Box 1, Bentley Library). The dishonoring of Rev. Hill by more militant black activists was an indication of the challenges awaiting clergy seeking to fuse integration and nationalist tactics or strategies in their quest for black empowerment.

Hidden in Plain Sight: Black Nationalism and the Council of Black Baptist Pastors

In 1964, a dispute arose in the city's largest black ministers' group, the Baptist Ministers Conference (formed in 1947), and some sixty to seventy dissenters eventually broke away to form a new organization, the Council of Baptist Pastors of Detroit and Vicinity (CBP). The split resulted over disagreement about the degree to which the council should use its collective resources to enhance the political autonomy of the group, thereby empowering itself and the church members it represented. One of the dissenters remarked:

> The BMC's leadership was actually exploiting its representative power for purpose of self-promotion. What we [dissenters] thought was unfair was the use of power of the Council in relationship to political candidates. We [black pastors] were not an economic force in industrialized Detroit, and so the political arena was the only place we could influence. The older view was that politics was ugly and dirty, and that religion had no business mixing with it. We aimed to de-align ourselves from the belief that politics is outside the arena of religion. . . . The Reverend T. S. Boone, whom I remember well . . . helped bring this new group into existence with the expressed intent of our becoming more socially and politically involved as a means of expressing our religious commitment. The new group aimed quietly and deliberately "to re-socialize blacks from old southern ways," which included, especially, emphasizing the significance of voting as a vehicle of group empowerment. (confidential interview, December 5, 1996)

That modernizing elites are more likely to engage in political activism that has the potential of empowering the group is evident among the more educated Baptist clergy. The new group differed from the older one in terms of having higher levels of education. Whereas the BMC members traditionally had grade school educations, the new group for the most part was college educated. For example, Rev. Charles A. Hill was a graduate of Cleary Business College, Lincoln University, and Moody Bible College. C. L. Franklin attended the Howe School of Religion and Lemoyne College and took courses at the University of Buffalo, and Rev. Jim Holley graduated from Wayne State University.

During its initial years, the CBP had difficulty in fulfilling its declaration to exert a church-based influence on city politics. Its members met from time to time with the Detroit mayors of this era, Jerome Cavanagh and Roman Gibbs, and were invariably provided a good "spread"—a term denoting food but that also carried broader symbolic overtones. A mayor would invite black clergy to dine with him as a gesture of courtesy, and not, typically, to discuss substantive changes for black racial equality. The "spread" was heavily criticized by Malcolm X and the Reverend Cleage in their sermons. Malcolm X labeled black clergy who attended these dinners "Uncle Toms" if they failed to press for policies to end police brutality and discrimination in the housing and employment sectors. Surely the creation of the Freedom Now Party signaled dissatisfaction with the symbolic spread. Black Baptist clergy were certainly aware of criticism from black radicals, but before 1973, they collectively showed little visible support for black self-determination. The political campaign of Coleman Young in 1973 would provide the CBP with an opportunity to use its resources to elect an African American who would provide blacks with control over the city government.

Rev. Charles Hill, Coleman Young, and the Politics of Self-Determination

Beginning well before his election as the city's first black mayor in 1973, Young came to embody the collective aspirations of the black community, and his political ascendancy would be partially assisted by activist black Baptist clergy. Young's involvement in city politics began in 1945 when he served as campaign manager for the unsuccessful candidacy of Rev. Hill for a seat on the Detroit city council, then known as the Common Council. Rev. Hill, while denouncing the "black power" movement, had earlier sought to increase black political and economic autonomy by founding the National Negro Congress (NNC) in the 1930s.

The NNC directly challenged the authority of white dominance, for example, at the Ford Motor Company factories where the Ford regime and UAW officials both supported racist employment practices that resulted in blacks getting the worst and most dangerous jobs. The racists' practices in factories would eventually be a leading cause of the formulation of the Dodge Revolutionary Union Movement or DRUM in 1968. It should be pointed out also that Rev. Hill was the protégé of Rev. Robert Bradby, who from 1910 to 1946 served as pastor of Detroit's Second Baptist Church, and was the city's most prominent black preacher. Throughout a long career, Bradby involved himself in helping the flood of newly arriving blacks settle into the city, and as president of the Detroit NAACP chapter he was in correspondence with Detroit civic leaders and factory managers, a novel role for a black man in the white-dominated, racist era.

Young notes that the NNC provided a progressive forum for black working people, and it naturally acquired a political accent. However, he states that it was Rev. Hill's simple passion, courage, and organizational skills that inspired young ideological upstarts like himself (Young and Wheeler, 1994: 43). It was thus under the tutelage of Rev. Hill that Young as a young man would involve himself in the leftist wing of Detroit's nascent industrial union movement. Although never a Communist Party member, he was at least CP identified. One of his assignments consisted of chauffeuring the prominent African American singer and social radical Paul Robeson around the inner city on the latter's periodic Detroit visits. Since Robeson was highly controversial, and also Communist identified, the local arrangements for these visits called for concealment of his appearances from general public view. Thus with Robeson beside him in the car, Young would pull up in front of a church at night to find the edifice darkened, and by all appearances deserted. Once inside, however, the two would find themselves in a large, well-lit room, thronged with well-wishers, all curious about Robeson and attentive to his message. According to Young's longtime confidant and press secretary, Robert Pisor, Young was deeply impressed by this experience, and he came to regard the church as an avenue into the "soul of the black community" (Pisor, interview, 1998).

The militant politics of Hill and Young would result in both of them—along with other civil rights and labor activists—being summoned to testify in February 1952 at hearings held in Detroit by the U.S. House Un-American Activities Committee. More specifically, this committee believed that the National Negro Labor Council, formed on October 27, 1951, was a communist front organization (Young and Wheeler, 1994: 116–17). On February 25, Rev. Hill was called to testify before the committee. Hill refused to answer whether or not he was affiliated with communist activists or organizations although he did state that his primary political objective was to accept the cooperation of anyone that sought to eradicate discrimination, segregation, and the second-class citizenship that plagues black communities. Hill also labeled the hearings an "affront" because of the lack of democracy in Georgia—the chair of the committee, Representative George Woods, was from Georgia. Hill also accused members of this congressional committee of being modern-day Pharisees, so as a result, he, like Jesus, must speak out against "injustice heaped upon the Negro and others because of their race and color." The Council of Baptist Preachers wrote a letter to the Un-American Activities Committee supporting the freedom of speech rights of Rev. Hill (Committee on Un-American Activities Hearings held in Detroit, Michigan, on February 15, 1952, Bentley Library). Young's political testimony on February 28 was also one of defiance. Young refused to answer questions dealing with Hill's union activism, and like Hill, asserted that he was fighting against racist political and economic policies and behaviors that harm blacks (Young and Wheeler, 1994: 119–28). Undeniably, Hill and Young were involved in resistance political efforts because they wanted to end political and economic elite decision making that limited the ability of blacks to have personal and collective dignity. Equally important, both engaged in political activities, selected strategies, and sought out allies that would improve the ability of the black community to have more political autonomy. Young's political involvement during this era provided him with political skills, knowledge, and church-based networks that would assist him in his electoral bids that would begin in the 1960s.

Young's first electoral bid ended unsuccessfully: he ran for Common Council in 1960 and was defeated. He ran for a Michigan House seat and was defeated in 1962. In his 1964 bid for a state senate seat, Young sought the endorsement of the Council of Baptist Pastors (CBP), knowing that their endorsement would increase the potential of gaining black votes. Young, realizing that he did not have strong religious credentials, felt it imperative that he gain the endorsement of prominent religious leaders such as Rev. Hill and C. L. Franklin. Their endorsements were critical in 1964 because neither Democratic Party leaders nor the major metropolitan newspapers were supportive of his campaign. Moreover, a special assistant in the FBI sent a memo to President Johnson about the Young campaign (Young and Wheeler, 1994: 164–65). With the support of the Council of Baptist Pastors and other progressive labor groups, Young was elected to the state senate in 1964. Young was able to overcome the skepticism of fellow Democrats and became the first black to serve as Democratic senate floor leader. That era ended when state senator Young entered the race to become Detroit's mayor.

Coleman Young's 1973 Election Campaign

In these terms, the 1973 city election was a watershed for both the city's black power movement and the politically active black-clergy-based organizations. That year's election was not the first in which a serious black candidate had offered himself; Richard Austin had run strongly against the successful white candidate, Roman Gibbs, in the city election of 1969. Never before, however, had the prospects for achieving a racial "first" appeared so promising, with blacks now a clear majority of the city electorate. In addition to the mayoral race, the ballot included approval of a new city charter, sponsored by a blue ribbon commission and proposing to expand greatly the new mayor's formal authority. (The proposed charter would enlarge by 50 percent the number of city officials filled by mayoral appointment while greatly reducing the city council's traditionally large role in appointments). In the end, the proposed charter was approved, and by a wide margin. Coleman Young was successful as well, but by a narrower margin, just 9,186 votes.

By endorsing Coleman Young in the 1973 campaign, the CBP, with a membership of around three hundred ministers, took another major step in its own political development. Rev. Hill's 1947 Common Council bid had received some support from progressive Baptist ministers; however, in 1973, the CBP acted as a collective body by endorsing Coleman Young's mayoral candidacy. The group's endorsement came largely because Charles Butler, pastor of New Calvary Baptist, whom Young considered his minister, used his influence as president of the CBP to urge members to endorse the Young campaign. The CBP endorsement was not widely publicized in the white media but was well known among activists in the black community. Still, it was a significant step, especially as it helped to legitimize the actions of those CBP members who more so than most were politically oriented and intent on promoting the idea that blacks should control the city government. One such member, Jim Holley, pastor of the Historic Little Rock Baptist Church, took the initiative in persuading a black city council member and potential Young rival, Ernest Browne, to avoid entering the race (interview, 1996).

Young, much like his mentor, Hill, pulled together a church-labor-liberal coalition, yet his primary supporters came from the black community. In addition to the CBP, Young's camp of supporters included Representatives John Conyers and Charles Diggs, and the Reverend Cleage, whose church, Shrine of the Black Madonna (formerly Central Congregational Church), had become a political force in the city. The white support was minimal, Young remarks:

> Frankly, there weren't a hell of a lot of white people behind me. Ted Kennedy gave me his blessing but didn't actively campaign on my behalf. I had token support from Henry Ford II, who also contributed to the Nicholas campaign. . . . Maryann Mahaffey, who had been on my side through many previous issues and campaigns, was with me again at the outset of the race but she was a candidate for city council and consequently coveted the endorsement of the United Auto Workers. When Maryann came to me and reported that she had a chance to receive the backing of the UAW, I predicted that union would ask her to repudiate me in favor of Ravitz, which it did, and she did. (Young and Wheeler, 1994: 199)

The electoral victory of Young in 1973 resulted in a higher visibility of black clergy; some were actually involved in the implementation of public policy. Rev. Charles Butler was appointed to the Police Commission, and Rev. Charles Adams (Hartford Memorial Baptist) was given a top post in the Head Start program.

The Black Church and Coleman Young's Later Years

Following his 1973 mayoral success, Coleman Young was subsequently reelected four times: 1977, 1981, 1985, and 1989, thus resulting in a twenty-year reign unprecedented in the city's long history. The Detroit city council over the period changed from majority white to predominately black, a development in which organized religion was prominent. For some clergy, this meant running and being elected to the city council. The first member of the clergy to serve on the Detroit city council since the mid-1960s was Nicholas Hood II, the pastor of Plymouth United Church of Christ (Detroit). He served on the council from 1965 until 1986, when his son, Nicholas Hood, III, who also succeeded him as church pastor, succeeded him on the council.

David Eberhard, pastor of Historic Trinity Lutheran Church (Missouri Synod), was elected to the council for the first time in 1969 and served until his departure in 1992. Erma Henderson, an activist church member, was first elected in 1973 and served until 1986. John Peoples, the pastor of Calvary Baptist Church (since renamed Cosmopolitan Baptist), served a single term on the council, 1982–86. Keith Butler, pastor of the Word of Faith Christian Center (since renamed Word of Faith International Christian Center), also served one term, 1986–92. So, at one point, 1982–86, three of the nine Detroit city council members were Protestant clergy, and a fourth was a church activist. While the clergy did not act as an interest group, their election to public office showed the prominent role that religion had in local political affairs. Race and religion would affect the city council also. The November 1977 election of Erma Henderson as city council president, the first African American and female in that post, was partially attributed to the political mobilization efforts of Rev. Hood II, who encouraged her to run for this position. In this same year, in the first mayoral election where both contestants were African American, Mayor Young defeated his most serious challenger to office, Councilman Ernest Browne Jr. (Detroit African American History Project, Wayne State University, www.daahp.wayne.edu/1950_1999).

Throughout his twenty-year mayoralty, Coleman Young enjoyed the overwhelming support of the black church and of black unionists. Yet over time the relative political significance of the two groupings shifted, with the union activists declining somewhat in perceived importance and that of ministers increasing. During Young's mayoralty, the number of active UAW members nationally declined by half—from 1,536,0000 members in 1974 to 866,000 in 1992 (Public Relations Department, United Auto Workers). One presumes that a correspondingly sharp decline also occurred in the UAW's central city Detroit membership, given the exodus of UAW members to the suburbs and to other locales elsewhere in Michigan and beyond. The UAW lost clout locally in proportion to these numbers. No such decline occurred, however, in black church membership, where the number of members remained immense.

The Council of Baptist Pastors was arguably the single greatest beneficiary of Mayor Young's increasing sensitivity toward black pastors and their congregations. By the 1980s, Young was making annual appearances before a CBP meeting to deliver what amounted to a "state of the city address." He was also consulting with the pastors informally, meeting with them from time to time at Manoogian Mansion, the mayor's official residence. It appears that Young came to regard the church as a political constituency second to none in its importance, and as one to be cultivated and exploited to the greatest extent possible. However, exploiting the black church was challenging, particularly in the context of the 1984 election when the Rev. Jesse Jackson ran for the Democratic Party presidential nomination.

In the summer of 1983, Jackson set out on a six-state campaign of "political Pentecostalism" through the South, largely to register blacks to vote. The campaign held up to forty rallies a week, mostly conducted, like the movement rallies in the region in the sixties, in black churches (Frady, 1996: 305). This voter registration effort was one of the building blocks of Jackson's 1983–84 Democratic Party presidential nomination bid. Jackson's presidential bid was kindled within the black church, and this is where it largely remained during the campaign. Even after Jackson announced his candidacy, Andrew Young, Julian Bond, and Coretta Scott King in Georgia, Richard Arrington and the Alabama Black Democratic Conference, Mayor Wilson Good of Philadelphia, Mayor Tom Bradley of Los Angeles, Mayor Young of Detroit, and Congressman Charles Rangel of New York remained loyal to Mondale (Barker, 1988: 45). Coleman Young did not view Jackson as a viable Democratic presidential candidate who could defeat Ronald Reagan, the incumbent president. When interviewed by a *Detroit Free Press* reporter in November 1983, Young remarked that Jackson did not have a chance to win the primary. Moreover, any votes that Jackson might attract would hurt the Mondale campaign (*Detroit Free Press,* November 1, 1983).

In addition, Young may have also remembered that Jackson refused to work for his first mayoral campaign unless Young paid him $50,000 (Young and Wheeler, 1994: 199). Walter Mondale, the Democratic senator from Minnesota who was the vice president in the Carter administration, was seen as a person who could attract voters across racial lines. Concerns over whether Jackson could win the nomination or defeat the incumbent president were not major concerns of Rev. Jim Holley, who was one of six Detroit pastors engaging in voter registration efforts. Holley remarked, "If Jesse Jackson runs, the people who feel rejected will have a voice" (*Detroit Free Press,* July 23, 1983).

In an attempt to win the 1984 Michigan Democratic caucus vote, Jackson held campaign rallies at Rev. Holley's church and other black churches in southeastern Michigan. In Michigan's March 17 caucuses, Jackson won 16 percent of the statewide vote. Black voters in Detroit, however, cast more votes for Mondale, who had Mayor Young's endorsement (*Detroit Free Press,* March 21, 1984).

Jackson's 1984 Democratic presidential nomination race merged integrationist and nationalist political strategies. This was done during black voter registration drives, proclaiming that "Our Time Has Come" at campaign rallies at predominately black churches. Jackson had first used this phrase in 1972 at the Black Power convention in Gary, Indiana. This convention of black elected officials, civil rights leaders, and community activists attempted to create a national umbrella organization that would be the independent voice of black America. Jackson was inspired by a poem written by black nationalist Amiri Baraka, and he told the delegates, "It's nation time, it's time to come together. It's time to organize politically" (Hampton and Faye, 1990: 576). Jackson also counted on the endorsements of black ultranationalists, including the Nation of Islam (NOI), for political support early in the campaign. This was a politically significant move given the religious ideology of the NOI, which endorsed racial separation and black economic self-determination. That Louis Farrakhan of the NOI would become involved in electoral politics suggest a willingness to explore the possibilities of integration and nationalism as strategies that could be used to enhance black self-autonomy. The Fruit of Islam provided security, and Farrakhan publicly endorsed Jackson's presidential bid at the Book Cadillac Hotel on May 5, 1984 (*Detroit Free Press,* May 6, 1984).

The political cleavage between Rev. Holley and Mayor Young is similar to the Cleage-Franklin split of 1963. By 1983, Coleman Young was a nationally prominent member of the Democratic Party; he therefore felt that blacks could gain more concessions from being inside the party system as opposed to being an independent political voice. This was not first time that Young opposed a black nationalist strategy. For Young, the politics of self-determination must have as its ultimate aim the integration of blacks into the mainstream of American politics. At the 1972 Black Power Convention in Gary, Indiana, Young led the Michigan delegation out of the convention because he believed that ultra black nationalists had taken over the meeting (Young and Wheeler 190). Rev. Holley in 1984, believing that he was in closer contact with the pulse of black Detroiters, favored a more independent political posture. Hence, just as Cleage had urged almost twenty years earlier, Holley was advocating that blacks use their voting strength to influence the Democratic Party platform. Holley's support for an independent political bid was not an isolated political gesture; a national survey of black adults revealed that 53 percent of blacks would have voted for Jesse Jackson, had he run as an independent presidential candidate in 1984 (Tate, et al. 43). Holley's backing of the

Jackson presidential bid did not signal the endorsement of the Council of Baptist Pastors. Nonetheless his backing, along with six other local pastors who spearheaded the Jackson campaign, provided Jesse Jackson with access to potential voters and volunteers. Thus, Rev. Holley, echoing the sentiments of those who organized the Michigan Freedom Now Party and by most delegates at the Black Power Convention in Gary, Indiana, felt that blacks should always be independent voters.

In 1988, Young supported Michael Dukakis, but he freed his formidable political organization to work for Rev. Jesse Jackson in the Michigan Democratic primary, which Jackson won (*Detroit Free Press,* November 2, 1988). Jackson's growing appeal to black voters may have driven Young to support Jackson, as might have support from black pastors such as Rev. Holley and Clyde Cleveland, a city council member (*Detroit Free Press,* November 2, 1988). Additionally, Jackson had done extremely well on Super Tuesday, which came before Michigan's primary. Jackson ran first or second in sixteen of the races. In the South, he finished first in five states and second in nine others, winning 27 percent of the popular vote, more than anyone else, and claiming almost one-third of the region's delegates (Frady, 1998: 391). Black church support and Young's indirect political endorsement may have contributed to Jackson's winning the Michigan Democratic primary.

Jackson did not win the national nomination: Dukakis was the Democratic presidential candidate in the 1988 general election. The black church would continue to play a significant role in the campaign. On October 13, Coleman Young brought together more than one hundred influential black ministers at a gospel-tinged, GOTV (Get Out the Vote) rally. Young's political concessions did not stop criticism from Jackson supporters. The Reverend Jim Holley criticized Dukakis for not connecting with blacks and stated that Jackson should be used more in the campaign to energize the black community. At one of the last campaign rallies in the Detroit metropolitan area, Young escorted Dukakis to Greater Grace Temple, where he spoke to more than two thousand Democratic supporters on Tuesday, November 1 (*Detroit Free Press,* November 2, 1988).

Young's political disagreements with the Rev. Jackson did not prevent him from appearing in public spaces with Jackson when political expediency called for it. In his last mayoral campaign, in 1989, Young ascended the pulpits of numerous packed city churches and repeatedly linked arms with Rev. Jesse Jackson and Aretha Franklin—renowned singer and daughter of the late C. L. Franklin, revered as one of Detroit's great black preachers and political activists. On those occasions, Young would quote the Bible and lead the singing of "We Shall Overcome" (*Detroit Free Press,* October 17, 1991). When Young's pastor, Rev. Charles Butler, introduced Young to audiences, he would allude to the great prophets or to Jesus himself to drive home the legitimacy of Young's leadership. "Like Jesus," he would intone, "he may be tortured and even humiliated, but he will not be defeated" (*Detroit Free Press,* October 17, 1991). It is ironic that Young would be linked to biblical prophets, given his low church involvement, yet it is not surprising that he would seek the endorsement of religious leaders given the centrality of black church support and opposition in his political career. Young was conceptualized as a populist black leader who represented the interest of blacks in the city. Young was viewed by ministers like Butler, therefore, as the leader of a black nation that is in a political struggle with a white nation. These two nations are in the same social space; thus Butler is implying that two co-national groups exist in the Detroit metropolitan community, black Detroit and the white suburbs.

The sweep of Coleman Young's power during his long tenure was of such magnitude that one is tempted to cast him as the dominant partner in the evolving church-city relationship. Clearly, there was a manipulative element in Young's dealings with the CBP and the black religious community generally. A leading analyst of the Young mayoralty, Wilbur Rich, makes this point tellingly:

> [Young] did not have to do anything to get the support of ministers, but accepted it because they wanted to be "players." One way to get attention was to have Mayor Young speak at your church. It was a game. Coleman Young stroked their egos in exchange for a platform to make campaign speeches and to rattle the local newspapers. . . . Relationships between Coleman and the ministers were never an even exchange. He gave them contributions and hired members of their churches. Black ministers never had the type of cohesive organization necessary to challenge Coleman even if they wanted to. (personal communication with Henry Pratt, November 11, 1996)

When, on occasion, the mayor sought voter approval in a city referendum for one of his favored projects—for example, on his 1989 proposal for a tax variance to permit expansion of the city's Cobo Hall Convention Center—he would turn to the CBP for endorsement and usually get what he wanted. While there was no way precisely to measure the electoral payoff of such political support, the general view was that CBP pronouncements counted for something in the black community.

Still, it would be a mistake to assume that mayoral influence over the clergy was without limits. The black pastors were amenable to mayoral manipulation but only up to a point. The CBP maintained its autonomy even at the zenith of Mayor Young's political strength. The church-city relationship that emerged during Young's tenure not only had minor disturbances in the 1984 and 1988 presidential elections, but it showed a great deal of strain on a highly controversial issue—casino gaming. The proposed introduction of casino gambling into the city—a scheme strongly favored, spearheaded even, by the mayor, was adamantly opposed by leading black Baptist clergy. In doing so, they were supported by the largely white Christian Communication Council of Metropolitan Detroit Churches, whose opposition to casino gaming amounted to a crusade.

Church leaders, black and white, based their opposition to gaming on moral grounds and on concern for the city's social cohesion and stability. In a series of citywide referenda on this issue beginning in 1975, the Detroit electorate was called upon repeatedly to decide on permitting casino gaming, and on five separate occasions during the Coleman Young years such proposals went down to defeat. While the churches were not solely responsible for this outcome, the pastors' opposition was clearly a key ingredient. Casino gaming was finally approved in a statewide referendum held after Young left office, and on that occasion the Detroit voters did, on balance, come down in favor of the proposal. Yet it remains true that the churches were chiefly responsible for delaying by a full generation the introduction of casino gaming into the city.

Mayor Young was clearly annoyed that casino gaming should be opposed from within his own political constituency notwithstanding his repeated efforts. More than once, he sought a reversal, or at least a softening, of CBP's stand on this issue. At one point, the mayor used the occasion of his annual CBP address to plead from the pulpit for the pastors' support. His critics promptly condemned such pulpit usage for a "political" message, insisting that it was "insulting," involved an unwarranted mixture of religion and politics, and was essentially a violation of the rules of the game (Rev. Jim Holley, interview, December 20, 1996). The mayor obviously thought otherwise and was prepared to risk the abuse of such critics in hopes of winning over converts.

He was bolstered in that hope by the fact that the then-CBP president, Charles Butler, and at least one other CBP member had voiced a willingness to be "flexible" on this matter. Butler proposed the appointment of a CBP study committee to look into the morality of gambling and to write a report, thereby signaling his hope that the CBP might change its stance (Hopkins, 1990: 57). Butler's proposal was not, however, well received by the CBP rank and file. A number of pastors proceeded to quit the organization, apparently in protest over the president's action, and total membership fell from over 300 in the middle 1980s to a low of around 200 at the end of Butler's term in the early 1990s. Others stayed with the organization and fought, however. The Butler plan ended up being shelved, and the group held fast to its original position. The mayor's attempted intervention had no apparent effect on the group's political outlook or behavior.

There is more to be said on this point, however. One of the participants in the above-described events later speculated that the mayor might have brought the pastors around on casino gaming if he had been more aggressive—making systematic use, for example, of his appointment power to "break off a certain number of pastors, appealing to their greed." It was a "close thing," the observer emphasized (confidential interview). There is clearly something to this view, since the pastors were not totally invulnerable, and their behavior might have shifted if the mayor had been prepared to pay a high enough political price. Evidently, the mayor weighed the costs involved and decided against making such an attempt, which, after all, might have failed. Still, the very possibility that the pastors might have been moved on this issue is noteworthy as further evidence of their intense, mutually interactive relationship with the mayor.

Council of Black Pastors (CBP) Organization and Structure

The preceding comments suggest the need for a deeper understanding of the Council of Baptist Pastors of Detroit and Vicinity, including its structure and essential strategy. The CBP is not a political organization as such, and its constitution confers no authority on its leaders to speak politically in the name of the churches; it is a religious, not a political, body. That fact carries with it a measure of organizational constraint. Government officials, in their dealings with CBP leaders, are occasionally frustrated by the latter's lack of authority. Coleman Young, for one, in an interview two years after leaving the mayor's office, remarked that as compared to the CBP, the Catholic Church is more hierarchical, and is therefore much easier for a mayor to deal with on matters of city policy. Comparing the archdiocese and the CBP, the former mayor lamented the latter's looser, less authoritative character (interview, November 26, 1996).

The CBP is also politically constrained by the existence of certain well-defined internal norms. The organization functions through a series of departments, all led by volunteers (the organization has no paid staff), and from the standpoint of politics, the one interest is the Department of Social and Political Action. This unit oversees the council's candidate-endorsement process and enforces certain rules relating thereto. Four such rules are noteworthy. First, in its "slating" of candidates, CBP rules require that all aspirants must first make an appearance at one of its monthly meetings to present their case. The group does not solicit candidate responses but instead reacts to candidate initiatives. ("All politicians come to us," as one member expressed it.) Second, recommendations for political endorsements are brought up at a special "called" meeting where they are voted on. Purely ad hoc endorsements are prohibited. Third, while the candidates finally slated are permitted to mention their CBP endorsement in literature and public statements, the council does not, as such, produce its own "slate." Finally, it is forbidden for pastors to accept money or other tangible benefits from any candidate.

Taken as a whole, these various rules are reflective of a cautious political involvement on the CBP's part, and that in turn is reflective of certain underlying realities. They include, for example, the often-diverse political opinions within the Detroit religious community. CBP leaders are wary of implying that their particular view on any given topic is the only genuine "religious" expression. Others views are possible, and when differences exist all voices are deserving of respect, so the consensus holds. Rev. Jim Holley, a former CBP president, has written on this point:

> In our contemporary society of diversity, with its growing number of religious traditions, the church is challenged to make a difference in the lives of persons . . . We must work toward the establishment of a public theology that does not seek to convert, but to make society whole. . . . This public theology cannot be Christian centered and Christian based. It must be a moral, ethical, and practical model. . . . To attempt to do much more will inevitably border on an effort at religious domination; an attempt at religious domination in a pluralistic society threatens the stability of that society. (Holley, 1995: 80)

The casino gaming issue is illustrative of the changing political status of black Baptist clergy. By the mid-1970s, the CBP was a power broker in a city governed by blacks. It could therefore openly express its political agreements or disagreements with the mayor of the city. Equally important, as Holley points out, in a democratic society, a public theology cries out for the moral and political development of citizenry. Hence, politically minded clergy, no longer impressed by a "symbolic spread" or "cries for racial unity," used their moral authority and links to black churchgoers to defeat Young's gaming proposals.

New York: Churches and the Black Quest for Political Acceptance

In New York, the rough equivalent of Coleman Young's political success of 1973 consisted of two successive events, namely Rev. Jesse Jackson's New York 1988 presidential campaign and David Dinkins' successful mayoral bid a year later. And as was true of Detroit, the black church played a part in those developments; equally important, the politics of self-determination would be part of the political landscape.

Dinkins' success in becoming the city's first African American mayor is an obvious achievement. His victory was the culmination of a long political career involving a slow ascent up the political ladder. As recently as 1977 and 1981 he had suffered defeat at the hands of a white Jewish rival, Andrew Stein, in bids for the borough presidency of Manhattan. (With the support of the city's Democratic machine, Dinkins kept himself in the public eye in these years by serving in the appointive post of city clerk.) When Stein vacated the borough presidency in 1985 in a successful bid to become city council president, the way was opened for Dinkins, whose persistence finally paid off; his borough presidency victory that year made him the city's highest ranking black official. In his various campaigns over the years, Dinkins had demonstrated a unique capacity to unite the city's black community, and with that as his base he was in a position to reach out to other constituencies, especially Hispanics, Jews, and white liberals. His draw to Jewish voters, who comprised a quarter of Democratic primary voters and a significant fraction in the general electorate, was critical to Dinkins' political attractiveness. His appeal stemmed from a long-standing and fervent opposition to anti-Semitism, a willingness to rebuke anti-Semitic statements from fellow blacks, and unstinting support for the state of Israel. Dinkins' successful mayoral bid started with his personal attractiveness but was assisted by a series of disasters that befell the incumbent mayor, Ed Koch, after the latter's inauguration to a third term in 1986 that continued with stunning regularity until the next mayoral campaign.

Given his general political attractiveness, Dinkins might have won the city's highest office in 1989 even without Jesse Jackson's presidential bid the previous year. But absent the earlier Jackson campaign, it would not have been the same. That candidacy was clearly a catalyst for the black community as well as for Dinkins.

Among other things, the mayoral tenures of Ed Koch, 1978–90, and Rudolph Giuliani, 1994–2002, demonstrate that mayors of New York have the capacity to win repeated reelection while remaining aloof from, and even disdaining, African Americans, the city's largest racial minority. As a student of New York politics, John Mollenkopf, pointed out, "minorities are weakly incorporated in New York City. Most crucially, Mayor Giuliani's electoral coalition does not rest on black or Latino votes. Instead, he views blacks as the opposition, as had Mayor Koch in the 1980s" (Mollenkopf, 1995: 4). The noninclusion of blacks and Latinos in the local political regime extends to the city council. From the late 1970s to the mid-1990s, minorities remained underrepresented on the thirty-five-member council, with but 29 percent of city council seats—seven black and three Latino—a percentage that contrasts with those ethnic groups' combined 42 percent share of the city's voting-age population. Not the least of the several causes of such underrepresentation was the internally combative nature of black leadership. Its various elites often contended with one another on the basis of borough residency, ideology, and degree of (Democratic) party loyalty. The city's exceptional size, unique borough configuration, and widely dispersed African American population have long constrained black leadership. Another contributing factor has been the highly competitive relationship between black leaders and their Latino counterparts. Such leaders' inability to work out a mutual accommodation has worked to the advantage of conservatively inclined white mayors.

The Jesse Jackson Candidacy

No single initiative could ever entirely overcome these handicaps, but the Jesse Jackson presidential candidacies of 1984 and 1988 demonstrated the potential for greatly alleviating their effects. Jackson's 1988 candidacy, in particular, succeeded as never before in integrating the competing forces in the black community. As Charles Green and Basil Wilson point out, the candidate brought together under one banner the black clergy—especially the Reverends Al Sharpton, Calvin Butts, and Herbert Daughtry—black nationalist leaders (both inside and outside the electoral arena), and black politicians with strong ties to the Democratic Party, David Dinkins included (Green and Wilson, 1989: 111). Significantly, Dinkins served as Jackson's 1988 New York campaign co-manager, along with the state's American Federation of State,

County, and Municipal Employees (AFSCME) president, Stanley Hill. Jackson also introduced a style of strongly issue-oriented politics, emphasizing class and power issues that were to some extent alien to the city's accustomed pragmatic, nonideological style. In raising such issues, the candidate positioned himself to appeal to the white working class, thus laying the basis for a biracial coalition. The results of these efforts were noteworthy. Even though he lost the statewide Democratic primary to Michael Dukakis, Jackson won a plurality (45 percent) in New York City, where he received 98 percent of the black vote, 63 percent of the Hispanic, and 17 percent of the white. The Jackson coalition "might not be able to make a new social order, but at least created a new complexion of state power" (Green and Wilson, 1989: 113).

While the Jackson campaign was positive from the standpoint of Dinkins' subsequent race for mayor, it also introduced an element of discord. In 1988, racial tensions in the city were as fraught as they had ever been, given the recent lynching of three black youths in the Howard Beach section of Queens by a white mob and the sensational charges (later disproved) brought by a black teenager, Tawana Brawley, of abduction and rape by white men. The mood of black-white racial antagonism in the city was overlaid with an upsurge in black-Jewish hostility. As Jackson campaigned throughout the city, he was shadowed by charges of anti-Semitism, which stemmed in part from his reference some years previous to New York as "Hymietown"—a derogatory reference to New York's large Jewish population—and a well-publicized photograph of him in an embrace with Yasser Arafat, the Palestine Liberation Organization leader (McNickle, 1993: 292). Jewish antagonism toward Jackson was deep, unforgiving, and persistent; in 1988, he received only 8 percent of the Jewish vote. These negative feelings became a factor in Dinkins' 1989 mayoral bid: to avoid being labeled "anti-Semite" took an extraordinary effort on his part. Dinkins' linkage to Jackson was a critical factor—New Yorkers such as Ed Koch viewed Jackson as an anti-Semite and a racist black nationalist. Jackson's inability to clearly distance himself from Minister Louis Farrakhan during the 1984 campaign clearly hampered his efforts to build a broader coalition in the 1988 campaign. Farrakhan was viewed within the white and Jewish community as an intolerant black nationalist leader. That Farrakhan was linked to the Jackson campaign made it even more difficult for Jackson to win Jewish and other white ethnic votes.

The Farrakhan controversy did not hamper Jackson's support among New York City black voters. Indeed, perhaps the most lasting impact of Jackson's 1988 candidacy in New York was its galvanizing effect on the black community. There he achieved a level of unity and enthusiasm previously unmatched by a political aspirant. Elizabeth Colton's account nicely captures the mood:

> Jesse Jackson was happiest . . . when he was out with his own people, "our crowd"—the blacks of Harlem and Queens and Brooklyn. They were his original constituents and they loved him . . . "Jesse! Jesse! Jesse!" they would shout at every stop in the poorer sections of the city. . . . They chased his entourage along the streets, and women cried and old men held back tears. Teenage girls grabbed at him. Parents held their infants up to him to kiss. Boys and young men reached out to shake his hand and look at him with awe. (Colton, 1989: 214–15)

David Dinkins, a cooler, more reserved individual, clearly benefitted from this enthusiasm when, a year later, his own campaign entered the same black neighborhoods.

Churches Feel the Effect

The city's black churches were impacted by the campaigns while also contributing to them. A brief reference to earlier times may be helpful in this regard. New York's ministers were involved to one degree or another in essentially all black political agitation and protest that took place in the twentieth century. In the 1930s, church leaders took part in the effort to integrate the workplace, and it was they, more than others, that spearheaded the formation of pro-integration groups, especially the Citizens League for Fair Play (1934) and the Greater New York Coordinating Committee on Employment (1938). As Green and Wilson point out, "The struggles against racism and for social change in Harlem invariably had black ministers in the forefront" (Green and Wilson, 1989: 62).

Among the several ministers involved in those campaigns, one in particular, Adam Clayton Powell Jr., stood out. In 1938, Powell emerged as the city's most influential black political figure, a role he would occupy until 1945 when he was first elected to Congress and proceeded to turn his attention away from city politics and more toward national concerns. Powell was minister of the Abyssinian Baptist Church in Harlem, a position inherited from his father and for which he had been carefully groomed. The church gave him a power base unrivalled by other activist groups, both black nationalist and Harlem Communist. Other black leaders had to rely on their ideological appeals; Powell could also rely on an institution. Abyssinian Baptist was large by any standard;

at more than fifteen thousand members, it was the biggest Protestant congregation in America. Its members were united and unstinting in support for their minister (Hamilton, 1991: 106; Haygood, 1993: 56). Powell's civil rights activism would include frequent visits to Detroit where he preached at both Rev. Charles Hill and C. L. Franklin's churches. Powell's call for Negro power or black power led him to invite Malcolm X to speak at his church, where Malcolm spoke on such themes as "Which Way the Negro" and "The Black Revolution" (Cone, 1991: 178).

Powell was not the only pastor to recognize the growing popularity of Malcolm X among city residents. Gardiner C. Taylor of Brooklyn's Concord Baptist Church, William Jones of Metropolitan Community Methodist Church, SCLC executive director Wyatt Tee Walker, and the Presbyterian activist-pastor Milton Galaminson appeared on platforms with Malcolm and attempted to address his criticism of them. As preachers responded to Malcolm and acknowledged the significance of this ministry to the black community, he tended to soften his critique and thereby create a better atmosphere for dialogue (Cone, 1991: 178). Some of the politically active clergy who engaged in dialogue with Malcolm X had been prominently involved in the post–World War II emergence of a new black political elite in Brooklyn. While this borough's first significant black politicians were secular in outlook, and either Caribbean-born or the children of Caribbean immigrants, the borough's large-scale wartime and postwar black migration from the South dramatically altered its black makeup. The new arrivals became the basis for the emergence of a new borough political elite. Militant ministers, especially Milton Galaminson, Herbert Daughtry, and Bill Jones, were among the leaders of an insurgency that initially placed the Caribbean elite under pressure and later helped engineer its displacement. The aftermath of this change saw an increase in the number of Brooklyn-based black elected officials. Brooklyn blacks and liberal whites now collaborated to secure state antidiscrimination legislation and pro–civil rights court rulings. (Sleeper, 1990: 57–59). Moreover, in 1958 Gardiner Taylor became the first black to be elected president of the sixty-year-old Protestant Council of the City of New York—a noteworthy racial breakthrough.

By the 1970s, 80 percent of New York blacks belonged to twenty-eight churches in Manhattan's Harlem and in Brooklyn's Bedford-Stuyvesant section, and such churches were commonly regarded as "brokers" between the black community and the wider community (*New York Times,* August 18, 1975). Yet brokerage did not necessarily imply power, and evidence existed that the black church, and more broadly the black community, still lacked for tangible power. John Mollenkopf cogently observes that even though black officeholders in the period from 1977 to 1991 were able to extract rewards from leaders of the white establishment, their cooperation was associated with relatively low levels of patronage, contracts, and similar benefits (Mollenkopf, 1995: 5). The city's minority interest was incorporated in a dependent, controlled way, and the city's governing regime was in no way dependent on black or Latino votes.

While prospects for changing this picture to the greater advantage of blacks and other minorities were not especially promising in the pre-Jackson, pre-Dinkins era, the city's obvious racial inequities and "crisis of powerlessness" nevertheless provoked a reaction. As discussed by Green and Wilson, six interfaith church-based alliances were organized in the city's various boroughs between 1974 and 1987 (Green and Wilson, 1989: 67–81). They adopted various names—"ministers conference," "people's Christian organization," "community and clergy coalition," and so on—but were alike in representing a new community thrust and commitment to political empowerment. These efforts had at least some tangible results. They included black church participation in Queens in a successful campaign to elect a black clergyman to Congress and involvement in the Bronx in forcing elected officials, city bureaucrats, and businesses to become more accountable to the local community. Yet these alliances were all somewhat parochial, being essentially neighborhood or borough-based, even in those cases where "metropolitan" was in the group's name. All lacked for paid staff, and none approached citywide status.

Citywide Interfaith Alliance

In 1989, as David Dinkins' mayoral bid was gearing up, a group of clergymen came together informally to help get the candidate elected. Dinkins stayed aloof from the city's more established black pastors, often referred to collectively as "the old civil rights ministers," and their main organizational expression, the Baptist Ministers Conference. He avoided attending their meetings and adroitly sidestepped their embrace. Instead, Dinkins reached out to a more diverse, more ecumenical group of clergy comprised of both Catholics and Protestants and drawn from all five boroughs, not just Harlem as had been the traditional New York pattern. This loose coalition of clergy supporters were fairly young and were more deeply concerned with black economic empowerment than with the political preoccupations typical of the "civil rights ministers."

Having first helped to secure Dinkins' victory, this younger clergy group were impelled to work toward his continuance in office and to help him build a record of accomplishment in line with the interests of African Americans. Thus, in the immediate aftermath of the election, the clergy members agreed to establish a formal organization, the New York African American Clergy Council, or NYAACC. A chairperson was designated for each of New York's four boroughs with substantial black-church membership—Manhattan, Brooklyn, Queens, and the Bronx. It is not insignificant that three of the borough chairs served churches affiliated with mainline, predominantly white denominations, namely United Presbyterian, United Methodist, and American Baptist. (The fourth borough chair, Herbert Daughtry, served a "nondenominational" church.) Black pastors serving in predominantly white denominations were widely reputed to be activist and militant on race-empowerment issues (Hunt and Hunt, 1975). Thus, although they served in a predominately white church hierarchy, these pastors sought to improve the collective power of blacks.

Seeking to further the mayor's political agenda, the new group remained close to the mayor and his aides. This meant several meetings at Gracie Mansion, the mayor's residence, and city hall. The group was especially active, and made perhaps its greatest impact, in helping to bridge the city's black-Jewish gulf, which it dealt with in collaboration with the New York Board of Rabbis. When a race riot occurred in the Crown Heights section of Brooklyn in the summer of 1991 involving Hasidic Jews and blacks, followed by further tension in 1992, the NYAACC stepped in to help calm the waters and to help resolve the underlying problem. It likewise worked with the Board of Rabbis in connection with the firebombing of a white (Jewish) owned store on 125th Street in Harlem. At one point, the NYAACC brought Jesse Jackson to the city for a return visit, again with a view toward enhancing black-Jewish understanding and acceptance.

It remained unclear, however, whether the NYAACC could maintain itself as a vital organization in the aftermath of David Dinkins' departure as mayor. One of its leaders, Rev. Glenn Messick (Church of the Master, Presbyterian) informed an interviewer in 1996 that the group had lately been fairly inactive, although he and the other activists were prepared to mobilize quickly if an incident or situation were to arise.

Conclusion

In summing up, it is useful to lay aside, initially, the political role of churches and instead to concentrate on the more general position of the black community in the two cities. In those terms, it is clear that a vast gulf separates New York and Detroit. In New York, blacks have remained essentially outside the city's governing regime. Ed Koch and Rudolph Giuliani, who together occupied the mayor's office for all but four years of the final two decades of the twentieth century, demonstrated the potential for white mayors to win and retain office in the absence of significant electoral support from African Americans. In Detroit, the election of Coleman Young to his first term in 1973 commenced a process of increasing black political strength, such that by his latter years in office blacks dominated the political system: the mayoralty, the city council, the board of education, the courts, and all other central-city political institutions.

The evidence presented indicates that the political strength of the black church has been, and remains, a function of a given city's basic regime pattern. Thus the black church has become a highly significant and stable factor in Detroit but fairly marginal and unstable in New York. Both cases testify to the importance, from a black-church standpoint, of the relative saliency of black nationalism and integration as dual mobilizing forces. In both cities, the political environment since the late 1960s provided political opportunities that allowed church leaders to play more direct roles in local and national politics. Adopting an integrative–black nationalistic political strategy resulted in black political unity in Detroit and New York when black candidates were running for highly visible public offices. Equally important, the presence of African Americans in the mayor's office was essential. Coleman Young and David Dinkins both found it advantageous to cooperate with black-church leaders and to solicit their support for their projects. White mayors were generally more distant from the black church, although such behavior was more obvious and sharp-edged in the New York case than in Detroit. As pointed out, Mayors Coleman Young and David Dinkins both made critical distinctions among groups of black-church pastors. The mayors' personal styles and policy preferences caused them to be drawn toward the more sophisticated black pastors, and to distance themselves from the more established ministerial types. Thus, Detroit's CBP achieved an enhanced level of importance with Mayor Young's election, and New York's NYAACC likewise benefitted enormously from the David Dinkins incumbency. The CBP and NYAACC were alike as well in partially filling the leadership vacuum produced by the declining presence of their city's established council of churches. Black ministers might conceivably have taken control of those citywide religious bodies and sought to convert them to their own ends, given that African Americans now predominated among the Protestant populations of both cities. Yet they chose instead to establish new institutions, leaving the church federations to fend for themselves with some, but limited, black-church support.

The above characterization of the New York black church as a marginal and unstable factor in the city's politics should be placed in context and not overstated or overgeneralized. Beginning in the 1930s, black pastors in the metropolis were involved to one degree or another in essentially every effort at black empowerment. Citywide church mobilization remained a problem for some years, but the formation of the NYAACC in the late 1980s finally demonstrated that it could happen. This group's fragility, flourishing during Dinkins' tenure but withering in the wake of his departure, testifies to Dinkins' inability, during his single term in office, to alter fundamentally the city's existing balance of forces in a manner beneficial to African Americans. Within limits, nevertheless, the clergy group exerted an influence.

The ministerial councils and conferences emphasized in this chapter are the rough functional equivalents of the two cities' older, more established church federations. Both forms exist, in part, to articulate their members' moral and social concerns on a citywide basis. Yet in some quite significant respects, the two organizations are functionally dissimilar. The federations typically maintain a headquarters with paid staff, while the ministers' groups do not. The federations represent churches as such; the ministers' groups speak for themselves individually. While these differences might be taken as an indication that the federation form is the stronger of the two, that is not necessarily the case. The evidence from these two cities can be interpreted as suggesting that the greater flexibility and spontaneity and essential simplicity of the ministers' council form represents an advantage, politically, as compared to the federation's typically more bureaucratic, internally complex character.

It is tempting to attribute the wide difference in institutionalized black-church power in the two cities to the contrasting proportions of African Americans in their respective electorates—over 76 percent in Detroit, just 20 percent in New York. Hence, a black nationalistic–integrationist approach may have more success in Detroit than New York because of the presence of a critical mass of blacks in the former city. Population differences are obviously important, but an analysis based on that factor alone would not be fully valid or persuasive. One must consider as well the basic, ongoing structure of each city's political system. Exploration of that aspect, to be addressed in the conclusion, draws attention to the basic theoretical issue raised by this analysis.

Conclusion

After sorting through the data from this study, I found them falling into meaningful patterns. Seven conclusions eventually emerged, and they are summarized here.

Four of the seven merit special emphasis, since they relate to more than a single historical era or to more than a single group or institution. First, in the late nineteenth and early twentieth centuries, urban government proved to be a disturbing element in the collective lives of city churches in both Detroit and New York—one of several disturbances that collectively inspired, and gave shape to, American Social Christianity. Church leaders, both Catholic and Protestant, responded to their unsettled environments partly by spearheading the formation of new citywide church bodies whose purpose can be interpreted as one of restoring a preexisting social balance. In subsequent years, with urban governments increasingly proactive and assertive, the fledgling church groups were not uncommonly recast in still more politically aware, public-policy-responsive molds. Second, the prevailing system of urban government—"reformed" in the Detroit case, "partisan" in the New York—has significantly impacted church-state relations in those communities, leading to contrasting patterns of political behavior. Whereas the two cities' politics remained closely akin through the first decade of the twentieth century, Detroit's adoption of a reformed charter in 1918 fundamentally altered its political regime and introduced an element of contrast between it and New York, whose system remained partisan-based. Third, at some point in the 1920s and '30s, church leaders came to accept the expanded municipal and state government as a given, and even, potentially, as a useful ally in their own ongoing efforts to maintain and stabilize citywide church structures. Fourth, Catholic and Protestant ecclesiastical bodies in the two cities have adopted contrasting styles for their urban government dealings. Protestant church groups have been the more socially activist and public policy sensitive, whereas the Catholic Church has been generally less activist, more risk-averse, and more behaviorally consistent on civic issues.

My summary also highlights three other conclusions, which are worthy of note even though they are less broadly applicable. First, citywide church groups occasionally committed themselves to campaigns aimed at influencing high-level city and state government appointments. The results of such partisan thrusts were, from a church standpoint, organizationally ambiguous—beneficial in some respects, destabilizing in others. Second, black ministers' conferences, which featured for the first time in both cities' politics during the final third of the twentieth century, are to some extent the political equivalents of the two cities' more established ecumenical councils of churches—now much diminished in stature in comparison to earlier years. In other respects, however, the ministers' conferences are functionally distinct and historically unique. Third, and finally, citywide church organizations continued to impact municipal government in the two cities during the latter years of the twentieth century. This finding is somewhat at odds with what might have been predicted on the basis of leading present-day urban politics textbooks, which typically pass over in silence any actual or potential church political role.

The above, in essence, are my main themes. The remainder of the chapter elaborates upon them. The themes have figured in the body of the text, and the reader will not, therefore, find them wholly unfamiliar. Yet my discussion up to this point has been mainly descriptive, with only occasional analysis. Henceforth, analysis becomes primary. Also, in what follows I drop the chronology of successive eras of urban policy development, used to organize the chapters, in favor of an approach centered on the several conclusions.

Disturbances

In the introduction of this study, I observed that the concept of "disturbance," initially developed by Truman, may have heuristic value in interpreting the emergence and early survival of urban church organizations active in the two cities. The published literature on Social Christianity, as summarized in chapter 1, demonstrates that the Progressive-era formation of councils of churches at the local, state, and national levels, and of numerous Catholic social action groups, stemmed in part from an anxiety-provoking urban situation. That environment was marked by mass European immigration, the rise of an industrial economy, the tragedy of child labor, the prevalence of slums and urban overcrowding, and the burgeoning of the labor movement and related labor-management strife. Yet this literature essentially disregards another apparent source of disruption, namely the existence at this point of expansive, increasingly proactive, urban government.

Chapter 2 documents the far-reaching expansions that marked urban government in New York and Detroit at that time and points out the relationship in time existing between that and the subsequent formation of several city-wide religious bodies. Government, it appears, contributed indirectly to the process of church-group formation. It is true that church leaders may not in all cases have perceived government in threatening terms. Some probably did while others may have developed mostly positive and congenial city hall relationships. Reliable data on this point are, unfortunately, lacking. Yet the larger picture remains fairly clear. Progressive-era expansions in the scope of the two cities' urban governments altered the churches' wider environments in ways that challenged their traditional survival and development strategies. The period was, after all, dynamic in important and tangible ways: taxes rose, city regulatory agencies were established, vast municipal projects were launched, burgeoning city bureaucracies were created, and affluent citizens began exiting the central city for newly established suburbs in places like Grosse Pointe, Scarsdale, and New Rochelle. This period was also significant in less measurable, more spiritual, terms. Church members could not be unaware of, or indifferent to, the reality of municipal corruption and moral decay—nicely captured by a leading observer of the time, Lincoln Steffens, in the title of a classic study, *The Shame of the Cities* (Steffens, 1904). Their concern also focused on other moral issues including, especially, the political sway of the liquor industry and the pervasiveness of anti-religious bias—especially as directed against Catholics and the Catholic Church. None of these matters were entirely novel; all had existed in one form or another for many years. Yet their significance was now magnified. The increasingly dense relations between ordinary citizens and their state and local governments presumably helped to heighten public awareness of urban problems and a desire on citizens' part for civic betterment and reform.

Also documented in chapter 1 are several instances of government-inspired change that had a disturbing effect on church interests, and the related responses of church leaders. In New York, there was the series of city and state probes of sectarian welfare institutions that began around 1910 and that eventuated in state officials' leveling charges of abuse and mismanagement against a number of such institutions, many of them Catholic. These actions, in turn, contributed to the archdiocese's eventual decision to reorganize its local charities under the newly formed "Catholic Charities of the Archdiocese of New York."

Equally telling are the examples of the 1895 decision to form a city church federation in New York, and that of 1918 to form such a body in Detroit.

Reform-minded citizens in both cities now generally concluded that their municipal governments were beyond citizen control and in thrall to various special interests. While this situation was not altogether new—indeed, it dated well back in time—the recent large-scale expansions of local governments lent it urgency. Obviously, church leaders in both cases could employ any of several avenues to voice their moral outrage: pulpit sermons, popular religious periodicals, letters to editors in the local press, or support for civic reform groups. (The storied reform career of New York's Rev. Charles Parkhurst is illustrative of the wide scope for such interventions.) Still, church leaders evidently regarded the formation of councils of churches as indispensable in furtherance of their moral-uplift objectives; only collectively could they bring their full weight to bear on civic concerns.

In the Depression of the 1930s, Detroit and New York churches continued to feel the disrupting effects of expanding government but with fresh behavioral consequences: less that of new group formation and more of alteration in existing-group priorities and programs. To an unprecedented degree, the Depression saw government officials placing demands on sectarian welfare providers, given the clear inadequacy of purely public resources in the current crisis. Social pathologies like unemployment, family breakup, and child neglect all cried out for attention, and city officials came to regard churches and sectarian welfare institutions as necessary elements in any overall remedy. As early as 1930, Detroit's new mayor, Frank Murphy, in his personal capacity as well as through his lieutenants, reached out to organized religion, the Catholic Church especially, thereby helping to forge a church-city government relationship that would endure through time. The Murphy administration helped stimulate the Detroit Archdiocese to an expanded awareness of its potential to provide assistance to needy families, even in the face of daunting financial problems and, in 1937, undeclared archdiocesan bankruptcy. The Detroit Archdiocese's late-1930s' decision to reorganize Catholic social service was, in part, governmentally related, given that Edward Cardinal Mooney had come to appreciate the value of tight administrative control over social service operations through his firsthand encounter with the federal government as chairman of the Administrative Board of the National Catholic Welfare Conference. In New York, Fiorello La Guardia, elected mayor in 1933 on a Republican/City Fusion ticket, demanded early on that the city's church federations and local sectarian welfare agencies should cease their internecine squabbling and join hands in common endeavor. His pleading was not without its effect on church leaders, especially Protestants, who altered their behavior, albeit slowly.

None of this is intended to suggest that government was alone responsible for the Depression-era changes in urban churches. The latter were responding to an obvious emergency, and no input from government was required to inform their leaders of the gravity of the situation. Yet there is evidence to suggest that proactive local and state governments were a factor in helping to raise the churches' consciousness. Analysts have long recognized that government can impact church behavior given certain conditions. For example, Timothy Byrnes argues that at the federal level the nation's Catholic bishops were profoundly affected by the public policy developments of the 1960s. He observes that the American bishops shifted at that time from a traditionally defensive stance, based on a wary regard for Catholic institutional interests, to a proactive and positive one, under the leadership of the then-newly-formed National Conference of Catholic Bishops (NCWC). The New Deal of 1930s, Byrnes observes, also had an impact on the American Church, but less than was true of the New Frontier/Great Society transformations of the 1960s (Byrnes, 1991: 44–53). I find Byrnes persuasive on this point. Yet the evidence from the present study leads me to conclude that in the nation's larger cities the reverse may have applied. Assuming that New York and Detroit are typical cases, the decisive twentieth-century change in church-state relations—not just for the Catholic Church but for Protestantism as well—appear to have come in the 1930s, with the '60s secondary in importance. The relationship that developed in the former of these decades evidently did not fade away with the ending of the Depression and American entry into World War II, but instead mostly persisted into the years to follow.

Regime Differences

As pointed out in the introduction, earlier analysts have noted a connection between a city's basic form of government, partisan or reformed, and its prevailing political style or ethos. The present findings suggest that this insight can be usefully applied toward a better understanding of the Detroit and New York cases. New York's "partisan" system affected relations between municipal government and various nongovernmental actors, the churches included, in ways fundamentally different from the same set of relations in Detroit.

New York's partisan system dictates that its politicians engage in ticket-balancing as a condition of winning and holding office. The arranging of balanced tickets has a tendency to push ethno-religious concerns to the forefront. It is not accidental, for example, that leading studies of New York politics often employ phrases like "ethnic politics in the city" (McNickle, 1993), "beyond the melting pot" (Glazer and Moynihan, 1963), and "an ethnic and racial history" (Binder and Reimers, 1995) for their titles or subtitles—a pattern not duplicated in historical interpretations of Detroit, where race may be emphasized but seldom religion or ethnicity. New York's churches, synagogues, and other religious bodies have served in part as agencies of ethno-religious expression and articulation. That applies especially to religious bodies comprised of persons not well represented in the city electorate, Protestants, for example. Such bodies may feel under a special obligation to act as ethnic-group advocates, given that politicians ordinarily feel little inclined to include their constituents in the ticket-balancing, ethnic-accommodation process (Pratt, 1970).

A partisan system may also tend to heighten interethnic tensions as each group struggles for its place in the sun, and as some see themselves as having lost out or gotten less than their fair share. Rudolph Giuliani, upon becoming mayor in the early 1990s, had no fewer than thirteen ethnic representatives on his mayoral staff, so sensitive were ethnic issues in the city's politics. Religion was never far from such calculations, and politicians often came to regard "church" not simply as a religious and spiritual institution, but as one among a range of local interests to be reached out to and, within limits, accommodated. That perception, while not unknown under a reformed system of government, is likely to be less pronounced there.

Finally, among the various ways that partisan government differs from reformed not the least important is the method employed for electing members of the city council: neighborhood- or ward-based in the partisan case, at-large in the reformed. A ward-based system tends to elevate the importance of neighborhood concerns, whereas an at-large one tends to accord greater emphasis to concerns of citywide scope. This contrast in electoral forms has implications for religious-group behavior. Under a partisan, ward-based system, church groups are prone to organize initially at the district or borough level and only later on, if at all, citywide, whereas in an at-large system the pattern tends to be reversed, with citywide organization coming first, and neighborhood or borough only later on, if at all. In other words, churches are typically more constrained in their attempt to exert citywide influence under the partisan system.

The above considerations appear useful in interpreting some otherwise anomalous aspects of the data. First, the difficulties encountered by New York's black pastors in their attempts to establish viable African American ministers' groups on a citywide basis, as documented in chapter 6, are not duplicated in Detroit, where citywide organizations of this type formed fairly easily.

On the other hand, several black ministers' groups have formed among New York's five boroughs, whereas in Detroit interparish neighborhood groups of this type have not featured prominently. The two cities' differing forms of government appear to be involved in this organizational contrast.

Second, Detroit's "reformed" governmental system has contributed to the city electorate's resistance to becoming divided along sectarian lines. If ever an incentive existed for a religious grouping to embrace a sectarian political outlook, it would be Detroit Catholics in the 1920s. As noted in chapters 1 and 2, anti-Catholicism was rampant throughout Michigan at that point, Detroit included. In the city elections of 1923 and 1930, various candidates exploited their religious identities in hopes of mobilizing an anti-Catholic vote, thus enhancing their electoral chances. Catholic voters had ample reason, had they been so inclined, to rally around a Catholic standard, seeking to elect their co-religionists in preference to others. But as pointed out in chapter 1, no Catholic defense movement of consequence in fact materialized, not then or later. Protestant candidates continued to achieve top elective offices in the 1920s, '30s, and beyond, even though Catholics at this time were an increasing numerical majority. Obviously, other factors also contributed to the Catholic reluctance to identify politically on a sectarian basis—for example, the assimilationist stance adhered to by Archbishop Thomas Foley. Yet the city's reformed governmental system clearly played a role. Local politicians were not required, at least not to any marked degree, to take religion into account in the slating of candidates for public office, and the at-large character of city council elections placed citywide appeal, not the ethnic character of neighborhoods or districts, at the forefront of attention. This, in turn, impacted churches and citywide church organizations.

The Detroit case was paralleled by that of Springfield, Massachusetts, as ably treated in a study by N. J. Demerath III and Rhys H. Williams. In 1960, Springfield shifted from a traditional ward-based, two-party bicameral system of governance to a "reformed" system—at-large, nonpartisan, and strong mayoralty. In Demerath's and Williams' words, this action was the city's "single most important change in [the twentieth] century" (Demerath and Williams, 1992: 273). As was true of Detroit after 1918, this change in the system of governance impacted relations between churches and the local political regime, including a newfound tendency to downplay religious differences. With leadership provided by the newly formed Springfield Central, Inc., a multireligious body comprised of corporate leaders, and the city's public-relations-savvy Catholic bishop, Joseph McGuire, who assumed office in 1977 following the death of his fairly combative predecessor, the Rev. Christopher Weldon, Springfield's traditional

Catholic-Protestant competitiveness and occasional animosity mostly dissipated (Demerath and Williams, 1992: 70–77, 274, 295).

Government as Source of Validation and Legitimation

As municipal and state governments came to play an increasingly large role in the lives of the two cities under discussion, local church leaders reassessed their relationship with the wider community and in certain cases concluded that government could serve, indirectly, as a source of validation and legitimation in the maintenance of their own citywide organizations. Caution is required in interpreting the linkages that developed between church leaders and local officials lest their importance be exaggerated or overgeneralized. In neither Detroit nor New York did the churches become an integral part of the city's ongoing political regime, nor did citywide church bodies ever become critically dependent on the state as a condition of their survival. Even such influential church leaders as New York's Francis Cardinal Spellman or the Rev. Dan Potter stood somewhat apart from their city's established secular power, a pattern undergirded by the nation's norm of church-state separation. Still, ongoing relationships of significance did develop and at certain points even flourished—as embodied in formal and informal contacts that were sustained over time and were evidently seen as advantageous by all parties. The existence of expanded, occasionally even highly proactive, urban government was now no longer a "disturbance" in any realistic sense, but instead a fixed element in the churches' wider community setting—one that, if approached correctly, could be used to their collective interest and advantage.

A leading example of such potential was New York City's tripartite Mayor's Committee of Religious Leaders, formed in 1957. This entity benefitted the Protestant Council, and presumably also its other religious members, by helping to enhance its legitimacy in the eyes of constituents and supporters, and by providing an input into municipal policy making. It also evidently benefitted New York's mayor, providing him with useful counsel and input in a political setting suffused with religious overtones and potential for sectarian conflict.

Another example of religious-group validation and support was implicit in the relationship in Detroit between black Baptist leaders and the Coleman Young administration. CBP leaders met with Mayor Young from time to time, and that relationship was evidently viewed as beneficial by both parties—by the mayor as a means of monitoring an important element in his political constituency, and by the pastors as a means of further enhancing their collective status and citywide standing.

Catholic-Protestant Disparities

In comparing the present data across sectarian lines, Protestant and Catholic, it is useful to begin by noting a fundamental point of contrast in ecclesiastical polity. The Catholic Church is an essentially hierarchical institution, with authority emanating from Rome and mediated through local bishops, archbishops, and other church officials before reaching its base in Catholic parishes and other entities at the local level. In contrast, American Protestantism is characterized by the (nonhierarchical) principle of congregational autonomy. It is true that some Protestant denominations, Methodism and Lutheranism, for example, employ a top-down formal structure, with a certain measure of authority vested in local bishops. Yet even in those cases considerable local autonomy is present, with church property typically held in the name of the congregation, not the denominational judicatory. This contrasting pattern has implications for urban church behavior. The Catholic Church typically acts on issues of concern to the wider community through the local diocesan (or archdiocesan) chancery, which is not a "voluntary" unit in any sense but an organic, canonically based facet of the church proper. Title to parish property is typically held by the diocese or archdiocese, and parishes are obligated to pay taxes to the diocese for the property's maintenance and development. Thus the chancery is not dependent on securing the approval of any membership or local constituency. Church officials can seek to influence city hall and otherwise promote the Catholic viewpoint in the wider community to the extent they deem most appropriate, but they are under no necessary obligation to politically represent their local flock. Protestant churches, on the other hand, in their quest for unity of purpose, often amalgamate as *voluntary organizations*—chiefly councils (or federations) of churches, or ministers' conferences—and, as is true of voluntary organizations generally, their leaders must remain alert to the possibilities for achieving and maintaining member approval and backing, which can be withdrawn at any point. For such leaders, social action on the wider stage often presents itself as a means of maximizing internal support, and this may explain in part Protestantism's greater tendency to issue pronouncements on public issues and to become otherwise involved in civic affairs.

This contrast has implications for church social action in the two cities. Throughout the twentieth century, the Catholic archdioceses in both Detroit and New York have behaved in a fairly steady, consistent manner in regard to a range of moral and ethical issues; as compared to Protestantism, they have been less critically concerned with sustaining a given level of city hall, or state house, political access. While no detailed assessment of the Church's wider urban agenda was undertaken for this study, it appears that the two archdioceses have generally had a narrower range of policy concerns, including, for example, opposition to legalized abortion, opposition to legalized birth control, and defense of Catholic education. Citywide Protestant agencies, for their part, have adopted a wider array of public policy stands and have been generally more vulnerable to the ever-changing political environment at city hall.

Catholic and Protestant churches were behaviorally more distinct in New York, with its partisan system of governance, than was true under Detroit's reformed system. Throughout the period of this study, New York Catholicism's access at city hall was partly a function of the presence or absence of a Catholic in the mayor's office. As noted in chapter 5, Cardinal Spellman succeeded in establishing very close ties with Mayors O'Dwyer, Impellitteri, and Wagner—all Catholics—whereas his relationship with John Lindsay, a Protestant Episcopalian, was cool and distant. (While the extent of his links with Mayor La Guardia, also an Episcopalian, are unknown, there is nothing to indicate that they were especially close.) In the case of Protestantism, New York City's council of churches felt itself under much greater pressure than its Catholic counterpart to act as a Protestant status group in the city. This tendency was most apparent in the 1950s and early '60s during the administration of Mayor Robert Wagner Jr., but hints of it were present at various other points throughout the group's existence. The council's fortunes have varied widely over time—socially prominent and affluent at some points, marginalized and nearly destitute at others. Without suggesting any direct, cause-and-effect relationship, it is noteworthy that the group was generally more organizationally successful during the occasional Protestant mayoralties than when the mayor's office was occupied by a non-Protestant. The modest upsurge in the council's fortunes during the David Dinkins era, noted in chapter 5, was illustrative of that tendency. Little of this applies to Catholicism, where the New York Church has been less critically affected by changes in the wider political setting.

On the other hand, in both Detroit and New York Catholicism appears to have enjoyed fairly sustained influence in municipal government, notwithstanding various sociological changes occurring at the time that arguably should have diminished or possibly undermined its political status. In Detroit, as noted in chapters 2 and 3, the archdiocese was closely in touch with Frank Murphy and Jerome Cavanagh, both Catholics, during their mayoral tenures but almost equally so, as documented in chapter 6, with Mayor Coleman Young, an ex-Catholic turned Baptist. In New York, as discussed in chapter 3, the archdiocese enjoyed excellent relations with Mayors O'Dwyer, Impellitteri, and Wagner—all Catholics—but almost equally so with Fiorello La Guardia, a Protestant Episcopalian, and Ed Koch, a Jew. The important role played by the archdiocese in connection with the 1975 fiscal aid package for New York City provided further evidence of a continued capacity for political influence.

Political Appointments Campaigns

Two of the groups covered in this study, the Protestant Council of New York City and the Detroit's CBP, at one time or another assumed responsibility for screening of candidates for public office and making known their candidate preferences. The two cases are not, obviously, precisely parallel. The PC's endorsements in the 1950s and early '60s applied essentially to *appointive* posts, whereas those made by the CBP subsequent to its formation in 1964 were concerned chiefly with *elective* offices. Also, the two groups differed in their degree of assertiveness, with PC leaders fairly proactive in this area and the CBP more inclined to confine itself to a role that limited its political exposure.

Such differences aside, however, a rough parallel exists between the two groups' political behavior. Both acted in response to the shared political ambitions of their constituents under circumstances of perceived bias—against Protestants in the New York case, against African Americans in the case of Detroit. The two groups were alike as well in that the results achieved often fell short of initial expectations. In the late 1950s, for example, when black New Yorkers first became assertive politically on a citywide basis, several black activists evidently entertained hopes that the Protestant Council, then involved in an aggressive campaign in the area of political appointments, would extend its reach to encompass the political aspirations of African Americans. Yet any such hopes were soon dashed, and the PC vehicle created to further this effort, the CPRPL, soon passed out of existence. Also, as previously noted, the PC's endorsement role made the group aware of the inherent problem involved in appearing to favor the ambitions of certain individuals over others of the same religious persuasion, all of them aspirants for the same appointive post. This problem proved especially vexatious in the case of political aspirants who had anticipated the endorsement by the PC based on their declared religious faith and record of church support, but whom the PC ended up deciding were not the best qualified for the office. Such individuals' frustrated ambitions were a source of potential trouble for the church federation, and in certain cases that potential became the reality.

In seeking to forestall such problems, leaders of the PC and CBP adopted defensive tactics. The PC was inclined toward secrecy, the names of its candidates generally being kept confidential in hopes of avoiding embarrassment or internal discord. The CBP elected to avoid direct political involvement or advocacy, and instead to limit itself essentially to a candidate-screening role. Its leaders stipulated that aspirants for its favor must first approach the conference to request its endorsement and must not expect any active CBP role beyond that of the endorsement itself. The organization thus limited its exposure while also fostering black political advancement.

As I observed in the conclusion to chapter 4, the Protestant Council's stresses related to candidate endorsement were illustrative of a more general problem, namely the assumption by an interest group of functions more typical of a political party organization, and for which party leaders, but not their interest group counterparts, are generally well prepared. The PC derived certain benefits from its city appointments campaign, but only up to a point and at some cost in terms of internal factionalism. The activity placed PC leaders at a disadvantage given that they were typically ill-equipped, on the basis of their prior training and experience, to cope with the organizational stresses almost certain to arise from this kind of group activity.

Black Ministers' Conferences

New York and Detroit politics are alike in one particular, namely that in both cities the black church asserted itself to an unprecedented degree beginning in the early 1970s. While the church had always played a central role in the two African American communities, and despite the deference traditionally accorded to such politically active black clergy as New York's Adam Clayton Powell and Detroit's Charles Hill, this decade constituted a watershed in terms of collective religious action. With black numbers expanding, both absolutely and as a percentage of city populations, and with African American politicians assuming prominent positions at both the city and state levels, it was not at all surprising, in one sense, that black ministers should seize this moment to assert themselves—politically, socially, and otherwise. Such assertiveness was not limited to any one city or region but was common in cities throughout the United States.

In the two cities under discussion here, this political emergence expressed itself chiefly in the form of groups comprised of black ministers. In the 1970s and '80s. New York witnessed the formation of several such groups on a boroughwide basis, whereas in Detroit the CBP and other such citywide clergy groups began to assert themselves. Such groups can be usefully compared, in functional terms, with the preexisting ecumenical councils of churches, which, even though they survived, they did so at a much-reduced level of activity and civic involvement.

Two points of functional resemblance emerge in such comparison. First, the black ministers' groups and the older church federations were alike as the *articulators* of church-member sentiments. In some cases such expression reflected a concern for the welfare of the urban community as a whole. For example, the black ministers' groups, even though comprised of African Americans, acted as more than simply race organizations when they spoke out on matters such as gambling, vice, and local tax-base augmentation. Likewise, the ecumenical church federations, even though mostly comprised of Protestants, were more than just Protestant in the sectarian sense when they spoke out on civil rights and support for the local public schools.

At the same time, however, both religious bodies in varying degree sought to advance their members' particular, status-group concerns. The CBP and its approximate New York counterpart, the New York African American Clergy Council, were committed to promoting black community welfare and advancement, and that aim remained central to those groups' self-defined missions. The Detroit Council of Churches tentatively accepted a status-group role for itself during its first five years, 1919–24—proclaiming itself as unequivocally Protestant—but later softened that stance as its outlook became increasingly ecumenical and accepting of local religious diversity. A more persistent status-group outlook characterized the New York Protestant Council in the 1950s and early '60s. The group's campaign to insure that the city balanced its Jewish and Catholic appointments with Protestant ones was symptomatic of a deep-seated Protestant anxiety related to its perceived exclusion from an accustomed wider-community role. The PC was responsive to certain obvious anxieties among its constituents and was prepared to do what it could to combat the problem.

Secondly, both groups *aggregated* sentiment and opinion within their constituencies. They were alike in helping to bridge certain differences that otherwise could have divided their communities along congregational and/or denominational lines. While such consensus-building efforts were not invariably successful, they were substantially so much of the time, and that in turn enabled the organizations to express fairly unified positions on issues of shared religious-group concern.

Yet the parallels between the two types of religious organizations appear valid only up to a point, and beyond that certain contrasts become apparent. Two, in particular, are worthy of note. First, in *structural terms,* as noted in chapter 6, a ministers' conference differs from a council of churches in that in the former churches are not, as such, the basis of representation; member ministers speak for themselves in pronouncing on civic concerns. That can make their collective voice appear as less broadly inclusive of shared sentiment within the religious community as compared to a church federation. (The Protestant Council, for example, long proclaimed itself "The Voice of New York's 1,700 Protestant Churches.") Secondly, the ministers' conference form is structurally distinct in its lack of a headquarters or paid staff, and reliance on volunteers for the performance of key functions. Such absence of group infrastructure could potentially limit the group's ability to research and carry through on its pronouncements, but it could also constitute an asset in terms of greater flexibility and spontaneity.

Churches' Urban Political Influence

Returning to a question posed in the introduction, is it the case, as some would contend, that churches have irreversibly declined as a political force in urban America? Is the urban politics literature—as summarized in leading textbooks on the topic—correct in implying that churches are no longer significantly involved in the governance of the nation's larger cities? While this question obviously cannot be definitively answered on the basis of two just cases, however representative, the present data do at least enable one to shed some light on this question and to offer a possibly fresh perspective.

The thesis that religious organizations of all kinds have greatly declined as a source of large-city civic influence has been forcefully presented by a political scientist, Paul A. Djupe, in a paper subtitled "The Decline in Importance of Religious Leaders in Local Politics" (1996). Basing his conclusions on data resulting from a search of the indexes for the *St. Louis Post-Dispatch* from 1975 to 1994 and the *New York Times* from 1969 to 1994, Djupe documents what he terms "the big slide." He reports that in both newspapers the years in question witnessed a decline in the number of stories devoted to general religious issues. This pattern applied to stories specific to the two cities, St. Louis and New York, and also to ones of national religious import. "It is clear," the author observes, "that local religious leaders have faded from public view" (Djupe, 1996: 4).

In seeking to account for this, Djupe tests five hypotheses, four of which in his judgement end up as valid to one degree or another: population shift, secularization of urban society, decline in the public linkage role of political parties, and emergence of persistently confusing and controversial issues whose effect was to remove ministers and other religious leaders from the political limelight. Even though urban churches remain well attended and well supported, Djupe remarks somberly in his conclusion, "what is missing is cohesion above the congregational level" (Djupe, 1996: 11).

Two observations seem appropriate by way of response to Djupe's commentary. First, as the author himself admits in passing, the two papers' coverage of "Catholic Issues" did not in fact support the "decline" thesis. In St. Louis, the author reports that newspaper "attention to the Roman Catholic Church has increased in recent years," while in New York, Catholic coverage in the *Times* remained fairly constant throughout the twenty-five-year survey period. Only with respect to "general religious" topics was any decline clearly evident. Secondly, the author underscores the "lack of cohesion above the congregational level" and society's diversification "into smaller and smaller functional units" as contributory factors in the churches' declining urban political strength (Djupe, 1996: 11–12), but he does not mention citywide church structures whose mission is to bridge such differences and to combat the imbedded lack of cohesion. This is not to suggest, necessarily, that Djupe's thesis would be undermined were the above points to be more strongly emphasized, but they do at least provide grounds for some doubt regarding the general validity of the "decline" thesis.

Djupe is definitely correct in noting the decline in religious coverage in the nation's leading metropolitan press. A study of the Detroit papers would likely reveal a similar overall trend, although, again, one should be wary of its applicability to Catholicism. In the post-1970 era, newspaper editors evidently did not regard religion as "news" to the same degree that applied in prior years. It is debatable, however, that one can validly extrapolate from that the conclusion that organized religion no longer occupies an important place in American urban governance. Have religious leaders in fact lost civic importance, as the declining press coverage of religion might seem to suggest, or could it be that the press no longer covers the religious scene to the same extent as in earlier years and therefore may tend to overlook the churches' actual role? The present data suggests the latter is a distinct possibility. One could easily overstate the significance of mainline ecumenical councils of churches' declining scale and societal visibility in recent decades. The scope of this decline was certainly dramatic. Yet despite their vicissitudes, church federations continued to act politically and to exert some measure of wider community influence. That role was implicit in the Detroit council's prominent role in the anti–casino gambling crusade, in the backing given to the David Dinkins mayoral campaign, in the unofficial backing given by the CCCNY to the David Dinkins 1989 mayoral campaign, and later to Dinkins as mayor. Furthermore, as emphasized in chapter 6 and earlier in this conclusion, to the extent that the declining strength of councils of churches opened up a new social space in the metropolis, that space was at least partially filled by African American religious groups, especially black ministers' councils. While one should be cautious in interpreting these groups' political importance—they were probably as much the objects of manipulation by local officials as an autonomous political force—groups like the CBP and NYAACC demonstrated a capacity to impact the political system on issues of concern to their members: racial exclusion, legalized gambling, city tax policy, and so forth.

Also worthy of emphasis is the continuing political clout, in the two cities under discussion, of the Catholic Church. Not only did Catholicism continue to command attention in the New York press, but its officials and representatives maintained their privileged access to elective and appointive city officials. It appears that Catholicism's views on public issues were mostly conveyed privately and without fanfare, thus tending to frustrate attempts by outsiders to determine their precise level and scope. Yet one should be wary of any suggestion that in either Detroit or New York the Catholic Church lost its former political influence during the latter years of the twentieth century, or even declined appreciably from earlier peaks.

The tendency noted at the beginning of this conclusion for scholars to minimize and disparage the importance of the black church from the standpoint of black community leadership may apply more broadly to churches generally. The urban affairs literature and other writings pertinent to the urban scene suffers from a tendency toward passing over too quickly relationships between church representatives and city officials that often go underreported and are for the most part poorly understood. Such a tendency could well be reinforced by the American norm of church-state separation, one effect of which could be to make church leaders and politicians wary of each other, and disinclined to affirm the scope and intensity of their collaboration, if any. If any of this is true, the present study should serve as a corrective. In the case of New York and Detroit, at least, the evidence presented indicates that throughout the century-long period surveyed the churches significantly impacted government and vice versa. It is reasonable to expect that subsequent research, focused on these or other large American cities, would provide additional support for the view that religious bodies remain a significant, ongoing aspect of present-day American urban governance.

Bibliography

Abell, Aaron. *American Catholicism and Social Action: A Search for Social Justice, 1865–1950.* Garden City, N.Y.: Hanover House, 1960.

Aberbach, David, and Jack L. Walker. "Political Trust and Racial Ideology." *American Political Science Review* 56, no. 4 (December 1970): 1199–1219.

Anton, Thomas J. *Federal Aid to Detroit.* Washington, D.C.: Brookings Institution, 1983.

Banfield, Edward C., and James Q. Wilson. *City Politics.* Cambridge, Mass.: Harvard University Press, 1963.

Barker, J. Lucius. *Our Time Has Come: A Delegate's Diary of Jesse Jackson's 1984 Presidential Campaign.* Urbana: University of Illinois Press, 1988.

Barr, Earl R. "Is There a Religious Test for Public Office" (mimeo). New York: Methodist East Conference, Board of Social and Economic Relations, January 1960.

Binder, Frederick M., and David M. Reimers. *All the Nations Under Heaven: An Ethnic and Racial History of New York City.* New York: Columbia University Press, 1995.

Blumberg, Barbara. *The New Deal and the Unemployed: The View from New York City.* Lewisberg, Pa.: Bucknell University Press, 1979.

Boggs, Grace Lee. *Living for Change: An Autobiography.* Minneapolis: University of Minnesota Press, 1998.

Bridger, Jeffrey C., and David R. Maines. "Narrative Structures and the Catholic Church Closings in Detroit." *Qualitative Sociology* 8, no. 3 (1998): 319–40.

Byrnes, Timothy A. *Catholic Bishops in American Politics.* Princeton: Princeton University Press, 1991.

Cahalan, [Msgr.] Florence D. *A Popular History of the Archdiocese of New York.* Yonkers, N.Y.: United States Catholic Historical Society, 1983.

Campbell, Angus, and Howard Schuman. *Racial Attitudes in Fifteen American Cities: January–March 1968, Black Data File Documentation.* Ann Arbor: Institute For Social Research, University of Michigan, 1968.

Catlin, George B. *The Story of Detroit.* Detroit: *Detroit News,* 1926.

Cavert, Samuel McCrea. *The American Churches in the Ecumenical Movement, 1900–1968.* New York: Association Press, 1968.

Cayton, Horace R., and Setsuko Nishi. *Churches and Social Welfare,* vol. 2. New York: National Council of Churches of Christ, 1955.

Chafets, Ze'ev. *Devil's Night and Other True Stories of Detroit.* New York: Random House, 1990.

Colton, Elizabeth. *The Jackson Phenomenon: The Man, the Power, the Message.* New York: Doubleday, 1989.

Cone, James, H. *Martin and Malcolm and America: A Dream or a Nightmare.* New York: Orbis Books, 1991.

Conot, Robert. *American Odyssey.* New York: Bantam Books, 1974.

Cooney, John. *The American Pope: The Life and Times of Francis Cardinal Spellman.* New York: Times Books, 1984.

Costain, Anne N., and Douglas Costain. "Movements and Gatekeepers: Congressional Response to Women's Issues, 1900–1982." *Congress and the Presidency* 12 (1985): 21–43.

———. "The Political Economy of Social Movements: A Comparison of the Women's and Environmental Movements." *Congress and the Presidency* 19, no. 1 (1992): 1–27.

Dahl, Robert. *Who Governs: Democracy and Power in an American City.* New Haven: Yale University Press, 1961.

Demerath, N. J., and Rhys H. Williams. *A Bridging of Faiths: Religion and Politics in a New England City.* Princeton: Princeton University Press, 1992.

Department of Christian Social Relations. *Departmental Report.* New York: Protestant Council of the City of New York, 1956.

Detroit Council of Churches. "A Bit of History." *Twenty-Fifth Annual Report.* DCC, 1944.

Djupe, Paul A. "From Limelight to Churchlight: The Decline in Importance of Religious Leaders in Local Politics." Delivered at the Annual Meeting of Midwest Political Science Association, Chicago, 1996.

Dolan, Jay P. *The American Catholic Experience: A History from Colonial Times to the Present.* Garden City, N.J.: Doubleday, 1985.

Douglass, H. Paul. *Protestant Cooperation in American Cities.* New York: Institute of Social and Religious Research, 1930.

———. *The Protestant Church as a Social Institution.* New York: Institute for Social and Religious Research, 1935.

Edsall, Thomas B., and Mary Edsall. *Chain Reaction: The Impact of Race, Rights, and Taxes on American Politics.* New York: W. W. Norton & Co., 1992.

Eichenthal, David R. "Changing Styles and Strategies of the Mayor." In *Urban Politics New York Style,* edited by Jewel Bellush and Dick Netzer, 63–85. Armonk, N.Y.: M. E. Sharpe, 1990.

Feinberg, Walter. "Nationalism in a Comparative Mode: A Response to Charles Taylor." In *The Morality of Nationalism,* edited by Robert McKim and Jeff McMahan, 66–73. New York: Oxford University Press, 1997.

Fine, Sidney. *Frank Murphy: The Detroit Years.* Ann Arbor: University of Michigan Press, 1975.

———. *Violence in the Model City: Race Relations and the Detroit Riot of 1967.* Ann Arbor: University of Michigan Press, 1988.

Flanagan, Sue. "A Contemporary Variation in the Pattern of Protestant Social Work: The Federation of Protestant Welfare Agencies of New York." Master's thesis, New York University, 1948.

Frady, Marshall. *Jesse: The Life and Pilgrimage of Jesse Jackson.* New York: Random House, 1996.

Fragnoli, Raymond. "Progressive Coalition and Municipal Reform." *Detroit in Perspective: A Journal of Regional History* 4 (spring 1980): 119–42.

Freedman, Samuel G. *Upon This Rock: The Miracles of the Black Church.* New York: HarperCollins, 1993.

Fukuzawa, David. "Developing a Strategy for the Urban Parish: The Lessons of the Church Closing in Detroit." *New Theology Review* 6, no. 1 (February 1993): 54–65.

Gartrell, Leland. "Religious Affiliation, New York and Its Metropolitan Region." Department of Church Planning and Research. New York: Protestant Council of the City of New York, 1959.

Glazer, Nathan, and Daniel Patrick Moynihan. *Beyond the Melting Pot: The Negroes, Puerto Ricans, Jews, Italians, and Irish of New York City.* Cambridge, Mass.: MIT Press, 1963.

Glazer, Sidney. *Detroit: A Study in Urban Development.* New York: Bookman Associates, 1965.

Gleiss, H. C. "Historical Sketch of the Detroit Council of Churches." In *Five Glorious Years, Five Cooperative Years, 1919–1924* (pamphlet), 5–10. Detroit: Detroit Council of Churches, 1924.

Gosnell, Harold. *Machine Politics: Chicago Model.* Chicago: University of Chicago Press, 1937.

Greater New York Federation of Churches. *The Churches United for Service: 1935 Annual Report.* New York: GNYFC, 1935.

Green, Charles, and Basil Wilson. *The Struggle for Black Empowerment in New York City.* New York: Praeger, 1989.

Gurin, Patricia, and Edgar G. Epps. *Black Consciousness, Identity, and Achievement.* New York: Wiley, 1975.

Hamilton, Charles V. *Adam Clayton Powell, Jr.: The Political Biography of an American Dilemma.* New York: Atheneum, 1991.

Hammack, David C. *Power and Society: Greater New York at the Turn of the Century.* New York: Russell Sage, 1982.

Hampton, Henry, and Steven Faye. *Voices of Freedom: An Oral History of the Civil Rights Movement from the 1950s through the 1980s.* New York: Bantam Books, 1990.

Hansen, John Mark. "The Political Economy of Group Membership." *American Political Science Review* 79 (1985): 79–92.

Harris, Fredrick C. "Something Within: Religion as a Mobilizer of African-American Political Activism." *Journal of Politics* 56, no. 1 (February 1994): 42–68.

———. "Religious Institutions and African American Political Mobilization." In *Classifying by Race,* edited by Paul E. Peterson, 278–310. Princeton: Princeton University Press, 1995.

"Historic Sketch." *Federation* (Journal of the Federation of Churches and Christian Workers in New York City) 4, no. 2 (1905): 1–23.

Holley, Rev. Jim. *A Saved City is a Safe City.* Detroit: Harlow Press, 1995.

Holli, Melvin G. *Reform in Detroit: Hazen S. Pingree and Urban Politics.* New York: Oxford University Press, 1969.

Hopkins, Carol. "Pulpit Power: Detroit Pastors Wield More Power Than Most Politicians." *Detroit Monthly* (December 1990): 57–61.

Hutchinson, John A. *We Are Not Divided: A Critical History of the Federal Council of Churches of Christ in America.* New York: Round Table Press, 1941.

Hutchinson, William H. "The Americanness of the Social Gospel: An Inquiry in Comparative History." *Church History* 44 (1975): 367–81.

Johnson, F. Ernest. *Economics and the Good Life.* New York: Association Press, 1934.

Jones, Bryan. *Governing Urban America: A Policy Focus.* Boston: Little, Brown, 1983.

Judd, Dennis. *The Politics of American Cities: Private Power and Public Policy.* Boston: Little, Brown, 1979.

Judge, David. "Pluralism." In *Theories of Urban Politics,* edited by David Judge, Gerry Stoker, and Harold Wolman, 19–34. Thousand Oaks, Calif.: Sage, 1995.

Kessner, Thomas. *Fiorello H. La Guardia and the Making of Modern New York.* New York: McGraw-Hill, 1989.

Kneier, Charles M. *City Government in the United States.* New York: Harper & Brothers, 1947.

Koch, Edward I. *Citizen Koch: An Autobiography.* New York: St. Martin's Press, 1992.

Laidlaw, Walter. "Ten Years' Federative Work in New York City." In *Church Federation: Inter-Church Conference on Federation,* edited by Elias S. Sanford, 299–312. New York: Revell, 1906.

Landis, Benson Y. *Must the Nation Plan? A Discussion of Government Programs.* New York: Association Press, 1934.

Lennox, G. Merrill. *Christian Unity and Mission: A History of the Advance and Achievement of the Metropolitan Detroit Council of Churches, 1919–1969.* Detroit: MDCC, 1969.

Lovett, William P. *Detroit Rules Itself.* Boston: Richard G. Badger, 1930.

Lowi, Theodore. *At the Pleasure of the Mayor: Patronage and Power in New York City, 1898–1958.* New York: Free Press, 1964.

———. "Europeanization of America? From United States to United State." In *The Nationalizing Government: Public Policies in America,* edited by Theodore Lowi and Alan Stone, 15–29. Beverly Hills, Calif.: Sage, 1978.

May, Henry F. *Protestant Churches and Industrial America.* New York: Harper & Brothers, 1949.

McClellan, George B. *The Gentleman and the Tiger: The Autobiography of George B. McClellan, Jr.* Philadelphia: Lippincott, 1956.

McNamara, Patrick. "A Study of the Editorial Policy of the *Brooklyn Tablet* Under Patrick Scanlon, 1917–1968." Master's thesis, St. John's University, New York, 1994.

McNickle, Chris. *To Be Mayor of New York: Ethnic Politics in the City.* New York: Columbia University Press, 1993.

Mollenkopf, John Hall. *A Phoenix in the Ashes: The Rise and Fall of the Koch Coalition in New York City Politics.* Princeton: Princeton University Press, 1992.

———. "New York: The Great Anomaly." Paper presented at the Annual Meeting of the American Political Science Association, Chicago, 1995.

Nathan, Richard P. *The Plot That Failed: Nixon and the Administrative Presidency.* New York: John Wiley, 1975.

Oates, Mary J. *The Catholic Philanthropic Tradition in America.* Bloomington: Indiana University Press, 1995.

O'Connor, John Cardialn. *His Eminence and Hizzoner: A Candid Exchange.* New York: Avon, 1989.

Orloff, Ann Shola. *The Politics of Pensions: A Comparative Analysis of Britain, Canada, and the United States, 1880–1940.* Madison: University of Wisconsin Press, 1993.

Orr, M., and Gerry Stoker. "Urban Regimes and Leadership in Detroit." *Urban Affairs Quarterly* 30 (1994): 48–73.

Parkhurst, Charles H. *Our Fight With Tammany.* New York: Charles Scribners, 1895.

Peller, Gary. "Race Consciousness." In *Critical Race Theory: The Key Writings that Formed the Movement,* edited by Kimberle' Crenshaw, Neil Gotanda, Gary Peller, and Kendall Thomas, 127–58. New York: Free Press, 1995.

Peterson, Paul. *City Limits.* Chicago: University of Chicago Press, 1981.

Pratt, Henry J. *Gray Agendas: Interest Groups and Public Pensions in Canada, Great Britain, and the United States.* Ann Arbor: University of Michigan Press, 1993.

———. *The Gray Lobby.* Chicago: University of Chicago Press, 1976.

———. *Ethno-Religious Politics.* Cambridge, Mass.: Schenkman Publishing Co., 1974.

———. *The Liberalization of American Protestantism: A Case Study in Complex Organizations.* Detroit: Wayne State University Press, 1972.

———. "Politics, Status, and the Organization of Ethnic Minority Group Interests: The Case of the New York Protestants." *Polity: The Journal of the Northeastern Political Science Association* (December 1970): 222–46.

Pratt, John Webb. *Religion, Politics, and Diversity: The Church-State Theme in New York History.* Ithaca, N.Y.: Cornell University Press, 1967.

Presthus, Robert. *Elites in the Policy Process.* New York: Cambridge University Press, 1974.

Ramsay, Maurice M. "Some Aspects of Non-Partisan Government in Detroit, 1918–1940." Ph.D. dissertation, University of Michigan, 1944.

Ramsay, Meredith. "Redeeming the City: Exploring the Relationship Between Church and the Metropolis." *Urban Affairs Review* 33, no. 5 (May 1998): 595–626.

Rauschenbusch, Walter. *Christianizing the Social Order.* New York: Macmillan, 1912.

Reed, Thomas Harrison. *Municipal Government in the United States.* New York: Appleton, Century, Crofts, 1934.

Rich, Wilbur. *Coleman Young and Detroit Politics.* Detroit: Wayne State University Press, 1989.

Roohan, James Edmund. *American Catholics and the Social Question, 1865–1900.* New York: Arno Press, 1976.

Salamon, Lester M. *Partners in Public Service: Government-Nonprofit Relations in the Modern Welfare State.* Baltimore: Johns Hopkins University Press, 1995.

Sayre, Wallace S., and Herbert Kaufman. *Governing New York City: Politics in the Metropolis.* New York: Russell Sage, 1960.

Schneider, David M., and Albert Deutsch. *The History of Public Welfare in New York State, 1867–1940.* Montclair, N.J.: Patterson Smith, 1969.

Sharp, John K. *History of the Diocese of Brooklyn, 1853–1953.* New York: Fordham University Press, 1954.

Shefter, Martin. *Political Crisis, Fiscal Crisis: The Collapse and Revival of New York City.* New York: Columbia University Press, 1992.

Shelley, Thomas J. "John Cardinal Farley and Modernism in New York." *Church History* 61, no. 3 (1992): 350–61.

Skocpol, Theda. "Emergent Agendas and Recurrent Strategies in Historical Sociology." In *Vision and Method in Historical Sociology,* edited by Theda Skocpol, 356–91. New York: Cambridge University Press, 1984.

Sleeper, Jim. *The Closet of Strangers: Liberalism and the Politics of Race in New York.* New York: Norton, 1990.

Smith, H. Shelton, Robert T. Handy, and Lefferts A. Loetscher. *American Christianity: An Historical Interpretation with Representative Documents.* New York: Charles Scribner's Sons, 1963.

Steffens, Lincoln. *The Shame of the Cities.* New York: Ameron, 1904.

Steichen, Edward. *The Family of Man.* New York: Simon and Schuster, 1955.

Stidley, Leonard A. *Sectarian Welfare Federation among Protestants.* New York: Association Press, 1944.

Stoker, Gerry. "Regime Theory and Urban Politics." In *Theories of Urban Politics,* edited by David Judge, Gerry Stoker, and Harold Wolman, 54–71. Thousand Oaks, Calif.: Sage, 1995.

Stone, Clarence. *Regime Politics: Governing Atlanta, 1946–88.* Lawrence: University Press of Kansas, 1989.

———. *Urban Policy and Politics in a Bureaucratic Age.* Englewood Cliffs, N.J.: Prentice-Hall, 1986.

Sugrue, Thomas J. *The Origins of the Urban Crisis: Race and Inequality in Postwar Detroit.* Princeton: Princeton University Press, 1996.

Sundquist, Eric J. *To Wake the Nations: Race in the Making of American Literature.* Cambridge, Mass.: Belknap Press, 1993.

Tamblyn and Brown, Inc. *The Protestant Federations of Metropolitan New York: A Survey and Recommendations,* 1941.

Taylor, Charles. "Nationalism and Modernity." In *The Morality of Nationalism,* edited by Robert McKim and Jeff McMahan, 31–55. New York: Oxford University Press, 1997.

Tentler, Leslie Woodcock. *Seasons of Grace: A History of the Catholic Archdiocese of Detroit.* Detroit: Wayne State University Press, 1990.

Thomas, J. M., and R. N. Black Jr. "Faith-Based Community Development and African American Neighborhoods." In *Revitalizing Urban Neighborhoods,* edited by W. D. Keating, N. Krumholz, and P. Star, 131–43. Lawrence: University Press of Kansas, 1996.

Thompson, Heather Ann. *Whose Detroit?: Politics, Labor, and Race in a Modern American City.* Ithaca, N.Y.: Cornell University Press, 2001.

Tilden, Jeff Todd. "Rev. C. L. Franklin: Black American Preacher-Poet." *Folk Life Annual* (1987): 86–105.

Townsend, John D. *New York in Bondage.* New York: (privately published), 1901.

Trattner, Walter I. *From Poor Law to Welfare State: A History of Social Welfare in America,* 5th ed. New York: Free Press, 1994.

Truman, David B. *The Governmental Process.* New York: Knopf, 1951.

Upson, Lent D. "Increasing Activities and Increasing Costs." *National Municipal Review* (October 1922): 317–20.

———. *The Growth of a City Government.* Detroit: Detroit Bureau of Municipal Research. April 1942.

Vinyard, JoEllen. *The Irish on the Urban Frontier: Nineteenth Century Detroit, 1850–1880.* New York: Arno Press, 1976.

Wilson, Carter. "A Study of Organized Neighborhood Opposition to the General Motors Plant Redevelopment Project in Poletown." Ph.D. dissertation, Wayne State University, 1982.

Wilson, James Q. *Negro Politics: The Search for Leadership.* New York: Free Press, 1960.

Wuthnow, Robert. *The Restructuring of American Religion: Society and Faith since World War II.* Princeton: Princeton University Press, 1995.

Wylie, Jeanie. *Poletown: Community Betrayed.* Urbana: University of Illinois Press, 1989.

Yates, Douglas. *The Ungovernable City: The Politics of Urban Problems and Policy Making.* Cambridge, Mass.: MIT Press, 1977.

Yinger, J. Milton. *Religion and the Struggle for Power.* Durham, N.C.: Duke University Press, 1946.

Young, Coleman, and Lonnie Wheeler. *The Autobiography of Mayor Coleman Young.* New York: Viking, 1994.

Zink, Harold. *Government of Cities in the United States.* New York: Macmillan, 1948.

Index

Books in the African American Life Series

Coleman Young and Detroit Politics: From Social Activist to Power Broker, by Wilbur Rich, 1988

Great Black Russian: A Novel on the Life and Times of Alexander Pushkin, by John Oliver Killens, 1989

Indignant Heart: A Black Worker's Journal, by Charles Denby, 1989 (reprint)

The Spook Who Sat by the Door, by Sam Greenlee, 1989 (reprint)

Roots of African American Drama: An Anthology of Early Plays, 1858–1938, edited by Leo Hamalian and James V. Hatch, 1990

Walls: Essays, 1985–1990, by Kenneth McClane, 1991

Voices of the Self: A Study of Language Competence, by Keith Gilyard, 1991

Say Amen, Brother! Old-Time Negro Preaching: A Study in American Frustration, by William H. Pipes, 1991 (reprint)

The Politics of Black Empowerment: The Transformation of Black Activism in Urban America, by James Jennings, 1992

Pan Africanism in the African Diaspora: An Analysis of Modern Afrocentric Political Movements, by Ronald Walters, 1993

Three Plays: The Broken Calabash, Parables for a Season, and The Reign of Wazobia, by Tess Akaeke Onwueme, 1993

Untold Tales, Unsung Heroes: An Oral History of Detroit's African American Community, 1918–1967, by Elaine Latzman Moon, Detroit Urban League, Inc., 1994

Discarded Legacy: Politics and Poetics in the Life of Frances E. W. Harper, 1825–1911, by Melba Joyce Boyd, 1994

African American Women Speak Out on Anita Hill–Clarence Thomas, edited by Geneva Smitherman, 1995

Lost Plays of the Harlem Renaissance, 1920–1940, edited by James V. Hatch and Leo Hamalian, 1996

Let's Flip the Script: An African American Discourse on Language, Literature, and Learning, by Keith Gilyard, 1996

A History of the African American People: The History, Traditions, and Culture of African Americans, edited by James Oliver Horton and Lois E. Horton, 1997 (reprint)

Tell It to Women: An Epic Drama for Women, by Osonye Tess Onwueme, 1997

Ed Bullins: A Literary Biography, by Samuel Hay, 1997

Walkin' over Medicine, by Loudelle F. Snow, 1998 (reprint)

Negroes with Guns, by Robert F. Williams, 1998 (reprint)

A Study of Walter Rodney's Intellectual and Political Thought, by Rupert Lewis, 1998

Ideology and Change: The Transformation of the Caribbean Left, by Perry Mars, 1998

"Winds Can Wake Up the Dead": An Eric Walrond Reader, edited by Louis Parascandola, 1998

Race & Ideology: Language, Symbolism, and Popular Culture, edited by Arthur Spears, 1999

Without Hatreds or Fears: Jorge Artel and the Struggle for Black Literary Expression in Colombia, by Laurence E. Prescott, 2000

African Americans, Labor, and Society: Organizing for a New Agenda, edited by Patrick L. Mason, 2001

The Concept of Self: A Study of Black Identity and Self-Esteem, by Richard L. Allen, 2001

What the Wine-Sellers Buy Plus Three: Four Plays by Ron Milner, 2001

Looking Within/Mirar adentro: Selected Poems, 1954–2000, by Nancy Morejón, edited and with an introduction by Juanamaría Cordones-Cook, 2003

Liberation Memories: The Rhetoric and Poetics of John Oliver Killens, by Keith Gilyard, 2003

What Mama Said: An Epic Drama, by Osonye Tess Onwueme, 2003

White Nationalism, Black Interests: Conservative Public Policy and the Black Community, by Ronald W. Walters, 2003

Bobweaving Detroit: The Selected Poems of Murray Jackson, edited with a postscript by Ted Pearson and Kathryne V. Lindberg, 2003

Churches and Urban Government in Detroit and New York, 1895–1994, by Henry Pratt with a Preface by Ron Brown, 2003

For an updated listing of books in this series, please visit our Web site at http://wsupress.wayne.edu